The DIASPORA
AND THE LOST TRIBES OF ISRAEL

Еврей юноша.
Un jeune homme juif.

Закаспійскіе Типы.
Types du territoire Transcaspien.

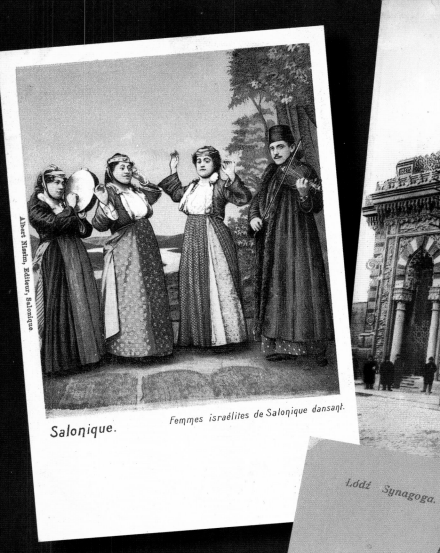

Salonique. Femmes israélites de Salonique dansant.

Albert Nissim, Éditeur, Salonique.

Lódź Synagoga. Lodz. Synagoge.

С. Петербургъ St. Pétersbourg

Синагога Synagoge

TANGER Femme juive en costume de céré...

48 SEDAN. — La Synagogu...

Typen

„Komme sofort nach Empf
und zahle die höchst

4. - KAISERSLAUTERN. - Synagoge
La Synagogue
Jewish Synagogue

M. H.

nue Philipoteaux — The Sy

Fillettes juives

Photo Garrigues Tunis - 100

Luzern 2/? 1902

Git Schabes.

Je regrette vivement que tu ne puisses
m'expedier la surprise par la poste. Tu
pourras m'envoyer en colis postal avec ce
que je t'ai demandé: Station Bortniki
Merci. Je t'embrasse Juilte

Synagoge.

Gruss aus
Dortmund.   le 5.9ber 1901

Cap

THE DIASPORA
AND THE LOST TRIBES OF ISRAEL

Amotz Asa-El

Hugh Lauter Levin Associates, Inc.

The Diaspora and The Lost Tribes of Israel

Copyright © 2004 Hugh Lauter Levin Associates, Inc.

PROJECT EDITOR AND
ILLUSTRATIONS RESEARCHER: Ellin Yassky

BOOK DESIGNER: Kevin Osborn, Research & Design, Ltd.,
                                 Arlington, Virginia

COPYEDITORS: Linda Bernstein and Deborah Zindell

DISTRIBUTED BY PUBLISHERS GROUP WEST

PRINTED IN CHINA

(PAGES 3–4)
YOUTHS CELEBRATE ON JERUSALEM
DAY AT THE WESTERN WALL.

(PAGE 8)
FACES OF JEWS THE WORLD OVER.

In memory of my father,
Zvi b"r Yaacov,
who sought his brethren
all his life.

Contents

HISTORY'S ULTIMATE NOMADS

"What's so pretty about this vista native Israelis so much adore?" my father once asked me in frustration, fanning his arm across the naked Judean Desert hills that rolled ahead of us, north of Jerusalem, all the way to the Dead Sea. Having grown up in interwar Czechoslovakia he never fully accepted the contrast between his native landscape's abundant lakes, rivers, forests, and snow-capped mountains, and his old-new homeland's Mediterranean climate and barren landscapes. Until his death, he quietly hoped that the arid land where his offspring were growing would someday be made to wear a gown of greenery much like the European vistas where his own parents initially thrived and ultimately perished.

And yet, despite his and many other Jews' lack of affinity to its desolation, heat, and solitude, the desert has been, and remains, a powerful metaphor for the Jewish nation's improbable survival through the ages. Like nomads wandering through inhospitable lands, the Jews have historically sojourned from land to land, country to country, continent to continent. Ever since the Exodus from Egypt, whether they lamented its wrath, embraced its solitude, or reached for its horizon, Jews could not remain indifferent to the desert, where their forefathers formed a nation while landless, impoverished, and in motion.

In fact, the Israelites' four-decade journey through the Sinai Desert's wilderness in a Sisyphean search for the Promised Land led anti-Semitic political economist Werner Sombart (1869–1941) to attribute the Jews' numerous migrations throughout history to the formative experience of rootlessness as it was handed to them by Moses. In *Die Juden und das Wirtschaftsleben*, Sombart traced the Jews' famous geographic mobility and mercantile agility to their collective shaping as nomads in an infertile land. Sombart, who ultimately joined the Nazi Party, also conceded that the Jews were a positive driving force behind the rise of European capitalism. "When Israel appears upon the face of Europe," he wrote, "the place where it appears comes to life; and when it departs, everything which had previously flourished withers away."

(ABOVE)

WINGED GENIUS AS ATLANTE.
HITTITE. FROM THE PALACE OF KING KAPARA, TELL HALAF, SYRIA. NINTH CENTURY B.C.E. LOUVRE, PARIS.
By the end of the sixth century B.C.E. the Israelite tribes had disappeared, while most of the Jewish nation had returned to Mesopotamia, home of their patriarch, Abraham.

(OPPOSITE)

THE SINAI MOUNTAINS.
The Israelites' forty-year journey to sovereignty through the desert has had a profound impact on their subsequent history.

LAND OF MANASSEH,
GOLAN HEIGHTS.
*When Moses begged to enter the
Promised Land about a fifth of the
Israelites remained outside of it
by choice.*

GATHERING OF THE MANNA
IN THE DESERT.
ARTIST: ANONYMOUS. SIXTEENTH CENTURY. STONE
RELIC. CHAPEL OF THE HOLY SACRAMENT, S. GIORGIO
MARTIRE, LOCOROTONDO (BARI), ITALY.

*Some rabbis contend that the Israelites'
receipt of the Torah while lacking a land
means that in Judaism observance is
more important than land.*

The wanderings of the Jews bore meaning not only to Gentiles but also to Jewish luminaries. Ultra-Orthodox Israeli rabbi Eliezer Shach (1898–2001), for instance, opposed risking human life for the sake of possessing biblical territories. A Lithuanian-born sage who inspired the establishment of numerous Talmudic academies in Israel, thus restoring some of what had been destroyed in the Holocaust, Shach contended that a nation that received the Ten Commandments in the desert can manage even without any land at all. Moses and the Israelites, he reportedly explained, got by for forty years while lacking any permanent land under their feet. Indeed, Rabbi Shach was merely echoing an age-old rabbinical view: The Jews were condemned to exile due to their sins, and will be redeemed from it only when the Messiah comes.

However, while the Israelites themselves resented that arduous forty-year trek from slavery in Egypt to sovereignty in Canaan, and missed their previous life in the fertile Nile Valley—"when we sat by the flesh pot, and when we did eat bread to the full"

(Exodus 16:3)—there is no arguing that their descendants emerged as history's ultimate nomads. For unlike the Bedouin, who merely roam the expanses of the one desert into which they are born, Jewish communities have for centuries been prone to appear, disappear, and reappear almost anywhere, arguably belonging simultaneously everywhere and nowhere.

THE FIRST EXILES

Contrary to conventional wisdom, the foundations for a Jewish Diaspora were laid well before Rome's conquest of Judea, when Jews built homes, farms, and businesses around much of the Mediterranean's tri-continental basin throughout the Second Temple period (538 B.C.E.–70 C.E.).

In fact, even the reluctance to unambiguously embrace the Promised Land already accompanied the Israelites as they made their odyssey from Egypt to Canaan. First, the

(ABOVE)
KADESH BARNEA OASIS, EASTERN SINAI.
While on their way to the Promised Land the Israelites longed for Egypt, "when we sat by the flesh pot, and when we did eat bread to the full." (Exodus 16:3)

(OPPOSITE)
THE BURNT HOUSE, JERUSALEM.
Ruins of a house that belonged to rich Jews before being burned by the Romans during the destruction of Jerusalem in 70 C.E. The Diaspora existed long before the Destruction.

spies who went to explore Canaan returned with a pessimistic report about its fortifications. Then, about a fifth of the nation—the tribes of Gad, Reuben, and half of Manasseh—chose to settle just outside Canaan, in what later came to be known as Transjordan. In other words, when Moses gazed longingly from Mt. Nebo into the Holy Land that he had so coveted but was barred from entering, there were within walking distance from him thousands of Israelites who were welcome to enter Canaan, and in fact were expected to do so, and yet preferred to shun it.

ELEPHANTINE ISLAND IN THE NILE, OPPOSITE ASWAM, EGYPT.
A Jewish colony existed here already in the sixth century B.C.E., possibly before the destruction of the First Temple.

By the time of the Temple's destruction in 70 C.E. and the Bar-Kochba Revolt in 135 C.E.—the dates frequently, and wrongly, mentioned as the beginning of the Diaspora—thousands of Jews, indeed the majority of the Jewish nation, were residing outside the Land of Israel.

Surely, the roots of this dispersed existence go back to the forced exile of the biblical kingdoms of Israel and Judah, mainly to Mesopotamia, in the eighth and sixth centuries B.C.E. respectively. Those exiles emerged in the aftermath of the destruction of the First Temple (which existed for four centuries after its construction by King Solomon in the tenth century B.C.E), and following the destruction in 720 B.C.E of the Israelite kingdom (which came into being after King Solomon's death, when his kingdom split into the rival monarchies of Judah and Israel).

Some passages in the Bible—such as Obadiah's prophecy concerning the restoration of "the children of Israel, that are among the Canaanites, even unto Zarephath, and the captivity of Jerusalem, that is in Sepharad," (Obadiah 1:20) or Jeremiah's address "to all the Jews that dwelt in the land of Egypt, that dwelt at Migdol, and at Tahpanhes, and at Noph, and in the country of Pathros" (Jeremiah 44:1)—allude to the existence of sizable Jewish communities across the eastern Mediterranean basin already before the Second Temple era.

In Egypt, the bulk of the Israelite population, including Jeremiah himself, resided in the Nile Delta. However, soldiers who originated in biblical Judah set up a colony some 1,500 kilometers south from there, near the current Sudanese frontier, on the river island of Elephantine (Greek for "City of Ivories"), near today's Aswan. Refugees from Judah established that colony—also known as Yev—shortly after Jerusalem's fall (in 586 B.C.E.), or maybe even earlier. Citing its Jews' apparent lack of Hebrew (they spoke Aramaic) some scholars concluded that the colony already existed well before

Jerusalem's destruction. Papyri found on the island during the first decade of the twentieth century indicate that the local Jews had a temple of their own and celebrated Passover according to the Jewish laws, including the ritual eating of unleavened bread (*matzah*) and the refraining from eating leavened dough (*hametz*) during that holiday's seven days. However, on other issues their norms did not reflect classical Jewish law. Women, for instance, could unilaterally divorce their husbands.

Still, the bulk of the early displacement was pushed north. The first exile, which began in the 730s B.C.E., settled in what today is northeastern Syria, as thousands of refugees from the vanquished Kingdom of Israel were forcibly relocated by the Assyrians to the Gozan region, now Tell Halaf, on the west bank of the Euphrates tributary known as the Habor River. The second exile ended up southeast of there, in the aftermath of Judah's conquest in 586 B.C.E. by the Fertile Crescent's new rising power, Babylon. That kingdom's defeat of Judah was preceded and followed by the exiling to Babylon of the Judean elite, beginning with King Jehoiachin himself, a decade before the First Temple's destruction.

And so, by the end of the sixth century B.C.E., the ancestors of what later became known as the Jewish nation were spread throughout Mesopotamia. Their dispersal echoed that vast landmass's own transition from the domination of its northern power, Assyria, whose center was in the city of Nineveh (on the Upper Tigris River opposite today's Mosul) to its southern counterweight, Babylonia. The hub of that empire was the city of Babylon—the largest metropolis in the world at the time— on the lower Euphrates River, some ninety kilometers south of today's Baghdad.

Thus, the first era of Israelite sovereignty in the Promised Land ended, ironically and symbolically, with Abraham's descendants scattered roughly along the erratic route of his own eventful biography. The Israelite patriarch, who was born and raised in Ur of the Chaldees, began his journeys there, near the mouth of the Euphrates and south of Babylon, where the kingdom of Judah was exiled; then proceeded north, to Haran, west of Gozan, where the Israelites were exiled; and finally, after already migrating to the Promised Land, Abraham proceeded farther south, albeit temporarily, to Egypt, which was also where Jeremiah ended up after witnessing the fall of Judah, which he so heroically tried and so tragically failed to prevent by preaching moral justice and political prudence.

(ABOVE)

HEAD OF A BULL FROM A HARP, TOMB OF QUEEN PU-ABI IN UR.
EARLY DYNASTIC PERIOD, 2450 B.C.E.
IRAQ MUSEUM, BAGHDAD.
The story of the Israelites began in current-day Iraq with the clash between Abraham and the prevailing pagan civilization.

CLAY CYLINDER, INSCRIBED IN
BABYLONIAN CUNEIFORM WITH AN
ACCOUNT BY PERSIAN EMPEROR
CYRUS (559–530 B.C.E.) OF HIS
CONQUEST OF BABYLON IN 539 B.C.E.
THE BRITISH MUSEUM, LONDON.

*The Cyrus Declaration, which allowed
the Jews to rebuild the Temple in
Jerusalem, did not bring an end to the
Diaspora's existence.*

THE SECOND TEMPLE ERA

Theoretically, the dislocation imposed on the Jews and Israelites by their Assyrian and
Babylonian conquerors could have ended abruptly in 538 B.C.E., after Cyrus—the
Persian emperor who conquered Babylon—declared the Jews' right to restore their land,
practice their faith, and rebuild their temple in Jerusalem.

However, while the temple was indeed reconstructed and a sizable immigration back
to the Land of Israel ensued, the Jews' geographical distribution throughout the 585-year-
long Second Temple period went far beyond the immediate vicinity of the Holy Land. In
fact, Jews lived throughout the entire Hellenistic-Roman universe, and transcended its
eastern horizon deep into the Parthian Empire, where large-scale Jewish communities
flourished in and around today's Iran and Iraq. Back in the Hellenistic sphere, Syria, Asia
Minor, Cyprus, and the Greek islands had sizable Jewish communities well before the
Temple's destruction, and Rome itself had a solid Jewish community already in the times
of the Maccabees.

In sum, the restoration that the tolerant Cyrus allowed, besides stopping short of
granting full independence, never came close to resulting in the entire Jewish nation's
return to its ancestral land. Instead, what gradually emerged was a model of numerous
disparate and far-flung communities, sometimes orbiting Jerusalem, at other times
challenging it. Clearly, many Jews—perhaps most— had grown comfortable abroad and
saw no imperative to return to the Promised Land.

(ABOVE)

THE HABAKKUK COMMENTARY.

QUMRAN. COPIED AT THE END OF THE FIRST CENTURY, B.C.E. THE SHRINE OF THE BOOK. THE ISRAEL MUSEUM, JERUSALEM.

The Judean prophet's timeless words, that the righteous shall live by their faith, later inspired Jews facing the challenges of survival in the Diaspora.

(LEFT)

THE TORAH NICHE ON THE WEST WALL OF THE DURA EUROPOS SYNAGOGUE.

C. 245, SYRIA. RECONSTRUCTION. BETH HATEFUTSOTH, TEL AVIV.

In its early centuries the Diaspora was attracted to the Hellenistic sphere.

There are testimonies that in Judea (as the former Judah was called by the Greeks who succeeded the Persians) the Jews steadily grew in numbers during the four centuries between the Cyrus Declaration and the rise of the Hasmonean dynasty (which followed Judea's anti-Hellenistic revolt that began in 167 B.C.E.). However, throughout those years the communities of Mesopotamia not only failed to disappear, but actually prospered. Relations between the Jews of Judea and Babylonia remained strong, due to their geographic proximity and frequent family ties, yet discord between local rulers would occasionally weigh on traffic between the two regions. Egypt, at the same time, remained on the whole more freely accessible and within the same geopolitical orbit as Judea. Because Jewish residents of fertile Egypt often enjoyed prosperity, the Nile basin once again attracted large numbers of Jews.

With the Jewish people spread across such vast territory, worship was also affected. Although the centrality of the Jerusalem Temple remained unchallenged until its destruction, communal houses of prayer began sprouting across the Diaspora well before the Temple's destruction. One of the most famous of these precedents was the Onias Temple, built at Leontopolis, east of today's Cairo, in the second century B.C.E. by Onias IV, son of the Jerusalem high priest Onias III. Unlike its predecessor at Elephantine, built half a millennium earlier on the other end of the Nile, the Onias Temple was centrally located, clearly emulated the Jerusalem Temple, and was led by priests who had actually officiated there.

A tower, wall, menorah, and other vessels much like those in Jerusalem transformed the shrine as Egyptian Jewry's alternative to Jerusalem's Temple, and sacrificial rituals were conducted much the way they are prescribed in the Book of Leviticus. In fact, the main questions this episode raises are not about the intention behind it—this temple clearly derived its inspiration from, and was meant to emulate, Jerusalem's—but how big its founders' pretension was to eclipse the original Temple, and what motivated them in the first place.

Some scholars contend that Onias merely sought to serve Egypt's sizable Jewish community while capitalizing on the Ptolemy dynasty's tolerance. Others note that the rival Hellenistic power, the Seleucid Empire, was persecuting Judaism at the time and defiled the Temple in Jerusalem. According to this camp, Onias's aim transcended the confines of his immediate community and actually sought to fill the gap caused by the Temple's desecration in Jerusalem. Josephus Flavius, on the other hand, claims it was actually built more than two centuries prior to the destruction of the Temple, and therefore also well before the Hellenistic attack on Hasmonean-era Judaism. The Talmud, for its part, though speaking from a distance of some 1,600 kilometers and four centuries, attributed the rise of the Onias Temple to personal rivalries between Egyptian and Jerusalemite priests.

Either way, the Onias Temple was summarily razed by Rome three years after the Jerusalem Temple's destruction. Whatever this temple may have meant for the Jews, to the

Romans it seemed to possess the same kind of religious power, and therefore also pose the same kind of threat to their authority, as Jerusalem's shrine had.

The Jews' geographical dispersal in the Second Temple era inevitably entailed cultural diffusion and diversity, a condition that was well expressed in their literary activity. The third-century B.C.E translation of the Bible into Greek, the Septuagint, like the later Greek-language works of Jason of Cyrene (in today's Libya), who chronicled in the middle of the second century B.C.E. the wars of the Maccabees, or the philosopher Philo Judaeus of Alexandria (c. 20 B.C.E.–50 C.E.), who wrote, among other things, commentaries on the Torah, reflected many Jews' weak Judean roots—in this case the failure to use, and maybe even know, Hebrew. However, these Diaspora scholars also had an unabashed attachment to other parts of their heritage and an urge to make them accessible and intelligible for a broad

audience, Jewish and non-Jewish. In the case of Philo, this desire to reach out was also complemented by the leadership he assumed in protecting Jewish values when he traveled to Rome (40 C.E.) to plead with Emperor Caligula against a decree to place that emperor's statue in Alexandria's main synagogue. While that particular effort to harmonize Jewish existence in a non-Jewish setting was successful, the overall relationship was far from perfect.

A mere seventy-five years after Philo's mission to Rome, Jewish communities in cities throughout the eastern Roman sphere rose up in arms against their Greek neighbors and Roman rulers. Though initially they had some victories, by 117 C.E.—two years after they rebelled—the Jewish insurgents were so severely defeated that the great Jewish communities along the North African coastline, including the one in Alexandria, all but disappeared, as did the entire, sizable community of Cyprus.

(ABOVE)
THE MOSQUE OF OMAR AND
AL-AKSA, THE SITE OF THE ANCIENT
JEWISH TEMPLES.
*Three years after its destruction Roman
troops destroyed a competing shrine in the
Diaspora, the Onias Temple in Egypt.*

(RIGHT)

THE PILLAGE OF JERUSALEM BY
ANTIOCHUS IV.

LOUF GUÉRARD, IN *De Bello Judaico* (JEWISH WARS),
BY JOSEPHUS FLAVIUS, TRANSLATED BY GUILLAUME
COQUILLART DE REIMS, PARIS. 1480–1485. PARCHMENT.
MS. 776, FOL. 21R. MUSÉE CONDÉ, CHANTILLY, FRANCE.

*The pillaging of Jerusalem by Antiochus
IV, who sought to forcefully Hellenize
Judea before the Maccabean Revolt of
165 B.C.E. In later generations scholars
like Philo Judaeus of Alexandria sought
to harmonize Hellenism and Judaism.*

(OPPOSITE)

MASADA.

*Less than a half-century after the Great
Revolt, Jewish communities throughout
the Roman Empire rebelled, but during
the upheaval, which ended with
Masada's downfall in 70 C.E., the
Diaspora apparently stood by idly.*

Just what motivated those rebels remains unclear. Some historians suggest they were inspired by messianic visions of overthrowing the existing political order. All scholars, however, agree that during Judea's Great Revolt of 66–70 C.E. the parents of those rebels and the rest of the Jewish Diaspora generally stood by idly rather than join the cause. Still, the entire Diaspora ended up lamenting the revolt's tragic aftermath no less than its direct victims—the Jews of Judea.

In all, during the seven centuries between the eve of the First Temple's destruction by Babylon and the aftermath of its successor's destruction by Rome, Jewish communities that sprouted thousands of miles away from each other managed to cohabitate with host cultures while clinging to their heritage and faith.

That is how the Diaspora saga began.

פירוש אברבנאל

אלהים מה להלן שנתן להם חפץ לדעת
נשמעה חף וירא את עניינו על זה
נאמר ומה מדרכו וידע ל
אלהים על תאמים ה
המטה לפי
סאין אדם
יודע מה בן לים
ולשתו כי לם אלהים ומרה
שנקרא תאמים המטה דרך ארץ כי
התשמים הוא מדרך הארץ שנאמר ואי
לין באלן לבא עלינו כדרך כל הארץ :

ויבן ערי מסכנות לפרעה את
פיתום ואת רעמסס : וירענו
עלינו עבודה קשה כמה שנאמר
ויעבידו מצרים את בני ישראל
בפרך

ואת

THE DIASPORA: BETWEEN IMAGE AND SUBSTANCE

Did the Promised Land's relative desolation play a role in the Jewish people's failure to effectively cling to it? It must have. After all, even Abraham—the national patriarch who had been personally commanded by God to settle in Canaan—at one point abandoned the famine-struck land God had promised him and his offspring. A similar struggle with famine later led his grandson Jacob and his twelve sons to Egypt, a fateful move that resulted in their staying put in that land of plenty, and their descendants suffering there through centuries of persecution. In any event, from the mist of the Exodus emerged a nation that would often seem averse to any territorial attachment, a nation that during three subsequent millennia was far more attached to the spiritual covenant its forebears were given upon their entry into the desert than to the earthly inheritance that awaited them beyond it.

In our times, the State of Israel's predominantly European-born founders counted the desert among their enemies and sought to tame and fertilize it, as they sought to restore the Jews' attachment to their ancestral land. Half a century later the ambition to extract the desert from the heart of the land of Israel seemed not much more realized than the quest to create that New Jew who early Zionists believed would abandon trade and embrace farming. Moreover, Israelis today concede what the first Israelis wanted to deny, namely, that the Jews remain the same inherently worldly people described by their biblical tormentors.

In the Book of Esther, when Haman the courtier plots "to destroy, to slay, and to cause to perish all Jews, both young and old, little children and women," (Esther 3:13) his pitch to Persia's King Ahasuerus was: "There is a certain people scattered abroad and dispersed among the peoples in all the provinces of thy kingdom, and their laws are diverse from those of every people." (Esther 3:7)

Some twenty-five centuries later this description of the Jews' condition remains as relevant and mind-boggling as it was back when Haman was consumed by his hatred for Mordechai, incidentally the first-ever literary character to be described as "the Jew."

(ABOVE)

THE ISRAELITES IN BONDAGE.

(OPPOSITE)

THE HEBREW SLAVES BUILDING STORE CITIES FOR PHARAOH.
FROM THE LEIPNICK HAGGADAH. ARTIST-SCRIBE: JOSEPH BAR DAVID LEIPNICK OF MORAVIA. 1740, ALTONA. VELLUM. SLOANE MS. 3173, FOL. 11V. THE BRITISH LIBRARY, LONDON.

The Hebrew slaves building the stone cities of Pithom and Ramses for Pharaoh as described in Exodus 1:11 are depicted as contemporary Jews at work in a German town.

(ABOVE)

BOOK OF ESTHER.

EIGHTEENTH CENTURY, HOLLAND. SCROLL NO. 34.
LIBRARY OF THE JEWISH THEOLOGICAL SEMINARY
OF AMERICA, NEW YORK.

*Shown in the panel on the right is the
hanging of Haman and his ten sons.*

The Jewish nation indeed is, and apparently has been practically since its inception, so geographically stretched and culturally fluid that its dispersion set it apart from other nations even more than its distinctive laws, rules, tradition, languages, and dress. This condition intrigued scholars already in ancient times. In his *Geography*, Greek historian Strabo (a contemporary of Jesus who gave the best surviving description of the Mediterranean basin during the Augustinian era of 27 B.C.E.–14 C.E.), wrote that the Jewish nation is to be found practically anywhere in the world.

If that was the case before the destruction of the Second Temple, the aftermath of that calamity altogether turned the Jews into the ultimate "People of the World." When, for instance, word of Messianic imposter Shabbetai Zevi's "appearance" traveled in 1666 from community to community, it crossed, within weeks, a Jewish universe ranging from the shores of the Atlantic to the doorstep of China. Seven centuries earlier, Jewish merchants sent caravans that linked Morocco with India and China. In the early Middle

(ABOVE)

SUPPORTERS AND OPPONENTS OF
MAIMONIDES DEBATE HIS WRITINGS
IN TOLEDO, SPAIN.
WALL PAINTING BY JUDE B. WATTS.
BETH HATEFUTSOTH, TEL AVIV.

*The monumental sage's life, which passed
through three continents, was not
uncommon for a medieval Jew.*

Ages, the rabbis of Baghdad corresponded with fellow rabbis in Persia, Spain, Germany, France, and the Ukraine. And the merchants who founded Franco-German Jewry in the early Middle Ages passed along thousands of miles of European roads and rivers, sheltered and assisted along the way by a chain of Jewish communities.

Indeed, while most Christians and Muslims seldom voyaged internationally altogether in pre-modern times, Jews were relatively frequently well traveled, and often also crossed continents. Shabbetai Zevi's travels, for instance, took him from Asia Minor and Greece to Egypt, the Land of Israel, and Syria. Thirteenth-century sage Moses Maimonides started his life in Spain, and then proceeded to Morocco and the Land of Israel before finally settling in Egypt. Fifteenth-century Mishnah commentator Obadiah Bertinoro left Northern Italy and continued through Sicily and Crete to Egypt before settling in Jerusalem. Alongside these notable personalities were numerous merchants and small-time educators who journeyed long distances habitually.

(ABOVE)

THE STORY OF THE TWELVE SPIES
(NUMBERS XIII).

1106, PROBABLY PERSIA. PARCHMENT. THE JEWISH
NATIONAL AND UNIVERSITY LIBRARY, JERUSALEM.

*The rivalry between the Promised Land
and the Diaspora goes back thousands
of years.*

(OPPOSITE)

EDAD ANTIGUA: COSTUMES
OF THE ANCIENT HEBREWS.
*Throughout the Middle Ages Jews were
distinguishable by their dress.*

In modern times this worldliness only intensified, as immigration reached mass proportions. By the twentieth century Jewish families frequently had at least second-degree relatives outside their own country of residence, and in most cases in a different continent, too. The Soviet Union is believed to have perceived the Jews as a threat because so many of them had relatives in the West.

Surely, during the Middle Ages contacts between far-flung Jewish communities were difficult to maintain, considering transport conditions and the relatively narrow geographic horizons that existed at the time. For instance, historians have questioned the authenticity of a correspondence between Jewish notable Hisdai ibn-Shaprut in tenth-century Muslim Spain and Joseph, king of the central-Asian Khazar kingdom, whose elite had converted to Judaism. Still, even if that document was forged, it was written by another medieval Jew, one whose very asking of a question like "Is there a Jewish kingdom anywhere on earth?"—as that document asks—echoes the Jewish nation's deep awareness of its anomalous dispersal, and a widespread thirst for information about fellow Jews.

EDAD ANTIGUA.—TRAJES DE LOS HEBREOS

זה ספר מסעות שחבר ר' בנימן כ"ר יונה מטורטושה נ"ע

זה ר' בנימין הלך ויחזור ועבר חמלה ולמו והלך וכו מדינות רבות
ומקומות מוסר הוא ומדרש כתוך מפרו וכל מקום שנכנסו בו כתב
כל הדברים שראה וששמע ודבר אנשי אמת ולא נשמעו בעיר ספרד
וכן כיון וזבר קלת החכמים והנשיאים שבכל מקום ומקום וכיון וספר הנה עשו כמו
ואיון קשוקלה פטונ"ל על תקקן. וכאו ר' בנימין הנזבר איש נבון ומשכיל וכעל תורה
והלכה ועל דבר שפרקנו אותו כדי לבשעט וחדי דביו פי'למו ותיקנום ואבותיו וכבים
בתולו כו הוא איש אמת ונהנו תחלת ספרן ◦

וזלה יצאתי וחבדרי מעיר סרקסטא וירדתי דרך חכן לערושאל
וישב הלתכר דרך שני ימים לעבר ורבטה הקדושה ובאו ביאל
ויברכו בקום יונעם לו ועלמו כנבין הבאו וכל הארן ואשר נפק זה
פים. וירחם שני ימים לבדלונה ויש שם קהל קדוש ונשלים חכמים
יום נדולים בכגוך חכמה. וג' שאלתיאל וג' שלמה וג' יוברהם בן חסדאי
יה וייגב של שתם ים וענדים אלוה בסחורה עובדים וכל מדיקומות מידון יוק
ה, לקכילה ויורן מסכנדריזה של ולעיים וכדן יומיל ואין חבריהה ול
עם יפה וחצל לשורה ובה קהל קטן ותהימדים ◦ וושם שלשה ימים,
ר קדושה ועבו ◦ וושם יצמה תורה ולו הראלות ובה חברים עבדלם
מיאש ר' קלונוש בן הנשריו הנדול וג' שרוים ויהויבוד וכטה במוטו
נחלות וקהקעות חיות אחשו העוד וין אדם ⟨…⟩ למושו וחנו בחונך ◦ וברויזם
ד' אברהם וחוש הליברב וג' וכר וג' יהודה ואחרים כנבץ ⟨…⟩ תלוידי חכמים ◦ ויש בה
היזם שלש מאות יהודים ◦ ◦ וונשם וירבת פרסואות לכרוד דיכד ונשם קהל ◦ וכה ת
תלוידי חכמים וכרושם י שלוה חלפתא וג' יוסף וז' נתטול ◦ ◦ וונשם שני ימים לחר
נטא הנקרין וונעו תשלו ◦ והוא ויקום יתב לסחורה קרוב וין הים כון פרסה ◦ ומה מלן
וכל ויקום לסחורה ◦ וונשם וישויעאלו ⟨…⟩ של עורה ולעבדריוה וליכות ומכה וכתה ⟨…⟩
מדן ולעיים וריך ישראל וריך יון ועכו ⟨…⟩ דה ויאכל טריא ויכו לשעות כעבים עלבדיס
שם אמויה על ידי כב ריונכבון ותמשון ◦ וונשם קלויר מבטרים חלוב בכד ונמשלם ל
ראוזן בב יונחש וג' נתן בם בכריה וג' שלויל הרב שלהם וג' שלוהר וג' וזרוכ, וים כנבחת
בתל וירדשות קבעצת לחלוור ◦ וים בנכתם עשירים ונטעי ◦עדך ◦ ◦ ומורדים סכץ לו הכדיו
◦ים ◦ וונשם ארבעת פרסואות לחלן ונשם קהל קדוש וישריאל וישריל ◦ ◦ ◦ נתעיה
זלה ◦ ונם ובוד ובין ◦וחולם ◦ הרב הנדול ◦ ◦ ◦ נחורשת בנו מטרים עבדים ◦ ◦ ◦ וג' יוסף וג' ימן
וג' יעקב וג' יוהדן וג' ◦ ◦ המברוט הנתדש ◦ ◦ יעו על הפכ אחום ולות ◦
וזתוספעה וירע ◦ ◦ חמם בשר וחם ◦ ◦ ◦ וג' משה ◦ ◦ וג' שמושל הדן וג ◦ ◦
וג' שלוה הכן וג' יהורה הנתפו בן ◦ חבדי ◦ ◦ ◦ ◦ הבדים ◦ ◦ ◦ ליוד תתה הל
ויכישן יתכן ◦ ◦ וריוזין יתן וזחרצן שם כבפה ◦ ◦ תיו קהל לו ◦ הי דיחון ◦ ◦
תחדרש ◦ ◦ ונש אנשים חכים ובועם קהלם ◦ ◦ בכלו ◦ ◦ עשורים סבן לו ◦ ◦
ותחקום ◦ ◦ ◦ וונשם שני פרסואות לביושקרש ◦ ◦

Seeking Their Brethren

Metaphorically, that inherently Jewish yearning for long-lost coreligionists and the curiosity concerning their travails are present even in the Pentateuch, when Joseph answered, "I seek my brethren" to a passerby who asked him, "What seekest thou?" (Genesis 13:15–16) or when Moses "went out unto his brethren and looked on their burdens." (Exodus 2:11)

It was that kind of seeking that characterized the journeys of Spanish Jewish merchant Benjamin of Tudela, whose wanderlust took him in the twelfth century through France, Italy, Greece, and Cyprus before he entered the Holy Land. That Jewish version of Marco Polo visited Antioch, Tyre, and Sidon, and went as far east as Mesopotamia and Persia after spending time in Syria and Egypt. Searching after his brethren and wondering about their lives, Benjamin of Tudela carefully recorded in his *Book of Travels* his generation's rabbinical figures, from France to Iraq, and their congregants' occupations—from dyers in southern Italy's Brindisi through farmers in Greece's Mt. Parnassus region to glaziers in Syria's Aleppo.

In Constantinople he noted that the Jews simultaneously enjoyed affluence and suffered oppression by the ruling Byzantines, who routinely assaulted them in the streets. He also mentions tellingly a physical wall that partitioned off the metropolis's five hundred Karaites (Jews who observed the Pentateuch only) and its twenty-five hundred Rabbanites (Jews who followed the legal interpretation of the Mishna and the Talmud). In Baghdad, whose Jewish population he estimated at fifty thousand (a figure scholars doubt), Benjamin of Tudela counted twenty-eight synagogues and ten Talmudic academies. In northwestern Persia, he said, there was a chain of one hundred Jewish communities in the Haftan Mountains.

Contacts between distant communities were not confined to the anecdotal journey of one inquisitive traveler, or to the correspondence of a curious courtier. In fact, Jewish books, ideas, and movements traveled during the Middle Ages through Diaspora communities thousands of miles away from each other, and sank roots so deep that they still bear fruit today. In Western Europe, scholars from Spain and their brethren of the Franco-German lands met on both sides of the Pyrenees, and generated a kind of intellectual cross-fertilization already well before the Expulsion of 1492. For instance, fourteenth-century French sage Rabbi Moses ben-Jacob of Coucy preached in Jewish communities in Spain, while the Spanish educated Maimonides (1135–1204) and Abraham ibn-Ezra (c. 1092–1167) were influential among French Jewish scholars.

A Worldly People

The Jews experienced globalization long before the term was coined. After the Iberian expulsions of 1492 and 1497 Spanish and Portuguese merchants shipped merchandise across the Atlantic and beyond it, benefiting from the existence of a network of *Marrano*

(OPPOSITE)
PAGE FROM BENJAMIN OF TUDELA'S BOOK OF TRAVELS.
The twelfth-century Spanish Jewish traveler's extensive journeys reflected a widespread thirst among Diaspora Jews for information about other Jews in distant countries.

communities on four continents. In the seventeenth century a network of court Jews spread throughout Europe's royal palaces, helping other Jews, and each other, when the need arose.

In the eighteenth century, Frankfort-based Jewish banker Meyer Rothschild, who had made his fortune as a currency and precious-metal trader, located each of his sons in a different European financial center: Nathan in London, Solomon in Vienna, Karl in Naples, and James in Paris, with Anschel succeeding his father as the head of the family's German branch. Economically, this strategy was visionary because it allowed the Rothschilds to mobilize and transfer large sums of money across the continent. Socially, the Rothschilds could embark on this kind of strategy because in each of the chosen destinations there was a Jewish community they could readily join.

In general, communities the world over allowed many Jews to establish themselves in new destinations with less difficulty than other immigrants might have met. That, in a nutshell, was the power of the Jewish Diaspora.

EXILE: THE ULTIMATE PUNISHMENT

The tension between the commitment to the Promised Land and the attraction to the rest of the world was already a defining experience for the Jews in biblical times. Not long after having uprooted himself from his native Haran in Mesopotamia in order to fulfill God's command to go "unto the land that I will show thee," (Genesis 12:1) Abraham moved on to Egypt. The cause of that emigration was momentary and mundane—a famine—but Abraham's grandson, Jacob, saw his twelve sons all migrate to Egypt, where they laid the foundations for the historic experience of Diaspora by staying put even after conditions back in Canaan had improved. Even more peculiar is the case of Moses. His role as the national founding father who delivered the Israelites from slavery and gave them their legal codex was hardly disturbed by his failure to ever set foot in the land of his ancestors and descendants.

Ironically, while they disagreed on almost everything else, pre-modern Jews and Christians agreed that the Jews' loss of the Promised Land was anomalous, deliberate, and part of a divine plan. The Jews' inherent homelessness, vulnerability, and humiliation were reminiscent of Cain's punishment for killing his brother Abel, "a fugitive and a wanderer shalt thou be in the earth," a curse about which Cain himself said: "My punishment is greater than I can bear. Behold, Thou hast driven me out this day from the face of the land; and from Thy face shall I be hid; and I shall be a fugitive and a wanderer in the earth; and it will come to pass, that whosoever findeth me will slay me." (Genesis 4:12–14)

The only difference between Jewish and Christian interpretations of the Jews' landlessness was that the Jews saw their dispersal as a disruption of history, an aberration that would be rectified in the days to come when their sins are atoned for, while Christian theology saw in the Jews' dispersal a punishment for their rejection of Christ and his

The Court Jews

Common myths concerning Jews ostensibly manipulating elaborate international networks could find some support in the rise of the court Jew as Europe entered the modern ages. An institution that emerged at a time when Central Europe was beset by severe economic, military, and political instability (mainly during the seventeenth century, but also before and after), the court Jew offered kings, princes, and dukes indispensable financial savvy and commercial connections that reached far beyond the horizon.

The needs of the time were immense. The Thirty Years' War (1618–1648) suddenly made wartime essentials such as horses, wheat, or gunpowder, not to mention credit, ever more scarce than they were ordinarily. The existing, privileged bureaucracy was often incapable of supplying the goods, certainly not quckly and cheaply. In many cases a local Jew was capable of, available for, and above all eager to be, rendering such services. Jews could mobilize the assistance of fellow Jews in other lands in order to provide what rulers were lacking. That is how the court Jew phenomenon gained momentum.

The court Jew came in handy for ruling powers not only because of the state of emergency in the their relations with neighboring states, but also because of the general transition in Europe from medieval to modern times. During these decades, European leaders, particularly in the German principalities, were at loggerheads with their respective nobilities and sought ways to bypass them and still wield power. The court Jew was ideal for that purpose, since in addition to the many services he could efficiently render as a supplier of credit and goods, he also offered unequivocal loyalty since his dependence on his patron was total.

Culturally, too, though the Enlightenment era and its tolerance had yet to dawn, hostility toward the Jews on the part of nonreligious leaders had

subsided considerably due to the war that devastated much of Central Europe. The Thirty Years' War, which pitted Protestantism against Catholicism, ended inconclusively with a general agreement that each state and principality would simply practice the religion of its ruler. In this kind of setting, the mobilization of Jews in government service was less of an oddity than it might have been during the fervently theocratic Middle Ages, when a powerful and unchallenged church spread among the people anti-Jewish doctrines and forced political leaders to conduct anti-Jewish policies.

For their part, the court Jews also gradually veered away from the traditional Jewish community's norms and shackles. In their dress, language, and culture they radiated a sort of affluence, cosmopolitanism, and broad-mindedness largely unknown to previous generations of Jews. Still, when Maria Theresa of Austria ordered the expulsion of the Jews of Prague in 1744, an elaborate network of court Jews waged a concerted effort to undo the decree. By 1745 the pressure bore fruit, and the expulsion order was reversed.

However, the court Jew's position was perennially precarious, and prone to end tragically. Such was the case of Charles Joseph Suess Oppenheimer. During Alexander of Württemberg's reign in the 1730s, Oppenheimer masterminded an administrative revolution based on meritocracy whereby the privileged classes were sidelined in order to make way for a council of professional ministers that would report directly to the duke. Determined to strengthen the military, develop local industry, and expand the tax base, Oppenheimer ultimately antagonized too many powerful people. When Alexander died, he was arrested and hanged. Though not a practicing Jew, he refused to convert, and died citing the age-old "Hear, O Israel," which Jews traditionally said when about to be murdered for being Jews.

In all, the court Jews shrewdly used relative advantages such as mobility, agility, and contacts, which Jews had developed during centuries of provocation, dislocation, and relocation. However, as Oppenheimer's case attests, their accomplishments by no means signaled the end of the historic Diaspora Jew's social isolation, political weakness, and personal vulnerability.

(ABOVE)

DETAIL OF THE MEDAL DEPICTING THE ARREST AND SHACKLING OF JOSEPH SUESS OPPENHEIMER.
1738, GERMANY. WATERCOLOR AND INK ON PAPER; AND METAL CASE. HEBREW UNION COLLEGE SKIRBALL MUSEUM COLLECTION, SKIRBALL CULTURAL CENTER, LOS ANGELES.

The famous court Jew's dramatic rise and abrupt fall became an emblem of the promise and perils ahead of modern European Jewry.

(OPPOSITE)

THE HANGING OF JOSEPH SUESS OPPENHEIMER.
EIGHTEENTH-CENTURY. ENGRAVING.

disciples' gospel, and a living testimony to Christianity's validity. Consequently, the Jews were not considered natural inhabitants of Christendom, even in lands where they and their ancestors had lived for centuries. Rather, they were simply considered as *servi camerae*, or servants of the king, which meant they would repeatedly obtain and renew permission from local rulers in order to dwell in their lands. As historian Jacob Katz has noted in his book *Tradition and Crisis,* the only controversy in this regard throughout the Middle Ages was over who constituted that authority. In the German lands, for instance, it could have been the Holy Roman Emperor or the burghers, and in Poland it might have been the king or the landed nobility.

That the Jews were guests at best, slaves at worst, went without saying, not only to Christians but to the Jews, too. The Jews prayed every day for the arrival of the Messiah, the ingathering of their distant exiles, and their collective return to Jerusalem, all of which served them as constant reminders that their dispersal was abnormal, divine, and temporary. But while that gave reason to hope for a dramatically different future, in the meantime the Jews saw nothing the matter with their treatment by the Gentiles as guests. "Obviously, the tax we pay for dwelling in their lands is like a rent fee," wrote the eighteenth-century chief rabbi of Bohemia, Yehezkel Landa. "What difference," he asked, "is there for me between paying rent for living in a house or living in a state? In turn for the rent we pay them they tolerate our presence in their midst." (Noda Bi'Yhuda, "Hoshen Mishpat," p. 22)

DESTRUCTION AND RENEWAL

The hardship endured by Jews over the centuries can hardly be exaggerated. "Please God," prayed the tenth-century rabbi Sa'adia Gaon, "let this be the end of your people's, the house of Israel's, captivity, and an end to our exile and mourning." (Sidur Rav Sa'adia Gaon) While they begged for salvation, the Diaspora's Jews continued to suffer, and Jewish communities incessantly fell, rose, and relocated. When Spanish Jewry's two main leaders failed in their last effort to rescind the Expulsion, one of them gave in to the pressure and converted, and the other traveled on. Few moments in Jewish history were so emblematic of the Diaspora's elusive distribution. When one regime persecutes the Jews in one place, explained seventeenth-century Dutch scholar Manasseh ben-Israel (1604–1657), another regime somewhere else will accept the Jews.

Paradoxically, the Jews always seemed to prefer gaining access to yet another horizon to waging eternal war on countries that once persecuted them. *Marrano* Jews, for instance, who had survived the Expulsion, soon helped Portugal obtain its independence. Centuries later, the State of Israel preferred to create formal ties with post-Holocaust Germany rather than foment enmity between the Jewish and German states.

PORTRAIT OF MANASSEH ben-ISRAEL.
REMBRANDT VAN RIJN. ETCHING, 1636. RIJKSMUSEUM, AMSTERDAM.

When Jews are persecuted in one place by one regime, other Jews in another place are being treated favorably, as was the 17th-century scholar from Amsterdam.

"SINAGOGA."
MASTER OF THE ST. URSULA LEGEND. GROENINGEMUSEUM STAD BRUGGE.

"Sinagoga" is the depiction of Judaism as a blindfolded woman supporting herself on a broken staff. Throughout the Middle Ages both Judaism and Christianity agreed that the Jews' dispersal was a divine punishment, which meant that the Jews were merely guests among the Gentiles.

BETWEEN ESCAPE AND MOBILITY

The Jews' ability to survive "rootlessly" made Gentiles embrace the "wandering Jew" stereotype, a character easily rendered as metaphor, which fascinated numerous writers from Goethe to Gorky. Based on a tale about a man who had personally hit Jesus on his way to the crucifixion and was consequently condemned to endlessly roam the world without ever having a patch of it to call his own, this myth haunted Jews and fascinated Gentiles for centuries. Some, such as Christian Schubart (1739–1791) in his *Der ewige Jude*, described the despair that overcame the wandering Jew after he failed to die in battle, fire, and tempest. Others, such as William Wordsworth—shortly after his return from an arduous walking tour of France, where he had an illegitimate child, among other tribulations—echoed through this character their own travails.

So pervasive was the myth about Ahasuerus the wandering Jew, that occasionally someone would claim to have personally seen him. The Schleswig bishop Paulus von Eitzen (d. 1598), for instance, fingered as the wandering Jew a bearded, barefoot, ragged beggar who in 1542 entered a Hamburg church, beat his chest, lowered his head, and sighed deeply whenever he heard Christ's name. Indeed, to medieval Christians, the Jews' lack of land, both collectively and individually, while orchestrated through legislation by the Church itself, nonetheless seemed as natural proof of *Synagoga*'s theological defeat by *Ecclesia*, a living proof of Christian doctrine's truth and God's punishment to those who denied it.

Centuries later, when a paranoid Joseph Stalin sought to deport millions of Jews to the wilderness of Central Asia—a catastrophe averted only by his death—the Soviet propaganda machine depicted assorted Jewish personalities as "rootless cosmopolitans." The way he saw it, the ties that Soviet Jewish actors, writers, and scientists had with the rest of the Jewish Diaspora (through the wartime Jewish Antifascist Committee) were proof that the Jews were an abnormal people and posed a danger to the future of the Soviet Union.

BRACING FOR EXILE

The quest for an apocalypse that would reshape Jewish history began during the times of the prophets and culminated in the Shabbetai Zevi affair, with the hope for the ingathering of the exiles looming large as a central facet of the Jews' anticipated redemption. However, during the struggle with Rome the main thrust of the messianic ideology was about cultural and religious independence, with moderates seeking mere secession from the Roman Empire and extremists espousing various forms of anarchy by altogether dismissing the very notion of human rule in a godly world.

Still, as the clash with Rome accelerated and the loss of the homeland seemed imminent, Rabbi Johanan ben-Zakkai (first century C.E.) was already hard at work equipping the Jews with a survival kit that would last for two millennia and sustain the myriad theological, social, and political challenges. Trapped in Jerusalem when the rationalists within its walls had already concluded that the war with Rome had been lost, ben-Zakkai, according to a Talmudic tradition, sneaked hidden in a coffin through the barriers set up by the Jewish zealots. Once outside the city's walls he met with the Romans—according to one source he met with the overall commander, and future emperor, Vespasian—and was asked what they could do for him. "Give me Jabneh and its scholars," retorted the sage, alluding to a town south of today's Tel Aviv, where he subsequently launched what historian Paul Johnson aptly described as a "great enterprise in social metaphysics."

Ben-Zakkai's self-imposed task was to create for his nation a spiritual compensation for its physical loss, a religious formula that would furnish the Jewish nation with a functional substitute for the Temple that had vanished. By ben-Zakkai's times the Temple had become so central in Jewish theology that many feared that with its disappearance there would be no meaning left to the Jewish faith. Without the sacrificial rituals that the priests used to perform on a daily basis in the Temple, many believed, there would be no vehicle for atonement before God and no place in which to properly practice the laws of the Jewish faith. Moreover, the Sanhedrin, the synod of sages that governed and legislated the Jewish nation's religious affairs, used to hold its sessions on the Temple Mount. What would now become of that?

To address these challenges, ben-Zakkai turned Jabneh into an alternative spiritual and legislative center, transplanting there the Sanhedrin and using it as the new place from which to announce the arrival of each new month to the entire Diaspora. Moreover, ben-Zakkai issued a series of decrees and regulations that made it possible to practice the Jewish faith not only beyond the physical Judea but indeed altogether without it. For instance, blowing the *shofar* is ordinarily forbidden on the Sabbath (as is any other form of playing music), but within the Temple's confines it was permitted, in fact obligatory, to blow the *shofar* on that exceptional Sabbath that would fall once in several years on the Jewish New Year. With the Temple gone, ben-Zakkai decreed that the *shofar* would be blown on such a Sabbath day anywhere, as if it were the Temple.

Similarly, while the Temple existed, farmers who lived within a day's walking distance from Jerusalem had to bring every fourth year's fruit to Jerusalem and eat it there. Ben-Zakkai decreed that such farmers, like those who lived farther afield, could redeem their pilgrimage through a payment.

In all, the ben-Zakkai reforms placed the scholar on a pedestal taller than the former Temple. The self-made sage, whose specialty was the issuance of legal rulings, would replace the Temple era's hereditary priest whose specialty was the performance of rituals. As it prepared for a future where it would lack a land and inhabit the entire world, the Jewish nation brought itself under the leadership of an intellectual elite of jurists whose

Sultan Mehmet II: Diaspora's Rule of Renewal

(ABOVE)

SULTAN MEHMET II.

GENTILE BELLINI. 1453. OIL ON WOOD. THE NATIONAL GALLERY, LONDON.

A generation before the Spanish Expulsion the Ottoman ruler urged Jewish immigrants to move to the newly conquered Constantinople. Gentile Bellini (1429-1507), who was called to Constantinople as a court painter in 1479, painted the portrait the year before Sultan Mehmet II's death.

The Ottoman capture of Constantinople in 1453 signaled a major turning point in the history of the Christian-Muslim balance of power. Never before or since has either of these rival faiths dealt such a severe blow to the other's possessions, confidence and prestige.

Named after Constantine the Great, the Roman emperor who formally recognized Christianity, this ancient Greek metropolis became the capital of the Byzantine Empire in 330 C.E. During the subsequent twelve centuries, that metropolis saw much turmoil, conflict, and siege, most notably between indigenous Greeks and invading Crusaders who for several decades during the thirteenth century established a Latin kingdom there. Throughout those centuries the Jews, while tolerated, were subject to systemic and institutional discrimination by hostile Christian regimes.

This chaos came to an abrupt end with the city's conquest by Sultan Mehmet II (1432–1481). Though ultimately known as "The Conqueror" due to his military campaigns, which nearly doubled the size of the Ottoman Empire, Mehmet was also an intellectual who mastered many languages, including Hebrew, and published a legal codex that laid the foundations for the empire that outlived him by nearly half a millennium.

As he set out to establish a new order in the newly conquered Constantinople, converting its churches into mosques and checkering it with ambitious construction projects, Mehmet also invited the Jews of his empire to migrate to his new capital. "Who among you," he is said to have proclaimed, "of all my people who is with me, may his God be with him, let him ascend to Constantinople, the site of my royal throne. Let him dwell in the best of the land, each beneath his vine and beneath his fig tree, with silver and with gold, with wealth and with cattle. Let him dwell in the land, trade in it, and take possession of it."

While apparently motivated by a desire to diminish the city's previous Christian character and stimulate economic activity there by enlisting Jewish commercial power as an alternative to the Greek elite's sway, Mehmet's move was received so positively by the Jews that it even prompted some to interpret the event in messianic terms. The proclamation indeed touched off a Jewish migration into the Ottoman capital, which, thanks to its combination of tolerance, affluence, and opportunity, quickly emerged as a choice destination for oppressed Jews. While one tax was imposed on the Jews exclusively, the Jews were also given permission to choose their own leader.

By sheer historical coincidence, a generation before the 1492 expulsion of Spanish Jewry Mehmet created a haven for its victims. As has happened so many times throughout the history of the Diaspora, the eclipse of one major Jewish center was compensated for by the rise of another.

Lavater and Lessing Visit
Moses Mendelssohn.
Moritz Daniel Oppenheim. 1856. Frankfurt-am-
Main. Oil on canvas. The Judah L. Magnes
Museum, Berkeley, California. Gift of Vernon
Stroud, Eva Linker, Gerta Nathan, and Ilse
Feiger in memory of Frederick and Edith Straus.

*German philosopher Moses Mendelssohn
with his Christian admirers, Johann
Caspar Lavater and Gotthold Lessing.
As the modern ages dawned, some Jewish
scholars began to tolerate and even
idealize the Jews' dispersal.*

source of authority was merit rather than genealogy. From here on the communal scholar would be the leader of the Diaspora, and the local synagogue would be the "modest sanctuary," or *mikdash me'at*, as Judaism would describe its soon-to-be ubiquitous prayer houses, based on God's consolation to Ezekiel in Babylon, some six centuries before ben-Zakkai's time: "Although I have removed them far off among the nations, and although I have scattered them among the countries, yet have I been to them as a little sanctuary in the countries where they are come." (Ezekiel 11:15)

Soon enough, in the aftermath of the Bar-Kochba Revolt of 135 C.E., as sages fleeing Rome's wrath relocated the Sanhedrin in the Galilean Mountains, the Jabneh model proved a viable alternative not only to Jerusalem but to any of its would-be successors as well. Over the next two centuries new Judaic academies sprouted in the Diaspora itself, between the Tigris and Euphrates rivers, where the study of Judaism reached unprecedented proportions, attracting thousands of students, scholars, and sages who within two centuries generated the monumental Babylonian Talmud. In subsequent centuries, the Diaspora-bred Talmud would be the foundation of Judaic scholarship in newer Jewish centers, first in medieval North Africa, Spain, and France, then in early-modern Central and Eastern Europe.

Thus, the physical destruction that initially seemed like a devastating blow to Judaism could now be seen more like a spiritual nuclear explosion, one that instead of deleting the Jews from human history actually spread them and their faith throughout the world. Nevertheless, the Diaspora experiment came at a prohibitive price, which made modern-day thinkers wonder what it meant, and whether it was worth upholding.

Diaspora as an Ideal

By the nineteenth century, with the Diaspora experience already more than two thousand years old and a brave new age of emancipation dawning across Western Europe, some Jewish thinkers began not only to tolerate the dispersal of their nation but even to idealize it. The way they saw it, the Jews' diffusion and lack of a homeland were indeed an act of Providence, yet one meant not as a punishment to the Jews but as a blessing to the non-Jews.

The roots of this attitude could be traced to the eighteenth-century founders of the Jewish Enlightenment movement who, led by Berlin-based philosopher Moses Mendelssohn (1729–1786), despaired of the prospects for the Jews' return to their ancestral land. Responding to linguist and theologian J. D. Michaelis's charge in 1755 that the Jews were inherently disloyal to the state due to their deep-seated, messianic yearning for another land, Mendelssohn said that the quest for Zion was mainly a matter of liturgy and that the Jews were obliged to defend their respective lands of residence, which he described as their "fatherland."

On another occasion, in 1770, Mendelssohn dismissed as unrealistic a proposal for the establishment of a Jewish state in Palestine. "My people," wrote the scholar who spent much of his time debating and fraternizing with Christian men of letters, "is not adequately prepared to undertake anything great.... The oppression under which we have been living for so many centuries has deprived our spirit of all its vigor ... the natural instinct for freedom has lost among all of us its active drive." (See I. E. Barzilay, "Mendelssohn and Jewish Nationalism," *Jewish Quarterly Review,* 52, p. 185.) Besides requiring financial and spiritual resources that he thought the Jews of his time lacked, Mendelssohn also believed that an attempt to restore Palestine to the Jews would be torpedoed early on by some superpower. Still, while he lost hope of rebuilding a political Zion, Mendelssohn did not lose his faith in the spiritual Zion. That mental departure would be the lot of his self-styled followers, the founders of the Reform movement.

Unlike Mendelssohn, who had not experienced emancipation and for whom messianic notions were theoretical if not altogether alien, Judaism's radical reformers believed the messianic age had actually dawned, in their time, with the victory of emancipation. The way they saw it, Christian society's expanding acceptance of the Jews as equal citizens, and Judaism's emerging legitimacy and respectability in the eyes of Christians, meant that the Jews' dispersal was now not only tolerable in terms of Jewish theology but indeed desirable. "The national existence of the Jews ceased when the Romans set the Temple aflame and destroyed Jerusalem," wrote David Philipson (1862–1949), an American historian and pioneer in the Reform movement. "The career in Palestine was but a preparation for Israel's work in all portions of the world.... Palestine is a precious memory of the past, but it is not a hope for the future." In 1885, a conference of Reform rabbis in Pittsburgh concluded that the Jews' scattering was part of a divine plan to disperse the Jews the world over "for the realization of their highly priestly mission." Kaufman Kohler (1843–1926), the German-born longtime leader of the U.S. Reform movement, hoped that those who still sought a return to Zion would recognize "the power, the hope, and the refuge of Israel in its God, and not in any territorial possession."

However, there were also secular voices idealizing the Diaspora. Foremost among them was historian Simon Dubnow. Born in White Russia in 1860, he later moved, initially illegally, to St. Petersburg, where he stayed until after the Bolshevik Revolution before proceeding to Berlin in 1922, only to leave it after Hitler's rise to power, and finally settle in Riga, Latvia. There, when the Germans invaded in 1941, he was murdered by a Gestapo officer who was once his student.

That this quintessentially exilic aftermath of discrimination, displacement, and dismemberment would befall a man who spent a lifetime idealizing the Diaspora was, of course, ironic. Still, as a scholar Dubnow disabused the Hasidic movement—an emblem of Diaspora life—of the intellectual disrepute to which it had been condemned by the

(OPPOSITE)
RABBI ISAAC MAYER WISE'S PLUM STREET TEMPLE B'NAI YESHRUN, CINCINNATI.
HENRY MOSLER. 1866. OIL ON CANVAS.
HUC SKIRBALL CULTURAL CENTER MUSEUM COLLECTION, LOS ANGELES.
Wise deleted from his prayer book references to the Jews' return to Zion.

founders of modern Jewish historiography. In his "great centers" thesis, Dubnow argued that throughout its history the Diaspora produced every several centuries a new hegemonic center that eclipsed its predecessor as the Jewish people's demographic, spiritual, and material center. Thus, the Hellenistic era's Land of Israel was eclipsed by Babylon, which then gave way to Spain and the Rhineland, which were later succeeded by Poland-Lithuania.

Dubnow's hope, that the next great center would be in the Polish-Russian sphere, proved tragically illusory. Yet the rise of the American and Israeli centers, along with the intrinsic weaknesses of assimilation in the former and war in the latter, still leave Dubnow's thesis as a thought-provoking challenge to classical Zionism's dogma, that the Jews' only future lies in their ancestral land.

Dubnow's pro-Diaspora attitude was further developed by historian Salo Baron (1895–1989), who was born in Galicia but spent most of his life in the United Sates. If Dubnow emphasized the Diaspora's bright future, Baron did the same to its past, by attacking in 1926 what he described as "the lachrymose conception of Jewish history." In Baron's view, the Jews' suffering since the destruction of the Temple was overly stressed by his predecessors. Moreover, historians such as Dubnow and Heinrich Graetz (1817–1891), he argued, went overboard in portraying medieval Jewry as historically passive.

Still, Baron's critique notwithstanding, Dubnow's thesis glorified the Diaspora, hailing it as a unique Jewish invention, a condition that may have originally stemmed from the constraints dictated by the loss of sovereignty, but one that ultimately rendered "statehood, land, military, all the external attributes of a national power" superfluous to the Jews.

The idealization of the Jews' dispersal even has some anecdotal support in early rabbinical sources. The Talmudic sage Rabbi Oshaia, for instance, said the Jews' dispersal actually saved them from complete annihilation, and therefore "God did justice with the nation of Israel in scattering them among the nations." Other sages compared the Jews to "a flask of perfume," whose good smell spreads only when dispersed into the air. (Shir Hashirim Rabba, I; 4.)

RECONCILING ZION AND BABYLON

Most Jews refused to formally part ways with their ancestral land, even if they were not prepared to actually move there. For the Jewish masses in Europe, not to mention those in the Middle East, the Land of Israel remained divine and inspiring. Still, even those who yearned for a return often agreed that transforming the Promised Land into a modern state that could accommodate millions was not feasible.

One such Jew, a scholar from Odessa named Asher Ginsberg, who became better known by his pen name Ahad Ha-Am (1856–1927), offered a formula that would

(ABOVE)

SIMON DUBNOW.

POSTCARD.

The great Jewish historian, who was murdered during the Nazi invasion of Latvia, believed that the Diaspora brought out the best in the Jews, and that the Jews learned to survive as a nation even without political power.

reconcile Zion's spiritual qualities while leaving the Diaspora intact. Palestine, he claimed, was no longer suitable as a place for the entire Jewish nation, and a Jewish state would inevitably become embroiled in the kind of power plays, wars, and plots that characterize the business of statehood. Still, the Land of Israel could play a role in modern Jewish history as a spiritual center for the Jews of the world. As such, it should host research and educational institutions where thousands of Jews would come from the Diaspora to create and study before returning to their respective countries. Alongside that spiritual center would be a permanent but compact community of scholars, farmers, and merchants.

In other words, if mainstream Zionism sought to rewind Jewish history to before the destruction of the Temple, when the Diaspora was inferior to Zion, spiritual Zionism made do with rewinding history to just after that time, when, under ben-Zakkai's leadership, Zion's scholars led the Jewish nation spiritually from its ancestral land, despite their lack of political control over it.

DIASPORA AS ANATHEMA

For most early Zionists, however, the Jews' dispersal seemed like a deformity whose only remedy was its abolition. In their view, the dispersal was the root of the Jews' tragic condition as a pariah nation, and the only way to offset that condition was to gather the Jews in their ancestral land. The Diaspora Jew's attempt to "belong" among the Gentiles had failed, asserted Leon Pinsker (1821–1891), a Russian Jew stirred to action in the early 1880s by the pogroms in southern Russia. "For the living," he wrote in his *Auto-Emancipation: A Warning of a Russian Jew to his Brethren* (1882), "the Jew is a dead man; for the natives, an alien and a vagrant; for property holders, a beggar; for the poor, an exploiter and a millionaire, for the patriot, a man without country."

Austro-Hungarian journalist and playwright Theodor Herzl (1860–1904) concurred, saying that the Jews' "honest attempts" to integrate with the nations among whom they lived had failed. "In vain do we exert ourselves to increase the glory of our forefathers by achievements in art and in science and their wealth by our contributions to commerce," wrote the Zionist movement's founding prophet in his groundbreaking *Der Judenstaat* (1896). "We are denounced as strangers." Indeed, the way Herzl saw it, the Jews' dispersal was so anomalous that it would always generate hostility, and that antagonism, in turn, would always keep the idea of a Jewish state both relevant and indispensable.

Even more sweepingly anti-Diaspora were the Lithuanian-born historian Joseph Klausner (1874–1958) and the Russian-born historian Benzion Dinur (1884–1973). The former advocated "a completely radical Hebrew movement, seeking a complete revolution in Israelite life—a revolt against *galut*, the Hebrew term for "exile" and Zionist code word for the Diaspora's historic humiliation and dehumanization. Dinur believed the Jewish people had been thrown out of their natural, historical orbit in the wake of

A. Ginzburg (Achad-Haam). (אחד-העם) א. גינזבורג

חברת „לבנון" פֿ 29 א

(ABOVE)

ASHER GINSBERG.
The Zionist thinker, who moved to Tel Aviv in 1922 and became better known by his pseudonym Ahad Ha-Am, thought that only a select few of the Jewish nation should actually reside in the Land of Israel.

their dispersal, and began "returning to history" only in the year 1700, when a relatively sizable group of Jews arrived in the Holy Land. Though that group was religiously motivated and led by the mystic rabbi Yehuda Hassid, Dinur believed it heralded the Jews' restoration of their sovereignty over their ancestral homeland, and, by extension, the Jewish nation's return to normality.

Ironically, this harsh critique of the Diaspora was shared by modern anti-Semitism. Canards such as the late-nineteenth-century forgery *The Protocols of the Elders of Zion*, which alleged that a secret, international Jewish leadership is working to seize control of the world, further fanned widespread beliefs that behind the Jews' disjointed geography lurks a very cohesive nationality whose leaders meet secretly and regularly in order to conspire against humanity. Marxist anti-Semites believed the most characteristic Jews were the Rothschilds, and capitalist anti-Semites saw in Bolshevik leader Leon Trotsky the quintessential Jew, yet both schools shared the blind belief that behind the Jews' ubiquity lurked a conspiracy to take over the rest of the world.

Ironically, and as if to both mock and vindicate the anti-Semitic belief in a global Jewish conspiracy, a multi-national group of Jews played a major role in inventing the bomb that ended the war that targeted their people.

First, Italian physicist Enrico Fermi (1901–1954)—whose study of nuclear reactions and discovery of radioactive elements generated by bombardment with neutrons were landmarks en route to the atomic bomb—was married to a Jew, Laura. The two were therefore compelled to flee the Nazi-Fascist sphere, proceeding in 1938 to the United States directly from Stockholm, where he had just received the Nobel Prize. In the United States Fermi eventually teamed up with Danish-Jewish physicist Niels Bohr (1885–1962), a fellow Nobel laureate, who in 1943 had fled Copenhagen to Sweden on a fishing boat.

Aided by information smuggled earlier by the German scientist Otto Hahn's Jewish companion, Lise Meitner (1878–1968), concerning the Third Reich's efforts in nuclear research, and joined by the Jewish Hungarian-American physicist Leo Szilard (1898–1964), who, while in London after fleeing Nazi Germany, had discovered the neutron chain reaction, these and other scientists, including prominent Zionist Albert Einstein (1879–1955), sent to President Franklin D. Roosevelt the letter that eventually produced the Manhattan Project. Based in Los Alamos, New Mexico, and led by Robert Oppenheimer (1904–1967), son of a German-Jewish immigrant to the United States, that forum ended up giving the Allies the nuclear bomb that dealt fascism its ultimate deathblow.

Thus, a group of Jews from Hungary, Germany, Italy, and Denmark who teamed up in the United States defeated the totalitarian axis that sought to eradicate their nation. In their origins, plight, cooperation, and accomplishments, these scientists and their supporters also encapsulated the Jewish experience of Diaspora.

(ABOVE)
DAVID BEN-GURION AND
ALBERT EINSTEIN.
The great physicist was part of a group of Jewish scientists from assorted countries who helped decide the outcome of World War II by participating in the invention of the atom bomb.

(OPPOSITE)
MOSES HANDS OVER
HIS ROD TO HERZL.
J. OLIVELLA. 1901. BUENOS AIRES, ARGENTINA. ILLUSTRATION ON THE COVER OF A BOOK OF PRAISES GIVEN TO HERZL BY MEMBERS OF THE ZIONIST ASSOCIATION AHVA IN BUENOS AIRES ON THE OCCASION OF THE FIFTH ZIONIST CONGRESS.
Herzl thought the Jews must have a state because assimilation had failed.

THE DIASPORA IN THE EAST

The destruction of the Temple in 70 C.E. abruptly ended the pilgrimages that used to bring Diaspora Jews to Jerusalem in throngs three times a year. That alone cast a shadow over the Judean sages' ability to maintain their religious leadership of the Jewish people. Still, having destroyed Jerusalem, the Romans did not immediately set out to storm Judea itself, nor its inhabitants. That would happen only in the wake of the Bar-Kochba Revolt, which began in 132 and ended three years later in colossal calamity for the Jews.

By the time the rebels lost their last outpost—Betar, just outside current Jerusalem's southwestern outskirts—the Romans had destroyed nearly a thousand Jewish settlements and killed more than half a million Jews, according to the Roman historian Dio Cassius's *Romaika*. Thousands of others who did not die on the battlefield lost their lives in the wake of the general mayhem caused by the war, and additional thousands were captured and shipped far beyond the Land of Israel. In the aftermath of the Bar-Kochba Revolt the Romans, under Emperor Hadrian, had become so suspicious of the Jews' potential for rebellion that they changed Judea's name—to Syria Palestine—and made of Jerusalem an idolatrous town called Aelia Capitolina, where Jews were forbidden not only to reside, but even to set foot. (This prohibition was eased only on the Ninth of Av, the annual fast day during which Jews lament the Temple's destruction.) A host of anti-Jewish decrees imposed only in the Land of Israel, from prohibitions on circumcising children to bans on rabbinical assemblies, further weighed on Judea's centrality in the Jewish people's life.

Thus, a physical crippling that both shrank the Jewish people as a whole and depleted the Jewish community in the Land of Israel itself now complemented the national catastrophe that began with the psychological trauma of the Temple's destruction. Judea itself was, by the second half of the second century, scorched earth that had lost the ability to host a large-scale, let alone universally inspiring, Jewish community.

(ABOVE)
IVORY POMEGRANATE.
EIGHTH CENTURY, B.C.E. IVORY. THE ISRAEL MUSEUM, JERUSALEM.
This piece is the only known object attributed to King Solomon's Temple. Solomon's foreign endeavors stretched from current-day Lebanon to the Horn of Africa, but the Jewish eastward migration only began in the wake of the Temple's destruction.

(OPPOSITE)
INTRODUCTION TO SECTION II FROM MOSES MAIMONIDES' *Guide for the Perplexed.*
C. 1470. MS. HEB. 685, FOL. 58. BIBLIOTHÈQUE NATIONALE, PARIS.
The philosopher, jurist, and physician widely seen as the Diaspora's greatest scholar ever, wrote in Arabic and was the product of the Muslim universe.

ARCH OF TITUS (DETAIL).

81 C.E. ENLARGED RELIEF OF THE ARCH OF TITUS AT THE ENTRANCE TO THE PERMANENT EXHIBITION OF BETH HATEFUTSOTH, TEL AVIV.

This detail portrays the Temple vessels, with the Menorah in the center, being carried in a triumphal procession by Roman soldiers in the street of Rome in 70. C.E. The most lasting blow to the Jewish presence in the Land of Israel came in the wake of the Bar-Kochba Revolt, sixty-five years after the Temple's destruction.

THE BABYLONIAN FLOURISHING

As historical coincidence goes, just when Mesopotamian rulers stormed westwards and southwards, trampling among others the biblical kingdoms of Israel and Judah, an altogether external power, Persia, was rising beyond Babylon's eastern horizon. Soon enough it swept and redefined all that lay not only between, but also far beyond, the Tigris and Euphrates rivers.

Cyrus, the great founder of the kingdom that would stretch from the Aegean Sea to the doorstep of India (and whose center was initially in Susa, or Shushan, as it is called in the Book of Esther, some 500 kilometers south of today's Tehran), did not share the Assyrians' and Babylonians' hostility toward foreign cultures and nations. In fact, he believed in the power of tolerance and the merits of pluralism, and set out to undo the legacies of the Mesopotamian conquerors by restoring exiled nations to their ancestral lands and encouraging them to practice their respective faiths. This policy breathed new Jewish life into the Promised Land and helped lay the foundations for a monumental Jewish center that would leave an indelible imprint on the history of the Jews.

(LEFT)
LINTEL WITH THE ARK OF
THE COVENANT FROM THE
CAPERNAUM SYNAGOGUE.
FOURTH-FIFTH CENTURY C.E. LIMESTONE.
*The Capernaum Synagogue is located off
the southern shore of Lake Kinneret.
Following the Destruction Judaism's
spiritual center first gravitated west, to
Yavne, then north, to the Galilee.*

In early historic times the exceptionally fertile land between the Tigris and
Euphrates became host to advanced civilizations (the Book of Genesis locates the Garden
of Eden here). This is where urban civilization began, where writing was invented (by the
Sumerians in the fourth millennium B.C.E.), where Hammurabi introduced his legal
codex (in the second millennium B.C.E.), and where the foundations for the sciences of
mathematics and astronomy were laid.

From a Jewish perspective, however, Babylonia's significance was in the political
counterbalance and cultural hinterland it ultimately offered the Jews during the late
Roman era and the early Middle Ages, as an increasingly Christian Mediterranean basin
was fast becoming hostile to the Jewish faith.

During the second century, when Jews along the eastern Mediterranean basin
rebelled against the Roman emperor Trajan, Mesopotamian Jewry also confronted the
Romans. However, they did so under much more favorable circumstances, since they
were not on the kind of bad terms that cast a shadow over Jewish-Greek relations in cities
such as Alexandria and Cyrene. In fact, Babylonian Jews joined their non-Jewish

(LEFT)

ISRAELITES BEING EXILED BY
THE ASSYRIANS (DETAIL).
FROM A RELIEF IN THE PALACE OF SENNACHERIB AT
NINEVEH, IRAQ. 701 B.C.E. BRITISH MUSEUM, LONDON.

*Throughout the ancient era, the Israelites
and Jews settled more solidly in the Land
of Israel's mountainous areas, while the
Diaspora developed mainly in cities and
along major trade routes.*

(OPPOSITE)

SARCOPHAGUS IN THE BEIT
SHE'ARIM CATACOMB.
THIRD CENTURY C.E. CARVED STONE.

The legal codex, the Mishna, compiled in this Galilean town the century after the Destruction, eventually governed much of the Diaspora's day-to-day life.

neighbors in fending off the Roman effort to ultimately reach the Parthian Empire. Moreover, in Mesopotamia the anti-Roman effort was crowned a success, as Trajan abandoned his plans to further confront Parthia.

When Constantine the Great recognized Christianity in 313, Babylonian Jewry—though not always relieved of its own share of hardship—remained unaffected by the rise of a religion that, with the backing of a superpower, set out to discredit the Jews and disinherit them of their faith. Babylonian Jewry, clearly benefiting from their acceptance by the surrounding population, had a respectable and powerful political leadership headed by an Exilarch—or *Reish Galuta,* at they were called in Aramaic—whom the Jews regarded as descendants of King David.

This situation did not change fundamentally after the fall in 224 of Mesopotamia to the Sassanians, though their impassioned Zoroastrian faith did, in the fifth century, lead to some religious persecution. That zeal, while generally focused on Christianity, led also to occasional anti-Jewish decrees, including at one point (in 455) a prohibition on the observance of the Sabbath.

On the whole, however, Jewish quasi-autonomy was left intact, as was the Exilarch's status as a senior official who was part of the Persian royal apparatus. While Christianity dawned elsewhere, in this part of the world the Jews generally suffered no persecution, whether through the imposition of special taxes or a prohibition on practicing various professions. The Jews of Babylonia, including many of the sages who wrote the Talmud, were largely farmers who made a living from tilling the famously fertile soils between the Tigris and Euphrates.

That was the general setting within which the great world of Babylonian rabbinical learning developed and flourished for the better part of the first millennium C.E. Here, from Nisibis in the north to Sura, Pumbedita, Nehardea, and Mekhoza some 500 kilometers south of there, near today's Baghdad, religious academies, or *yeshivot,* flourished beginning in the third century C.E. In many of these cities the Jews constituted the majority of the population, and when combined they added up to such a dominant force that the Mishna uses the generic exile to refer specifically to Babylonia.

Clearly, the destruction that was wrought on the Land of Israel in the wake of the Bar-Kochba Revolt generated a refugee movement, particularly of members of the spiritual elite who had the most to fear as long as they remained within reach of Rome's long arm. Such individuals, once in Mesopotamia, gradually led a previously unassuming community to a Judaic prominence that has been monumentalized by the voluminous Babylonian Talmud, edited in the fifth century. Ultimately the Babylonian diaspora reached such heights of intellectual accomplishment that it actually challenged, and indeed overpowered, the Land of Israel's rabbinical elite.

The major path-breaker in the making of Babylonia's scholarly leadership was Rabbi Abba bar-Aivu, who was known simply as Rav (Rabbi), because he was—in the words of

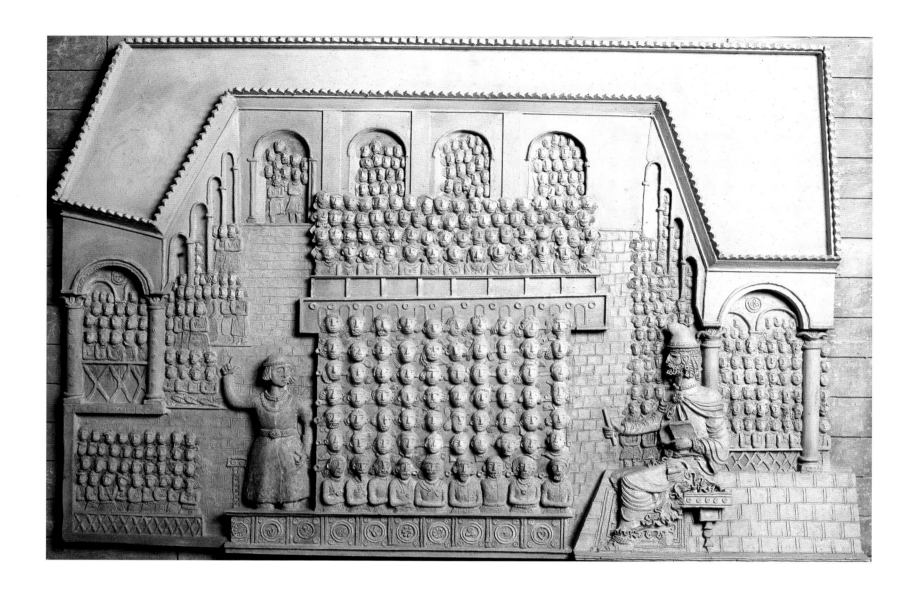

medieval sage and commentator Rashi (1040–1105)—"the grand teacher of all sons of the Diaspora." Born roughly a generation after the Bar-Kochba Revolt in the southern Babylonian town of Kafri to a prominent family that traced its origins to King David, the young Rav went to study Jewish law in the Lower Galilee village of Beit Shearim, just east of today's Israeli seaport town Haifa. His teacher was none other than the great compiler of the Mishna, Rabbi Judah ha-Nasi.

The Roman destruction of the Land of Israel's Jewish towns had been less systematic and comprehensive in the Galilean mountains, which fell to the Romans early in the Bar-Kochba Revolt. As soon as Emperor Hadrian died in 138 C.E. and the pressure against practicing Judaism eased, new centers of scholarship sprouted in various northern towns, from Bet-Shearim in the west to Tiberias in the east, each succeeding in its turn Rabbi Johanan ben-Zakkai's spiritual center of Jabneh. Even the forum that decided when a new month actually began—a crucial function that affected all Jewish observance throughout the Diaspora—migrated from the Judean to the Galilean mountains.

The sages, synagogues, and religious rulings that gradually became the mainstay of Jewish existence without a Temple were joined by what would become the Diaspora's ultimate spiritual road map: the Mishna. Edited in the Lower Galilee by Rabbi Judah ha-Nasi, this work added up to a codex of the laws transmitted orally during previous centuries. Researchers are not sure whether Rabbi Judah ha-Nasi (135–220) actually wrote the codex, as Moses Maimonides (1135–1204) and others have claimed, or whether later scholars did the actual writing, as Rashi believed. Treating all legal aspects of a ritual, moral, individual, and communal Jewish life, from civil and criminal law to holiday observance, daily prayer, and ethical behavior, the Mishna would become the basis for centuries of Judaic scholarship.

In a profoundly symbolic encounter, the Galilean-based editor of the Mishna and the Babylonian-based founder of Talmudic scholarship studied together in the Land of Israel, where the latter came for a period of study.

Upon his return to Babylonia in 219, Rav went to Nehardea but soon enough he proceeded south, to Sura, a town just outside today's Baghdad, which had already become home to thousands of Jews who were largely removed from the spiritual leadership of the established academies farther to the north. Soon enough, Rav's new academy had twelve hundred permanent students, who helped establish Rav's status as the undisputed spiritual leader of Babylonian Jewry.

In the following decades, Rav's Sura Academy and his soul-mate Shmuel's Nehardea Academy were joined by Rabbi Judah bar-Yehezkel's Pumbedita Academy. Together this sort of Jewish Ivy League formed along the Euphrates River an intellectual powerhouse where Judaism's sacred laws, texts, and traditions were interpreted and taught by generations of sages until they were compiled in writing, in the Sura Academy, while it was headed by Rabbi Ashi (371–427). That work became known as the Babylonian Talmud and overpowered the

(OPPOSITE, TOP)
"STUDY MONTH" AT THE SURA ACADEMY, BABYLONIA.
FIFTH CENTURY C.E. BETH HATEFUTSOTH, TEL AVIV.
The relief depicts the structure of the Babylonian Academy and its hierarchy, and the many visitors who came to participate in the study month. During the third century C. E. there were some 1,200 students in this academy alone, and thousands more in a series of academies along the Euphrates River.

(OPPOSITE, BOTTOM)
BET ALPHA SYNAGOGUE FLOOR MOSAIC.
SIXTH CENTURY C.E. UNEARTHED 1929, JEZREEL.
The rise of Babylonian Jewry was enabled by Christianity's failure to conquer Mesopotamia at a time when the practice of Judaism in the Land of Israel was becoming increasingly difficult. The best-preserved synagogue floor with a tripartite composition, Bet Alpha is also significant because the artist is identified. An inscription states that Marianos and his son Hanina made this floor during the reign of Emperor Justinian (518–527). The liberal approach to making art at a time is evidence by the elaborate iconographic program and the use of the human figure. The mosaic includes a depiction of the binding of Isaac, the zodiac cycle, and an iconographic program with the Ark of the Covenant and Temple implements.

The Great Eagle: Moses Maimonides

Few individual life stories encapsulate the experience of medieval Jewry in the Middle East as does that of twelfth-century philosopher, doctor and rabbinical giant Moses Maimonides (1135–1204).

Geographically, Maimonides spanned an extensive swathe of his time's Muslim universe, having hailed from its westernmost reaches in Spanish Cordoba, and later journeyed between Fez, Morocco, where he spent the second half of his twenties; the Land of Israel, where he spent a few months before settling down in Egypt; and Fostat, Egypt, where he spent the last, and best, four decades of his life. Moses' brother David, an international merchant, sailed much farther, and in fact was on his way to Islam's easternmost corner, Sumatra, when he drowned in a shipwreck.

Politically, Maimonides experienced first-hand both Islam's tolerance and intolerance toward Judaism. Initially, he and his family were forced to practice their faith in secret, after Cordoba's conquest by the Almohad sect. The family therefore moved to Fez, hoping it could more efficiently hide its Jewishness where it was anonymous. However, when one of Maimonides' teachers, Judah ibn-Shoshan, was executed for practicing Judaism, the chose to move on.

In Egypt, by contrast, Jews were free at the time to practice their faith provided they never previously adopted the Muslim faith. Indeed, Maimonides' faith was no obstacle to his appointment as personal physician to the great Muslim conqueror and Egyptian ruler, Saladin.

Economically, Miamonides' fate was emblematic of Middle Eastern Jewry's reluctance, in the era following the Babylonian academies' golden age, to bestow privileges on scholars. After his brother's death, which left Maimonides destitute, he supported himself as a physician. Though made when he was already in his thirties,

that career choice quickly earned Maimonides the reputation that soon landed him in Saladin's court.

However, what immortalized Maimonides was his religious writing, a massive corpus whose scope, depth, and impact are considered, until today, unique in all of Jewish history. Having studied extensively, already in Spain, the Mishna, Talmud, Greek philosophy, medicine, and astronomy, Maimonides was only sixteen when he wrote his first work, *Milot ha-Higayon*, a study in the terminology of the philosophy of logic and metaphysics, and thirty-three when he completed, after a decade's work, his commentary on the Mishna. Written in Arabic, the commentary included introductory essays, as well as the Thirteen Articles of Faith, a pioneering attempt to summarize in a few paragraphs what Judaism expects its followers to believe.

Yet Maimonides' most monumental work was the comprehensive legal codex Mishneh Torah ("A Torah Review"), which was written over the next decade, in Hebrew. This work served as the basic term of reference for Joseph Caro's *Shulhan Arukh*, which was written in the Land of Israel nearly four centuries later.

In philosophy, Maimonides' major work, *The Guide for the Perplexed*, took fifteen years to write and was completed in 1191, when he was fifty-six. Written in Arabic and aimed at reconciling faith with science and philosophy, it was later translated into numerous languages and left a profound impact on religious thinking, both within and beyond Judaism, though initially it was greeted by conservatives with suspicion, and at one point (after Maimonides' death) was also banned and even burned as heresy. Like his medical guides, Maimonides' philosophical writings remain relevant, and widely studied, even today.

Despite his extensive intellectual activity and medical practice, Maimonides was also involved in actual leadership. In a letter written during his

Moroccan period he offered solace and advice to Jews facing pressure to convert, ruling that they should emigrate to tolerant countries but adding that a certain (unnamed) rabbi who was being harsh with those who chose to observe Judaism underground and Islam outwardly, was in no position to pass such criticism since he had not himself faced their predicament. Decades later, when he was already established as Egyptian Jewry's leader, he helped Yemenite Jewry confront pressured to convert. Yemenite Jews consequently became so indebted to him that during his lifetime they mentioned Maimonides' name whenever reciting the Kaddish prayer. Indeed, Maimonides' leadership was felt throughout much of his time's Diaspora, and he corresponded with numerous rabbis and communities, from Iraq to France. In Egypt itself it is unclear to what extent Maimonides actually led the local Jewish community, but Arabic sources described him as "leader of the Jews," while Jews across the Diaspora called him "the Great Eagle." Apparently, Moses Maimonides wielded as much pan-Jewish moral clout as medieval circumstances could allow.

(OPPOSITE)
LETTER SIGNED BY MAIMONIDES REQUESTING FUNDS TO REDEEM HOSTAGES.
1170. EGYPT. MS. 8254. LIBRARY OF THE JEWISH THEOLOGICAL SEMINARY OF AMERICA, NEW YORK.
Despite his extensive intellectual activity, Maimonides was also involved in actual leadership. The hostages at stake here were captured in November 1168 in Bilbays, Egypt, by Amalric I, the crusader king, who was in Jerusalem. The letter's scribe was Mevorakh ben Nathan.

parallel work compiled in the Land of Israel (now known as the Jerusalem Talmud). The Babylonian Talmud became the mainstay of Jewish learning and went with the Jews throughout their arduous journeys among countless cities, countries, and continents.

The Babylonian academies were well-organized institutions, with a strict internal hierarchy whereby the first few rows in an academy's main auditorium were reserved for its seventy leading scholars, followed by several hundred permanent students, and closing with a number of rows where classes were given to occasional students. The academies received inquiries from across the Diaspora about Jewish observance, generally attesting to their universally accepted intellectual prominence.

By the Arab conquest in the seventh century, however, the material condition of Babylonian Jewry began gradually deteriorating. In the following centuries, Baghdad's demise as the epicenter of the Islamic world and the simultaneous rise of new caliphates from Persia and Egypt to Morocco and Spain generated a Jewish emigration that, by the eleventh century, effectively ended Babylonia's dominance over the Diaspora.

The Talmud says that before bidding farewell to his great disciple, Rabbi Judah ha-Nasi authorized Rav to make financial and ritual rulings without consulting other sages, including those of the Land of Israel. We can only wonder whether the mentor nd his disciple realized that they were, in effect, passing on the baton of Judaic scholarly leadership from the Land of Israel to the Diaspora, where it would remain until the Holocaust.

THE DECLINE OF THE HOLY LAND

Perhaps the most symbolic landmark in the Land of Israel's declining role in Jewish history was the effective abolition of the *ne'siut*, or patriarchy, by a rapidly Christianizing Roman Empire. That institution, through which Rome delegated to the Jews some functions of tax collection and spending, was led by a dynasty that traced its origins to Kind David. When the patriarchy lost its taxation privileges following a decree by Emperor Theodosius II in 429, the land the Romans called Palestine was being dotted by dozens of monasteries and churches. Collectively, these heralded a potent de-Judaizing era in the Holy Land. Replete with legislation, propaganda, and pogroms aimed at assaulting the nation and faith that Christianity accused of killing Christ, the Byzantine period saw the culmination of the disengagement between the Jews and their ancestral land. That is how the uprooting by pagan Romans determined to crush Jewish independence and prominence began. That effort was later intensified by Byzantine Christians bent on humiliating the Jewish faith.

By the time the Muslims conquered Jerusalem in 637–638, following two centuries during which synagogues were routinely burned down and building new ones was legally forbidden, Palestine's Jews had been humiliated and persecuted to such an extent that their numbers, stature, and spirit deteriorated beyond repair.

(ABOVE)

MODEL OF BAGHDAD'S GREAT SYNAGOGUE, SLAT-LI-KBIGHI.
THE BABYLONIAN JEWRY HERITAGE CENTER, TEL AVIV.

According to local tradition, the synagogue was built with ashes brought from the ruins of the first Temple in Jerusalem. The decline of Babylonian Jewry in the Middle Ages did not stem from Jewish circumstances but from Baghdad's decline as the center of the Islamic world.

(ABOVE)

SUCCESSIVE BATTLES FOR
JERUSALEM WAGED BY THE
PERSIANS (614), BYZANTINES (629),
AND ARABS (638).
WALL PAINTING. BETH HATEFUTSOTH, TEL AVIV.
*Of all the Holy Land's numerous rulers,
from Rome to Britain, the crusaders
dealt the most severe blow to
Jewish settlements.*

Yet the ultimate blow to the Jewish presence in the Land of Israel was dealt much later, by the Crusader kingdom of the twelfth century. Scholars believe that fewer than two thousand Jews lived west of the Jordan River during this period of time. Still, that void was not created overnight but rather was the aftermath of a lengthy period of steady decline.

Indeed, throughout the 450 years of Muslim rule that bridged the Crusader and Byzantine periods, the Jews' overall presence in the Land of Israel continued to shrink. Even the lifting of the Christian ban on Jewish residence in Jerusalem soon after Jerusalem's conquest by Caliph Omar I (637–638) and the subsequent opening in Jerusalem of the Talmudic academy Eretz Ha-Tzvi ("Land of the Deer") did not signify a true rehabilitation of the Jewish presence in the Land of Israel.

Paradoxically, this decline took place not despite but because of the Muslims' relatively indifferent attitude to the Holy Land. Unlike Christianity, which in all its

נגמר ספר הראשון באש חהוא ספר המדע יהמנהב

הלכות יסודי התורה עשרה פרקים הלכות רעות שבעה הלכות תלמוד תורה שבעה פרקים הלכותען שם עשר פרקים
הלכות תשובה עשרה פרקים וגושן פרקים של ספרזה ששה וארבעים

יבהיאהבתיתורתהר בלהזם היא אשיהתי ספר שיניהוא ספר

הלכתיו שש וזה סדריו הלכותקריית שוזוע הלכות תפליה וברכת הזמם הלכות תפלין ומזווה וספר תורה הלכות ציצת הלכן
הלכות פסות הלכות מילה

הלכות קריית שמע

פרק ראשון

וארם

versions attributed a special significance to the Promised Land, for the great Islamic caliphates it was but another region in a landmass that stretched from Central Asia to Western Europe. The result was a marginalization that left the land—particularly after the Muslim center of gravity shifted farther east, from Damascus to Baghdad—too commercially provincial to support a substantial Jewish restoration. If anything, the Muslim universe's vast expanses, and its newly cohesive trade and travel routes, resulted in massive Jewish immigration to North Africa. This further diminished the Land of Israel's already fading share in the Jews' geographic distribution.

The clash between Christianity and Islam, which came to a head with the Crusades of the eleventh through thirteenth centuries, further depleted the Holy Land of its Jews. With the conquest in 1099 of Jerusalem by Godfrey of Bouillon, the local Jews who fought alongside the city's Muslim defenders were burned alive in the synagogue where they sought refuge. Soon afterward the conquering regime renewed the Byzantine prohibition on Jewish settlement in Jerusalem.

However, the Crusaders also nurtured the coastal plain as a gateway to the outer world and turned Acre into a bustling, cosmopolitan port city, particularly after their loss of Jerusalem to Saladin in 1187. In this seaport, as well as in Ashkelon in the south and Tyre in the north, Jewish communities continued to exist. Travelers from across the Jewish world passed through Acre, and in some cases stayed. Biblical commentator Moses Nahmanides (c. 1194–1270), who was originally from Girona, Spain, settled in Acre in 1263. Two years later Moses Maimonides toured the Holy Land before proceeding to Egypt. Most notably, some three hundred rabbis from France and England arrived in Acre in the first decade of the thirteenth century. A generation later they were followed by a group of German rabbis.

Saladin's conquest marked a turning point in the Jews' status in Jerusalem, and a nascent community began gathering there from various Muslim and Christian countries. Yet the Mamluk Muslims, whose conquest of Acre in 1291 ended once and for all the Crusader chapter in the Holy Land's history, inadvertently dealt a blow to the prospects of the Promised Land's struggling Jewish community.

Traumatized by the ease with which European invaders had initially overrun the Holy Land two centuries earlier, the country's new rulers systematically razed the coastal plain's settlements and ports, including, of course, Acre. This action put an abrupt end to the life of a vibrant Jewish community where European, Asian, and North African scholars had a rare opportunity to rub shoulders. The obliteration of Acre and the coastal towns also severely limited travelers' and potential settlers' ability to access the Land of Israel from the sea.

The Holy Land's coastal population was now pushed east, to the mountains of Galilee, Samaria, and Judea, and the Jews were no exception. In 1267, Nahmanides found in Jerusalem two Jewish brothers, both wall painters, "who gather in their house a quorum for Saturday prayers." Though the Jewish community would grow slightly during more

(ABOVE)

SARCOPHAGUS TOPS WITH
HEBREW INSCRIPTIONS.
MUSEUM OF GIRONA, SPAIN.
Spanish Jewry's scholars were
influential throughout the
Mediterranean basin's Diaspora.

(OPPOSITE)

MISHNEH TORAH.
LATE FIFTEENTH CENTURY. NORTHERN ITALY
(LOMBARDY). VELLUM. COD. ROSSIANA, MS. 498,
FOL. 43V. BIBLIOTECA APOSTOLICA VATICANA.
The second of the fourteen-volume
Maimonidean code, Mishneh Torah,
deals with the ways to worship God.

than two centuries of Mamluk rule, it would not be until the influx of Spanish Jewish refugees, following the 1492 Expulsion, that the Land of Israel would once again have an impact on Jewish life throughout the Diaspora.

In all, Christian discrimination and Muslim provincialization left the Holy Land on the fringes of medieval Jewish history. Only a fraction of the world's Jews alive in that era actually saw their ancestral land, let alone lived there, or even met someone who had seen it. Moreover, with the Jerusalem Talmudic academy but a memory and with Jewish scholarship's center of gravity having sailed west, to North Africa, Spain, France, and Germany, the Land of Israel transformed into a mostly abstract concept rather than a tangible factor in the lives of Diaspora Jews.

TUNISIA: BEYOND THE RIVERS OF BABYLON

Paradoxically, once finally victorious in its centuries-long struggle with Jerusalem, Babylonia soon began losing its hegemony. As would often happen in Jewish history, even while one great demographic and spiritual center was blossoming, another center, often thousands of miles away, would already be well on its way to succeeding it. In practically all these transitions the Jews' geographic distribution would reflect broader transfers of political, economic, and military centers of gravity, which in turn accompanied the rise, expansion, and decline of cities, regions, and entire empires.

That is what happened to the glorious community of Babylonia as the rise of Islam gradually saw the Mesopotamian basin's magnetism give way to burgeoning new centers. For one thing, the Arab conquerors neglected the sophisticated irrigation system along the banks of the Tigris and Euphrates rivers, thus inadvertently hampering the entire farming sector and encouraging the transition from farming to commerce, as well as migration from village to town. Beyond this, the emergence of a vast, geographically contiguous and culturally harmonious landmass stretching from the Persian Gulf in the east to the Atlantic Ocean in the west, coupled with a tendency to delegate power to local rulers, breathed life into varied international commercial routes, checkered with bustling metropolitan centers in today's Tunisia, Morocco, Spain, and Egypt.

One such major center was Kairouan (in modern north-central Tunisia). After having been the springboard from which the invading Muslim armies conquered northwest Africa in the seventh century, this city served the Aghlabid and Fatimid dynasties as the capital of the entire Maghreb region (the western part of the Arab world). Between then and its abrupt decline in the wake of Bedouin assaults in the eleventh century, Kairouan became a major Jewish center. It attracted merchants and scholars from Babylonia and other communities in the Mashraq (the eastern part of the Arab world, including the Land of Israel) as well as from Morocco, Spain, Italy, and other countries.

As would befit those dwelling in a bridge between east and west, Kairouan's Jews maintained solid ties with their brethren in Spain, Babylonia, and Jerusalem. Some of

BEN EZRA SYNAGOGUE, FOSTAT (OLD CAIRO).
Originally built in the tenth century C.E., it was destroyed in 1013 along with the rest of Egypt's synagogues and churches. Two decades later it was rebuilt and remained fairly intact until the 1890s, when it was entirely reconstructed.

their Talmudic academies were influenced by Babylonia, others by Jerusalem, but ultimately the Kairouan school asserted its independence under the leadership of Rabbi Hananel, whose Talmudic commentary is studied in Talmudic academies even today.

Still, correspondence and social ties between Kairouan's scholars and the great traditional centers was extensive, as evidenced in documents found in the Cairo Geniza, a treasure of medieval Jewish sources found more than a century ago in Egypt's capital. The Kairouan rabbi Nissim ben-Jacob, for instance, tutored the Spanish poet Solomon ibn-Gabirol, and his daughter married the son of Shmuel ha-Nagid, the leader of Muslim Spain's Jews in the first half of the eleventh century.

EGYPT: BACK TO THE HEART OF THE MIDDLE EAST

The destruction of the Kairouan community in 1057 by Arab armies that advanced westward from Egypt pushed its survivors farther west, to Morocco and Spain. However, the great Torah center that Kairouan's decline helped create was some 1,600 kilometers

(ABOVE)
SOLOMON SCHECHTER STUDYING
GENIZAH FRAGMENTS AT
CAMBRIDGE UNIVERSITY,
ENGLAND, 1898.
The treasure of Jewish sources found accidentally in Cairo has helped shed new light on Jewish history.

to its east, in Fostat, which is part of today's Cairo. Thus, the land that had historically been an epicenter in the Middle East once again arose as a major Jewish hub.

Egypt's ascent to prominence as a center of Jewish legal leadership was marked by the presence in the eleventh century of sages such as Kairouan's Nahrai ben-Nissim and Spain's Isaac ben-Samuel. Its status, which had already been confirmed because monumental sage Rabbi Sa'adiah Gaon (882–942) received his early education there, peaked with the arrival of Maimonides in the twelfth century.

Actually, Egypt emerged as a major medieval Jewish center because thousands of Jews had migrated there from Mesopotamia in the tenth century. The Arabs' extensive conquests allowed Egypt's Jews to restore their broken ties with the Talmudic academies of Babylonia, while Jews throughout the evolving empire found new commercial horizons in a Muslim universe that stretched from western Africa to the doorstep of China. Egypt's conquest in 969 by the Fatimids, who allowed non-Muslims to build new houses of worship and join the civil service, turned the Nile basin into a major haven for Jews. Though disrupted once (from 996 to 1021) by a period of oppression, the Fatimid era marked the high point in the history of the Jews in Egypt.

Interestingly enough, the Cairo community's internal structure preserved the veteran rivalry between Babylonia and the Land of Israel. Expatriates retained their original communal identities through distinctive synagogues where they congregated separately. The Karaites (a fundamentalist sect that probably had its origins in the opposition trends of the Second Temple Period and rose to prominence during the twelfth to fourteenth centuries in Byzantium, and today still has several thousand adherents in Israel) worshiped in synagogues of their own. Even so, during the Fatimid era, Egypt's diverse Jewish community established a sort of umbrella organization that was headed by a political, rather than religious figure, who took the Hebrew title *nagid* (governor). Often a physician chosen by the community elders and approved by the authorities, the nagid would appoint judges, collect taxes, pass various decrees, and enjoy the aura of a semi-sovereign.

The tolerance and prosperity enjoyed by the Jews of Cairo for some three centuries came to an abrupt end with the rise in the middle of the thirteenth century of the Mamluks, who often persecuted non-Muslims. Sometimes this mistreatment meant a sudden imposition of exorbitant taxes, sometimes the closure of synagogues, and in some cases it also led to pogroms, like the one that occurred in 1354 and others that followed in the fifteenth century. Commercially, too, the Mamluks sought ways to confine the Jews, most notably by barring them from Cairo's elaborate trade with India and China.

The Ottoman conquest of 1517 initially renewed the Jewish expansion in Egypt, which had already been fueled by the previous century's influx of refugees from the Spanish Expulsion and was further reinforced in the middle of the seventeenth century by the arrival of Jews who survived the Chmielnicki massacres in the Ukraine. However,

(ABOVE)
THE GREAT SYNAGOGUE, ALEXANDRIA, EGYPT.
Unlike the Second Temple era, when Alexandria was a major center for Jewish scholars and merchants, in the Middle Ages Alexandria's Jewry lived in the shadows of Fostat.

(OPPOSITE)
MARRIAGE CONTRACT (*Ketubbah*).
1853. ISTANBUL, TURKEY. PAPER, GOUACHE, GOLD POWDER, PEN, AND INK. COLLECTION OF THE ISRAEL MUSEUM, JERUSALEM. PURCHASED BY COURTESY OF FUNDS IN HONOR OF ARI ACKERMAN, 1987.
During the Ottoman era Middle Eastern Jewry declined along with the broader Muslim world's self-imposed introversion at a time when European Christians were exploring, and conquering, the New World.

Safed: An Improbable Renaissance

TOMB OF RABBI ISAAK LURIA.

1534–1572. SAFED.

During a short-lived renaissance immediately after the Spanish Expulsion, the remote Galilean town produced two major Judaic turning points: Joseph Karo's Shulḥan Arukh *legal codex, and Luria's version of Jewish mysticism, each of which quickly influenced practically the entire Diaspora.*

The generally marginal role played by the Holy Land in Jewish history was briefly, but lastingly, interrupted by the rise of two monumental sixteenth-century sages who were active in two separate spheres of Judaic scholarship: law and mysticism.

Following the Spanish and Portuguese expulsions, some newly arrived Jews settled in picturesque Safed. Armed with the worldliness that was the hallmark of Iberian Jewry, traumatized by the Expulsion experience, and inspired by the serene vistas of the Upper Galilee, the rabbis of Safed studied intensely all fields of Judaism and interpreted their generation's tribulations as echoes of the Messiah's approaching footsteps.

The first of these notable men, Jacob Berab (1474–1541), tried to restore the Land of Israel's long-defunct rabbinical authority vis-à-vis the entire Diaspora to the place it held until the decline of the Sanhedrin, more than a thousand years earlier. Berab had many immediate and pressing questions to address, especially those arising from the return to Judaism of former *conversos* (Jews who, back in Spain, had outwardly converted to Christianity in order to survive the Inquisition's persecutions). However, Berab and his circle were mentally preoccupied by their belief that the Messiah's arrival was imminent. Thus, the way they saw it, the Holy Land community's authority to ordinate rabbis—a prerequisite for the Messiah's arrival, according to tradition—had become both feasible and imperative. Relying on a ruling by Maimonides—that if the Land of Israel's sages arrived at a consensus they could ordain rabbis who in turn would collectively issue rulings for the entire Diaspora—Berab set about his task. He first ordained four of his disciples, who in turn ordained an additional seven scholars, and then set out to enlist the support of Jerusalem's conservative rabbis. However, Berab's initiative was soon thwarted by

indigenous Jerusalem sage Levi ben-Habib. Besides being a scholar and a mystic, Berab was an affluent merchant who traded in Morocco, Egypt, and Syria, which made him politically vulnerable. Ultimately, Berab was forced out of the Holy Land by the Ottomans after some of his opponents convinced a local governor that he was a threat to the regime.

Still, post-Expulsion Safed's messianic fervor and intellectual confidence survived the failure to restore the ordination, and soon enough produced a book and a movement that would influence the entire Jewish world—until today. The book was the legal codex *Shulḥan Arukh* and the movement was Jewish mysticism.

In 1538, shortly after Berab's forced departure to Syria, Rabbi Joseph Caro (1488–1575) remained as the towering sage of the Galilean town. Born four years before the Expulsion, apparently in Toledo, Spain, Caro ended up in Istanbul, from which he proceeded, through Greece and Egypt, to Galilee. While still in the Balkans, and already in his early thirties, he began working on a definitive codex of Jewish law. By the time he completed its condensed version, in 1555 in Safed, the printing press had become ubiquitous, and the *Shulḥan Arukh* quickly spread across the Diaspora. Coupled with an annex written in Cracow by Moses Isserles, which explains the differences between European and Middle Eastern traditions, Caro's codex still remains the foundation of Jewish Orthodoxy. It is a tool through which to study, teach, and issue rulings on anything and everything, from how to slaughter a chicken or conduct a morning prayer to how to observe the Sabbath, build a tabernacle, or divorce a spouse.

Yet even more profound than its impact on an observant Jew's daily conduct was the Safed circle's development of a new approach to Judaism and the explanations it offered for the Jews' continued anguish.

Led by Isaac Luria (1534–1572), Safed's mystics developed the school of Kabbalistic thought, which revolved around complicated theories about secret meanings of Jewish texts, and was meant for only a small group of initiates. In fact, upon his deathbed, at age thirty-eight, Luria told his primary disciple, Rabbi Haim Vital, not to share his secrets, but Safed's mystics violated their mentor's will.

The son of a European father and a Middle Eastern mother, Luria was born in Jerusalem and raised in Egypt. In legends about his life, Luria emerges as a charismatic and sensitive leader who was loathe to scold sinners and keen on instilling faith in believers' ability to hasten the Messiah's arrival. He also derived his own.

Possessed by an urge to understand the evil in the world about them, obsessed by the desire to see the their people's exiles ingathered, and inspired by their proximity to the burial site of second-century sage Shimon ben-Yohai—to whom they ascribed Kabbala's basic text, the Zohar—Safed's mystics explained the Jews' dispersal and suffering as part of failures that occurred in the Creation itself, and whose end would be part of a universal redemption. The Safed Kabbalists also contended that mending Creation's deficiencies was up to mankind, and that the sooner Jews would accelerate their repentance the sooner will Redemption arrive. Historically, perhaps the most significant thing about this development was its popularization of mysticism and its instilling of a faith that Redemption was imminent, and up to the believers to unleash. It followed, that the sooner Jews accelerated their repentance the sooner Redemption would arrive. Indeed, the Safed mystics' most important innovation was the popularization of the Kabbala, and the spreading of their belief in Redemption's imminence.

Like Caro's codex, popular Kabbala also benefited from the invention of the printing press and innovations in maritime navigation, both of which enabled its teachings to spread through the Jewish world at an astonishing speed. One of the Safed circle's most tangible and lasting impressions

was the writing of the prayer for the greeting of the Sabbath. Quickly adopted by communities in Asia, Africa, and Europe and chanted even today in practically any synagogue, its composition was inspired by the Safed sages' custom of walking on around dusk on Fridays to the foothills of Mt. Meron, where they would meditate in nature's solitude as they greeted Judaism's holiest day.

Sixteenth-century Safed's spiritual renaissance may have been more lasting had the Ottoman Empire not begun its spiraling economic decline the following century. The town's wool industry—which for several decades competed efficiently with Venice and supplied a significant portion of the Ottoman Empire's demand—gave way to its French and British competitors. Moreover, by the seventeeth century, security in the Galilee was deteriorating, control by the Ottomans was lax at best, and local wars flared. Ultimately, a mere century after Caro finished writing his monumental legal codex, the Jews abandoned Safed.

Even so, less than a century after Luria's death, the movement that began in off-the-beaten-path Safed swept the Jewish nation off its feet with the appearance of Shabbetai Zevi, whose Messianic aspirations and popular following were inspired by the Safed circle's legacy. The following century the Safed legacy inspired yet another movement that conquered much of the Diaspora: Hasidism.

(ABOVE)

WOODEN ARK.
FROM THE EIGHTEENTH-CENTURY HA'ARI SYNAGOGUE, SAFED.

Unfavorable political and economic conditions, typical of remote Ottoman provinces, led to Jewish Safed's quick decline.

a mere few generations after their conquest of the Nile basin, the Ottoman rulers' lack of developmental drive also resulted in the region's, and the local Jewish community's, steady decline. Though it remained sizable until the State of Israel's establishment, Egypt's Jewish community never regained the confidence, prosperity, influence, scholarship, and centrality it enjoyed during the Fatimid period.

YEMEN: IN THE SHADOWS OF GREAT DIASPORAS

As a regional center, Egypt spread its influence not only west, to the Maghreb, but also east, to Yemen, where two millennia of Jewish existence were often characterized by relative isolation and highlighted by special ties to the Land of Israel. Jews arrived at the southern end of the Arabian Peninsula no later than the twilight of the Second Temple period, according to clear archeological evidence. Tradition traces their origins centuries beforehand, to the First Temple period.

(ABOVE)
A TRADITIONAL YEMENITE WEDDING CEREMONY.
BET SEAN, ISRAEL.
The Yemenite community in Israel has been more concerned about, and successful at preserving, its traditions than some other immigrations.

(OPPOSITE)
SILVER AND GOLD TORAH FINIALS.
TWENTIETH CENTURY. SAN'A, YEMEN,
THE ISRAEL MUSEUM, JERUSALEM.
Yemenite Jews became expert gold-smiths, a side effect of the elaborate Arabian-Indian trade traffic that harbored in Yemen.

MARRIAGE CONTRACT (*Ketubbah*).
1794. SAN'A, YEMEN. PARCHMENT, GOUACHE, PEN AND
INK. THE ISRAEL MUSEUM, JERUSALEM.

*While there are numerous instances of
images of the bridal couple depicted on*
ketubbot, *it is quite unusual for figures
to appear on a Yemenite* ketubbah. *The
figures are rather primitive, making the
simplistic handling of the flower vines in
the borders seem much more sophisticated.
The meaning of the scene is unclear,
although it has been suggested that it is
the wedding banquet.*

A YEMENITE WOMAN.

Like the Yemenites themselves, the Jews were split, demographically and culturally, between the region's two main urban centers, Sana and Aden. The former, located on the trade route that straddled the Arabian Peninsula's north-south axis, was some 150 kilometers east of the Red Sea coast, while the latter, situated on the shores of the Indian Ocean, was on the main Egyptian-Indian trade axis, and as such was more cosmopolitan. Documents such as those found in the Cairo Geniza indicate that maritime traffic between Egypt and India, largely overseen by Jews, harbored in Yemen, where it accelerated local production of metal products, a skill Yemenite Jews preserved until the modern era.

Even so, Yemen was for centuries relatively detached from the political intrusions and cultural influence of the Near East's two great poles, Egypt and Mesopotamia. During the Roman era, it thrived as an alternative trade route to an increasingly dangerous Red Sea, and during the dawn of Christianity, it was invaded by Ethiopian armies.

At that time there was a Jewish kingdom in south Arabia called Himyar, ruled by Yusuf Dhu Nuwas. After defeating the Ethiopians in a battle in 523, he was destroyed two years later, along with his Jewish kingdom, by a joint Byzantine-Ethiopian army. Until that debacle Judaism was so powerful in Yemen that it successfully resisted its opponents and even attracted converts. All that ended with a one-two Christian-Muslim blow: first, the defeat of the Himyar kingdom, and then, in the following century, the advent of Islam—which in Yemen's case was led by Mohammed himself—ended the Jews' ownership of land and subjected them to special rules and regulations and to *dhimi,* that is non-Muslim or alien, status.

Throughout this period Yemen's Jews maintained ties with the great communities of Babylonia. However, as Mesopotamia declined politically and economically, and as they gradually lost access to the distant north, Yemen's Jews increasingly gravitated toward the Egyptian community. That trend was later enhanced by the special concern for Yemen demonstrated by Egypt's greatest-ever Judaic luminary, Maimonides. In a famous letter addressed especially to the Jews of Yemen (c. 1170), which was read in communities throughout southern Arabia, the great sage wrote local Jews that the pressure they faced at the time to convert to Islam would ultimately pass. In the meantime he instructed them to either emigrate or seek ways to practice their faith despite the hardships. When the pressure to convert eased, Yemenite rabbis got hold of and embraced Maimonides' extensive legal and philosophical writings, which over the centuries became a mainstay of Yemenite Jewish scholarship.

The Jews of Yemen still experienced extreme hardship in subsequent centuries, both before and after the Ottoman departure from the region in 1635, as they got caught in the crossfire between local and foreign powers. Most memorably, a 1676 decree by Imam Ahmed ibn Hassan el-Mahdi ordered the destruction of all synagogues and the expulsion of the entire Jewish community. By the time the Jews were allowed to return, many of them had died as a result of their dislocation and dispossession.

93

בר דאר זרן מרדכי דה פוסרא
המן לעש רא

רולת צו דמיק חאר בחשר
גם רא ברל תה פאר ביאשר
מגן
שאר שוד זהר דם כמן
צו כסתה כי שאר גרדר או

Historical documents indicate that at least since the thirteenth century there was a steady trickle of Yemenite immigration to the Land of Israel. Perhaps most notable among those immigrants was Rabbi Shalom Sharabi (1720–1777), a mystic who established in Jerusalem the Beth El Kabbalist seminary. In an uncanny coincidence the next century, several hundred Yemenite Jews journeyed in 1881 on donkeys and camels to the Land of Israel, completely unaware that at the same time other Jews in Europe were setting out to settle the Holy Land after anti-Semitic pogroms swept across southern Russia.

Several more thousand Yemenite Jews moved to the Land of Israel before and after World War I, but the big mass—nearly fifty thousand people—came after the establishment of the state of Israel in the first-ever demographic airlift carried out by the new state, an operation that came to be known as "Magic Carpet." A subsequent emigration, from Aden in the aftermath of the 1967 Arab-Israeli war, reduced Yemenite Jewry to merely a few thousand, some of whom moved during the 1990s to the United States and Israel.

PERSIA: TWO MILLENNIA OF JEWISH LIFE

While the Diaspora originally spread from the Land of Israel to its immediate surroundings, namely, the Fertile Crescent from Babylon to Egypt, these contours had been expanded, already in biblical times, to a triangle that stretched from Asia Minor in the west to Persia in the east and Yemen in the south. The Persian Diaspora originated no later than 727 B.C.E. with the exile of the Israelite tribes by the Assyrian Empire to "the cities of Media and Persia," and saw additional influxes in the subsequent deportations. These culminated in the fall of Judah to Babylon in 586 B.C.E.

The Book of Esther's portrayal of a solid Jewish community not only in the heart of the Persian Empire but also "among all peoples of the Persian empire" probably echoes a historical reality, even if the book's specific plot has been widely interpreted as allegorical rather than factual. Apparently at the same time that some Jews returned to their ancestral land, in response to the Cyrus Declaration in 538 B.C.E. that allowed the reconstruction of the Temple, others veered east, where Persia's newly consolidated empire offered uncharted commercial horizons as well as opportunities in the civil service. Indeed, that is also the context of the Esther story, where a Jew (Mordechai) and a Gentile (Haman) lock horns while vying for influence in the imperial court, and the backdrop against which biblical figures Zerubbabel, Ezra, Nehemiah, and Daniel rose to prominence under Persian rule.

Still, in the longer term the Persian Diaspora lived in the shadows of Babylonian Jewry, dwarfed by it and never challenging its scholarship and sway. This relative marginality reflected the Persians' failure to sustain their overextended empire, which by the fifth century B.C.E. stretched from Afghanistan in the east to the doorstep of Greece in the west, and from the Nile in the south to the Danube in the north. Alexander the Great's effective expulsion of the Persians from the Euphrates and Tigris basins and the

(OPPOSITE)

MARRIAGE CONTRACT (*Ketubbah*).
1898. ISFAHAN, IRAN. PAPER, WATERCOLOR,
PEN AND INK, COLORED PAPER. THE ISRAEL
MUSEUM, JERUSALEM.

*Despite the traumatic encounter with a
succession of Shi'ite regimes since the
sixteenth century, Iranian Jewry has
known protracted periods of tolerance
and prosperity.*

subsequent spread throughout the Fertile Crescent of Hellenistic civilization largely
stemmed the Jewish Diaspora's eastward thrust.

However, by then the Jewish presence across Persia already added up to a critical mass
that would survive continuously for two millennia, and which exists until today, albeit in
small numbers. In fact, under the usually tolerant Sassanians, who ruled Persia and
practiced Zoroastrianism, the Jews expanded and consolidated their presence throughout
the country. Of course, they also survived periods of severe persecution, most notably,
according to a Persian source, the killing of half the Jews of Isfahan and the enslavement
of their children in 472 C.E. This alternation between periods of tolerance and
oppression would also characterize Persian Jewish history after the Arab conquest
and Islam's defeat of Zoroastrianism in 637.

The rise of Baghdad in the second half of the seventh century as the capital of the
Muslim world intensified the Jews' urbanization in Persia. Cities such as Shiraz and
Isfahan attracted sizable numbers of Jewish merchants who conducted hefty international trade and, by the tenth century, played a major role in the development of
banking services, particularly for the government.

What distinguished Persian Jewry in subsequent centuries were the traumatic
encounter with Shi'ism, on one hand, and the unveiling of Central Asian and Far Eastern
prospects, on the other. The dawn of the Shi'ite era with the rise of the Safavid dynasty in
1501 saw the demise of the previous centuries' tolerance. The newly ruling theology's
insistence that infidels were profane had a profound effect on Persia's attitude toward its
minorities. For the Jews this meant the beginning of severe persecution of a sort that
until then was much more characteristic of the Jewish experience in Christendom. At
one point, during the reign of Abbas II in the middle of the seventeenth century, Persian
Jews even faced harsh pressure to abandon their faith and embrace Islam. Many
converted, many others were killed. Still others converted outwardly while practicing
Judaism in secret, much the same way the *Marranos* had done in Iberia.

Persian-Jewish relations reached their lowest ebbs (until the 1979 Islamist Revolution)
with the 1797 mass murder of the community of Tabriz and the 1839 forced conversion
of the community of Meshed. The twentieth-century Khomeini revolution's famous
hostility toward Israel and the Jews can be understood better against the backdrop
of this legacy.

Still, in between these periods of severe social discrimination, cultural intolerance,
and political violence, Persia also saw protracted periods of tolerance, pluralism, and
cosmopolitanism from which the Jews benefited greatly. Shah Mozaffar od-Din's
openness toward the West led him to allow in 1898 the establishment in Tehran of an
Alliance Israélite school, the first of several that soon were opened across the country.
In 1907 the Jews were formally emancipated, and in 1925 Reza Shah formally abolished
the special taxes imposed on the Jews.

Until the 1979 revolution Jews dwelled in Iran in relative security. Shah Mohammed Reza Pahlavi, who seized power in 1953 backed by the United States, established formal ties with the state of Israel as part of a foreign policy aimed at challenging Arab hegemony in the Middle East. Throughout that period, the Jewish community in Tehran remained sizable, prosperous, and confident, while surrounded by smaller and less vibrant communities elsewhere in Iran. All this was dealt a severe blow with the rise of Ayatollah Khomeini's regime. Many of Tehran's fifty thousand Jews fled the country in panic (usually to the United States). The show trials in 2000 of a group of Iranian Jews as alleged collaborators with the United States and Israel made Iran loom ominously as the world's last bastion of state-sponsored anti-Semitism.

CENTRAL ASIA: ALONG THE CARAVAN TRADE ROUTES

Its long history of cultural intolerance notwithstanding, Persia was a bustling meeting point for merchants, due to its location on the major trade routes that linked Mesopotamia with India and China. Consequently, Jewish communities emerged along the historic caravan routes leading from the Near East to the Far East.

Mentioned already in the Talmud, Central Asia is believed to have attracted Jews as early as the time of Cyrus the Great (d. 529 B.C.E), whose vast empire opened new opportunities for trade. (Tractate Avoda Zara 31B says the early-fourth-century sage Samuel bar-Bisna lived in Margwan, which is in today's Turkmenistan.) In subsequent centuries Jewish merchants frequently ventured into, and even beyond, Central Asia's punishing deserts, endless steppes, and snow-capped mountains. Gradually they planted communities east of Persia, through India, all the way to China. Most of these groups were within the broader Persian cultural sphere that stretched across Central Asia, northeast of modern-day Iran, from today's Uzbekistan in the north to Afghanistan in the south. Here, beyond the all-but-impassable Karakum and Kyzylkum deserts and not far from the foothills of the nearly impassable Pamir Mountains, the sizable, durable, and vital communities of the Jewish Diaspora reached their easternmost extent.

Why the Diaspora did not proceed east of here is not fully clear. Daunting geographic barriers must have been a major reason, but cultural circumstances—namely, the titanic clash between Islam, Buddhism, and Hinduism that took place just east and south of Central Asia—might also have made those locales undesirable. For some reason, a major trading junction such as Kashgar, on the eastern foothills of the Pamir Mountains and just inside the Takla Makan Desert, which leads from Central Asia into China, apparently never had a Jewish community.

The most solid and influential of the Central Asian communities was in Bukhara, an oasis city some 1,000 kilometers east of the Caspian Sea, in what today is Uzbekistan. A thriving Jewish community apparently flourished in the twelfth-century Bukharan khanate on the eve of the Mongol invasions that trampled Central Asia. The great

BUKHARAN WOMAN.
A Jewish community apparently already flourished in Bukhara in the twelfth century, on the eve of the Mongol invasions.

(OPPOSITE)

MEN'S AND WOMEN'S CAPS FROM AFGHANISTAN, BUKHARA, AND UZBEKISTAN.
COTTON, SILK METAL AND THREAD EMBROIDERY. THE ISRAEL MUSEUM, JERUSALEM.

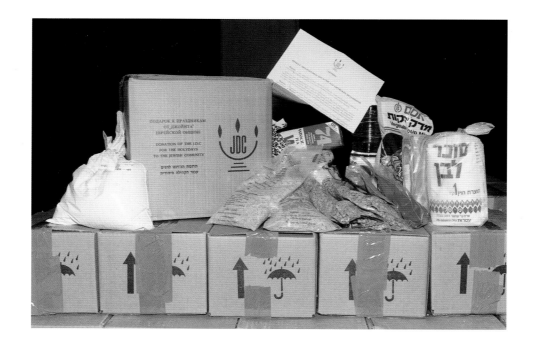

thirteenth-century Jewish traveler Benjamin of Tudela is believed to have exaggerated when he claimed that two generations before the Mongol destruction, Samarkand alone had fifty thousand Jews. Still, his account clearly conveys a Jewish prominence that impressed contemporary visitors and endured in a politically volatile region.

During the sixteenth century, when the Uzbek Shaybanid dynasty broke away from Persian dominance and expanded Bukhara southwest to northern Persia and southeast to Afghanistan, the newly cohesive and commercially bustling region attracted more Persian Jews. These numbers included people who fled the fighting between Persian Shi'ites and Central Asian Sunnis. However, within a short time unfavorable political and cultural circumstances would prevent Bukharan Jews from capitalizing on their demographic growth.

Politically, the rise in the eighteenth century of an independent Afghan kingdom further disjointed the region's Jewish communities, due to the enmity between Bukhara and Afghanistan. Culturally, repeated attempts to forcibly convert Jews to Islam took their toll. Many chose to practice their Judaism in secret; others were altogether lost to the faith. Ultimately, Bukharan Jewry became spiritually depleted and its members all but ceased to study and teach Judaism.

However, in the eighteenth century, an accidental visitor, Rabbi Joseph Maman Maghribi, stemmed this decline. Born in Morocco, Maman arrived in Bukhara in 1793 to raise funds for the community of Safed in the Land of Israel. Without initially planning to do so, he ended up staying in Bukhara for three decades and restoring its community's largely lost knowledge of Judaism. Maman's efforts, highlighted—according to some sources—by the establishment of a Talmudic academy, were aided by a new tolerance on the part of business-minded local rulers. They allowed the Jews of various cities, including Bukhara and Dushanbe, to reside beyond the confines of the special Jewish quarters, the *mahalla*, to which they had been consigned since the early seventeenth century.

Consequently, Bukhara became the natural haven for the newly persecuted Jews of Meshed, many of whom moved east after fleeing the forced conversions that awaited them in their native Persian town. In the twilight of their rule, Bukharan leaders allowed the Jews to elect local leaders, who in turn were allowed to exercise authority in civil affairs involving Jews.

As the nineteenth century approached, Russia increasingly cast its immense shadow on Central Asia, allowing local Jews to serve as involuntary agents of integration between Moscow's European domains and Asian horizons. Thus, even before the 1865–1868 conquests of Bukhara, Tashkent, and Samarkand by Czar Alexander II, Central Asian Jewish traders were allowed to reside outside the Pale of Settlement and take part in Russia's large trade fairs. Following their region's conquest, Central Asia's Jews became even more privileged, since the czars believed them to be a trustworthy minority among an otherwise hostile population. Bukharan Jews were allowed to receive Russian

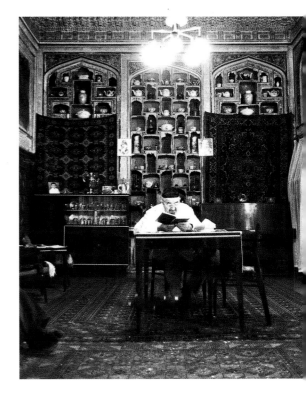

(ABOVE)

A MAN STUDYING AT HIS FATHER'S OLD HOUSE IN BUKHARA.

1990.

Bukharan Jewry's level of Jewish knowledge deteriorated in the eighteenth century due to region-wide instability, until 1793, when Rabbi Joseph Mamman Maghribi, an accidental tourist who came to raise funds for the Jews of Safed, changed his plans and stayed in Bukhara as a spiritual leader.

(OPPOSITE, TOP)

NEWLY ARRIVED IMMIGRANTS FROM THE FORMER SOVIET UNION CARRYING GAS MASKS AT BEN-GURION AIRPORT DURING THE GULF WAR OF 1991. *Prohibitions on the practice of Judaism were less strictly imposed in the Soviet Union's Asian regions.*

(OPPOSITE, BOTTOM)

FOOD PACKAGES FOR THE JEWISH HOLIDAYS. *One of the many recipients of help sponsored by the Joint Distribution Committee are Jews still living in the Former Soviet Union.*

citizenship and even purchase land in Russia proper, provided they engaged in Russian-Asian trade.

From the 1870s Bukharan Jews became key agents in leading Central Asian silk and cotton to Russia and assorted Russian goods into Asia. Still, the Jews' new prosperity was overshadowed by the hostility of frustrated Bukharan rulers, who attributed to the Jews a role in their decline. Eventually Bukharan governments raised the taxes for the Jews, and many migrated to nearby Tashkent and Samarkand. At the same time, Russian bureaucrats and regional governors made it difficult for Bukharan Jews to obtain Russian citizenship and reside on major trade routes.

However, all these hardships dwarfed in comparison with what Bukharan Jewry lost after the Bolshevik Revolution. The first shock to the community came in the 1920s, when even its many artisans and merchants were largely forced out of their businesses and maneuvered into joining new industrial and agricultural cooperatives. Most synagogues were shut down and religious education was banned. By the late 1930s nonreligious Jewish cultural activity, from publishing to education, was also obstructed. However, during World War II the region, particularly Samarkand and Tashkent, attracted thousands of Jewish refugees. These comprised the bulk of Central Asian Jewry when the Soviet Union disintegrated in 1992. By 2000 these Jews had emigrated, by and large, to Israel.

THE CAUCASUS: OFF HISTORY'S BEATEN PATH

The Caucasus, on the other end of the historical Persian sphere of influence, has had sizable Jewish communities at least since the Byzantine era. In Georgia, tradition claims the Jewish population descended from the Ten Tribes. Proof of this supposedly lies in the community's lack of priests (*kohanim*) and Levites, who would have come from Judea and were common in the rest of the Diaspora.

During the Byzantine period, when the Caucasus was split between Persians and Christians, the Jews gravitated to the region's non-Christian south, in today's Azerbaijan. After the Arab conquests in the eighth century, the greater Caucasus region was relatively reintegrated, but Jews were occasionally also persecuted by local Muslim rulers. Many fled to the trans-Caucasus area, where the Khazars welcomed them even before its ruling class adopted the Jewish faith in the eighth century. Recent archeological findings indicate that a solid and affluent Jewish community existed also in Armenia in the thirteenth century, and that Jews there even owned land, a privilege that was inconceivable at the time in Europe.

The decline of the Khazar kingdom in the tenth century, and the Mongol destruction in the thirteenth century of the lands to their north and west, largely cut off Caucasian Jewry from the west. Still, it clearly continued to exist throughout the centuries, benefiting from the region's fertility and isolation. Only in the nineteenth century, with

(ABOVE)

A BUKHARAN WOMAN LIGHTING SABBATH CANDLES.
Most of Bukharan Jewry has immigrated to Israel.

(OPPOSITE, TOP)

JEWISH HIGH SCHOOL GIRLS FROM THE CITY OF KUBA, AZERBAIJAN.
1960.

Working in the nearby Kolkhoz is a part of their education. Jews first arrived in Azerbaijan during the Byzantine era, when they gravitated to the region's Persian sphere.

(OPPOSITE, BOTTOM)

A GRANDMOTHER AND GRANDSON IN FRONT OF THE SYNAGOGUE GATES IN OGUZ, AZERBAIJAN.
Russian Jews arrived in the region as it fell under czarist sway.

(RIGHT)

A YOUNG JEWISH BOY IN FRONT OF A
SYNAGOGUE IN TIBLISI, GEORGIA.
*The Georgian Jewish community was the
most solid in the entire Caucasus during
the twentieth century.*

(OPPOSITE)

A JEWISH WOMAN FROM THE
CAUCASUS.
*The so-called mountain Jews managed to
preserve their close-knit patriarchal
society even under the Communists.*

the czarist encroachment on the region, did Russian Jews begin visiting the Caucasian
communities and reporting about them in the Jewish press. Though obstructed by the
czarist regimes, a modest migration movement from the Pale of Settlement also began to
trickle south, mainly to Tbilisi and mineral-rich Baku. There, Jews played a leading role
in building the Caspian shore's prospecting, drilling, and transshipment industries, while
in Tbilisi Jews were leaders in its thriving trade sector. Another Jewish element in the
Caucasus were the so-called Mountain Jews, whose rural communities dated back
centuries—possibly to the Khazar Kingdom—and whose close-knit patriarchal social
structures largely endured even the challenges posed by the Communist era.

The Georgian Jewish community in general, and Tbilisi's in particular, were the most
solid in the entire Caucasus region throughout the twentieth century. However, when the
Brezhnev regime allowed partial emigration from the USSR in the early 1970s, Georgian
Jews comprised a disproportionate share of those let out. After the Gorbachev era's
complete lifting of travel restrictions, emigration from Georgia further intensified,
and the newly independent republic was severely depleted of its Jews, as was the
rest of the Caucasus.

Today the region's Jewish future seems more uncertain than ever before in its
history of at least 1,500 years. And yet, some synagogues in Tbilisi are still active,
and their worshippers still pray facing south, toward Persia, to where for centuries their
ancestors had sought Judaic leadership.

BRIDGES TO THE WEST

A fter having initially spread mainly throughout the ancient Near East, the Diaspora gradually gravitated toward Europe, which by the nineteenth century emerged as home to 90 percent of the world's Jews. During the Middle Ages, European and Near Eastern communities developed in very different ways linguistically, intellectually, liturgically, and politically.

During the Middle Ages, two countries linked the Diaspora's east and west: Italy and Spain. The former, because of its maritime position as Europe's leading bridge to the Near East, and the latter because of the centuries in which it hosted simultaneously Christianity and Islam.

ITALY: THE MOST DURABLE EUROPEAN DIASPORA

Very few countries have hosted a Jewish community uninterruptedly from antiquity until modern times. In Europe, only Italy can make this claim. The Jewish presence there was sparked by the confluence during the first century B.C.E. of Rome's rise as a major metropolis and the empire's expansion to the eastern Mediterranean basin. For more than three subsequent centuries Jews lived across the Italian peninsula, from Milan and Ravenna in the north to Naples in the south and Sardinia in the west. Historians believe their numbers were relatively high, and that on the whole they benefited from Rome's general religious tolerance.

However, as Christianity expanded, Italian Jewry faced increasing discrimination, particularly in the parts of its south where Byzantium ruled. Yet even so, in the early Middle Ages new communities sprang up in northern Italy, where Jews were merchants, doctors, and farmers, and Talmudic academies grew in various places across the country. Because these settlements were close to major seaports, Italian Jewry maintained relatively close ties with the Jews of Mesopotamia and the Land of Israel.

By the thirteenth century, however, discrimination against Italian Jewry, including the demand (passed by the Fourth Lateran Council in 1215) that they wear distinctive dress, had been formalized. In Naples in 1290, the Jews were forced to convert. Some who refused were executed, while others observed their faith in secret. The papal prohibitions on Christians to charge interest for money lending and on Jews to own land maneuvered Italian Jews into the practice of only a select few professions, mostly in finance and medicine.

The advent of the Renaissance, which made many Christian thinkers appreciate Jewish scholarship, and the simultaneous arrival in Italy of prominent scholars who survived the Spanish Expulsion influenced Italian Jewry markedly. Jews now worked in government and academia and became the world's major printers of Hebrew literature. Italian Jewish communities became a magnet for refugees from France, Germany, and Spain, although they also suffered bouts of persecution and even occasional expulsions.

(ABOVE)
VIEW OF THE CAMPO DEL GHETTO VECCHIO IN VENICE.
The ghetto was first created in Italy as a way to protect the Jews, but as it spread to other places it turned into a tool for blocking their growth.

(OPPOSITE)
TEMPIO ISRAELITICO, FLORENCE.
The construction of such expensive and impressive synagogues was common in post-emancipation Western Europe, and reflected the Jews' emergence from the ghetto, both physically and mentally.

In the second half of the sixteenth century, as the Vatican reacted to the rise of Protestantism, Jews were forbidden to employ Christian servants or possess the Talmud and were forced to live in the Italian-invented ghettos.

Between the eighteenth and nineteenth centuries, as Italy tilted back and forth between liberal reforms and conservative reaction, the Jews were gradually emancipated. The ghettos were abolished, all bans on professional practice were lifted, and government positions were open to Jews no less than to Christians. However, during this liberal era, Italian Jewry declined spiritually and demographically. The community's medieval accomplishments in the various Judaic disciplines all but disappeared, and its physical growth lagged behind the more politically stable and economically vibrant centers in Austria, Germany, England, and America.

Nevertheless, Italy continued to accommodate its Jews for another two hundred years. In fact, even Mussolini's Fascist regime tolerated the Jewish community up until the eve of World War II, when it finally followed Germany's lead and passed anti-Jewish laws. During the Holocaust, seventy-five hundred Italian Jews were murdered, while an estimated seven thousand converted to Christianity. Still, though it dwindled from nearly fifty thousand before the war to fewer than thirty thousand in its aftermath, Italian Jewry survived even under those harsh circumstances in the land it has never left since at least the times of Caesar.

IBERIA: THE TRAGEDY OF TOTAL DESTRUCTION

When the Talmudic sages wanted to indicate that something was farfetched, they would say it was like "dreams in Spain." Despite that adage's implication that the Iberian Peninsula was indeed far from the Near East (where most Jews lived during the first millennium C.E.), Jews actually inhabited that area during Roman times, possibly even well before the destruction of the Temple.

From the late Roman era and for the next five hundred years, Jews thrived in Spain. Usually they lived in towns that were originally Roman centers of government along the Mediterranean coastline, where they were often farmers. In all, Jews lived in Spain for nearly a thousand years. For many generations, that unique diaspora was unusually prosperous, secure, and fertile. But its saga ended abruptly amid a trauma almost on a par in Jewish history with the Temple's destruction and the Nazi Holocaust.

In 587 Spain officially adopted Christianity when the Visigoth king Recarred converted, and soon afterward he started legislating draconian laws against the Jews. These included a ban on Jewish ownership of real estate and employment in government as well as an exceptional prohibition on intermarriage. During the seventh century there were attempts to prohibit circumcision and observance of the Sabbath and to forcibly convert all Spanish Jews—thus igniting an emigration movement to North Africa. By 694 the Jews had been officially defined as Christianity's slaves, whose children must be forcibly turned into Christians.

At that point Islam assaulted Western Europe. The subsequent struggle across Spain between Muslims and Christians gave the theologically neutral Jews political opportunities and economic leverage. Soon enough Spanish Jewry enjoyed a material prosperity and cultural fertility unparalleled at the time elsewhere in the Diaspora.

The favorable change in attitude toward the Jews surfaced almost as soon as the Muslims arrived, when the new conquerors placed various fortresses under their custody. The Jews also benefited from the Muslim rulers' determination to assert their independence from the caliphate in Baghdad, by conducting their own policies vis-à-vis minorities. In Spain, unlike the rest of the medieval Muslim world, Christianity posed a constant and tangible threat to the survival of any Muslim ruler. The need for local allies, and the Jews availability for that function, made Muslim Spain's leaders ignore anti-Jewish attitudes that occasionally prevailed in the Muslim Middle East.

(OPPOSITE)
BASIN WITH TRILINGUAL INSCRIPTION—HEBREW, LATIN, AND GREEK.
FIFTH CENTURY. TARRAGONA. MARBLE. MUSEO SEFARDI, TOLEDO.
Jews settled in Spain centuries before its adoption of Christianity, and may in fact have been there already before the Second Temple's destruction. The Hebrew inscription reads in part, "Shalom al Israel" (May there be peace on Israel). Though the imagery—the seven-branched menorah and what can be interpreted as a tree of life, and perhaps even a shofar, ram's horn— along with the Hebrew inscription clearly mean that this basin had a Jewish connection. Its use is unknown.

INTERIOR OF THE SANTA MARIA LA
BLANCA SYNAGOGUE IN TOLEDO.
*Built in the thirteenth century, the
synagogue still offers a glimpse of Spanish
Jewry's affluence.*

SINAGOGA DEL TRANSITO, TOLEDO. *Built in 1354–1357, the synagogue was part of an effort led by Pedro I and his treasurer, Rabbi Samuel Halevi, to restore Castille following the Black Death. However, in a sign of Spanish Jewry's decline, three years after the synagogue's completion Halevi was abruptly put in prison, where he died.*

HAVDALAH SERVICE FROM THE SISTER HAGGADAH. FOURTEENTH CENTURY, SPAIN. VELLUM. MS. 14761, FOL. 26V. THE BRITISH LIBRARY, LONDON.

Spanish Jewry's distinctive liturgy was preserved by Sephardi diaspora that emerged in the aftermath of the Expulsion.

By the tenth century, the Jewish leader Hisdai ibn-Shaprut was appointed the Córdoba caliphate's foreign minister and became Spanish Jewry's as well as world Jewry's undeclared leader, pleading at one point with Byzantine leaders on behalf of an oppressed Jewish community in Italy. On another occasion, his deep Jewish awareness and broad political horizons made him seek a correspondence with the distant and mysterious Khazar kingdom's leaders, whom he asked about their commitment to the Jewish faith. Ibn-Shaprut's precedent, a Jew rising to political prominence in one court, was emulated many times later and elsewhere, in both Muslim and Christian Spain. Eventually, this political tolerance, and the material opportunity with which it came coupled generated by the eleventh century a massive Jewish immigration to Muslim-ruled Spain.

Eager to depart the rapidly declining caliphates east of the Mediterranean, thousands of Jews were attracted to the Muslim universe's westernmost frontier. Here they sought opportunity much the same way modern-era immigrants gravitated to the New World. Jews also increasingly returned to own and farm Spanish soil, benefiting from the Muslims lack of an anti-Jewish agenda as fierce as medieval Christianity's, and from the

הָעוֹלָם בּוֹרֵא מְאוֹרֵי הָאֵשׁ

בָּרוּךְ

אַתָּה
יְיָ אֱלֹהֵינוּ
מֶלֶךְ

הָעוֹלָם הַמַּבְדִּיל בֵּין קֹדֶשׁ
לְחוֹל בֵּין אוֹר לְחֹשֶׁךְ בֵּין
יִשְׂרָאֵל לָעַמִּים בֵּין יוֹם הַשְּׁבִיעִי
לְשֵׁשֶׁת יְמֵי הַמַּעֲשֶׂה בֵּין

שֶׁטְפֵן כָּסָא וּמוֹזְגִין חַמְרָא וְגַם כֵּן בִּרְכַּת הַיַּיִן

וְקִדּוּשׁ הַיּוֹם וְאוֹמ בָּרוּךְ

אֱתָה יְיָ אֱלֹהֵינוּ מֶלֶךְ הָעוֹלָם בּוֹרֵא פְּרִי

הַגָּפֶן בָּרוּךְ אַתָּה יְיָ אֱלֹהֵינוּ מֶלֶךְ

הָעוֹלָם אֲשֶׁר בָּחַר בָּנוּ מִכָּל עַם וְרוֹמְמָנוּ מִכָּל

לָשׁוֹן וְקִדְּשָׁנוּ בְּמִצְוֹתָיו וַתִּתֶּן לָנוּ יְיָ אֱלֹהֵינוּ בְּאַהֲבָה

מוֹעֲדִים לְשִׂמְחָה חַגִּים וּזְמַנִּים לְשָׂשׂוֹן אֶת יוֹם

חַג הַמַּצּוֹת הַזֶּה זְמַן חֵרוּתֵינוּ בְּאַהֲבָה מִקְרָא

קֹדֶשׁ זֵכֶר לִיצִיאַת מִצְרַיִם כִּי בָנוּ בָחַרְתָּ וְאוֹתָנוּ

קִדַּשְׁתָּ מִכָּל הָעַמִּים וּמוֹעֲדֵי קָדְשֶׁךָ בְּשִׂמְחָה

local Christians' need to compete with the local Muslims over the Jews' sympathy and services. Consequently, the Jews' legal status was so solid that they were on a par with Christians even when confronting them in civil suits, a situation that was unthinkable in medieval Christendom.

The initial phase of the Jewish renaissance in Spain overlapped the first three centuries of Muslim presence in Iberia. During this period the Umayyad dynasty consolidated its rule over most of the peninsula, except for the Barcelona enclave in the northeast and the entire northwest between the kingdoms of Navarre and León. Toledo, Saragossa, Córdoba, and Granada in the Muslim sphere, and Barcelona and Navarre in the Christian one, were among the great new Jewish centers that coalesced during those centuries.

It was under these conditions that one of the most monumental eras of Jewish spiritual creation arose. Benefiting from the relative freedom created by the peninsula's rapidly shifting political alliances, Jews produced there some of the most original and lasting works on the Bible, Jewish law, philosophy, philology and liturgy, as well as original poetry and literature. The constant interaction with non-Jews also generated considerable secular writings by Jews.

Initially, Spain's Torah scholars had no contacts with their Franco-German peers across the Pyrenees. However, in the generation immediately following the 1096 massacres, ties were established with the academies of Provence. By the thirteenth century promising Talmudists from Spain were studying in Germany, and, upon their return, promoting the study of the Torah according to Franco-German methods.

The consequent blending of the Spanish tradition, which stressed the practical search for a legal ruling, and the Franco-German tradition, which emphasized the intellectual challenge of the legal deliberation regardless of its outcome, became the hallmark of Spanish Talmudic scholarship. Rabbinical luminaries Shlomo ben-Aderet, Aaron ha-Levi of Barcelona, and Nissim of Girodni produced classic commentaries that have been studied through the centuries in Talmudic academies from the Middle East to North America.

In the eleventh century, Muslim Spain began disintegrating into local kingdoms amid much anarchy and mayhem. Invasions from North Africa of religious fanatics such as the Almoravids and the Almohads proved that Islam could be as hostile to Judaism as Christianity. Forced conversions encouraged Jewish emigration or the secret observance of Judaism by Jews who outwardly adopted Islam.

Still, Spain remained for the Jews a land of opportunity. When Muslim persecution became intolerable, many found in the Christian north a haven no less attractive than others had in the more moderately Muslim North Africa. In essence, as long as Spain was politically disjointed, socially volatile, and religiously diverse, newly dispossessed Jews could find a place where they could restore their political rights and seek personal fulfillment somewhere within it.

BURGOS BIBLE.

1260, SPAIN. PARCHMENT. MS. HEBR. 4° 790, FOLS. 309V–310R. THE JEWISH NATIONAL AND UNIVERSITY LIBRARY, JERUSALEM.

Spanish Jewry's scholars dedicated much of their work to poetry, literature, and biblical commentary, unlike their successors in East Europe, who focused on the study and interpretation of Jewish law.

SEDER SCENE FROM THE BROTHER HAGGADAH.

THIRD QUARTER OF THE FOURTEENTH CENTURY CATALONIA. ADD. MS. OR. 1404, FOL. 8V. THE BRITISH LIBRARY, LONDON.

Jewish migration to the Christian north intensified as instability grew in Spain's Muslim south.

Shmuel ha-Nagid (993–1056), for example, one of Spanish Jewry's greatest scholars and leaders, was a refugee from Córdoba, Umayyad Spain's political, economic, and cultural capital. In 1013, when the city fell to the Berbers after a protracted siege, the poet and scientist turned warrior and statesman moved south, to Malaga. There he rapidly rose in political prominence and ultimately led, for thirty years, Granada's domestic and foreign affairs, under King Habus and his son Badis. In a series of poems he sent to his son Joseph after 1043, ha-Nagid described the battles he led, attaching discussions of their political contexts and military tactics. Yet even while being so deeply immersed in affairs of state, he headed a Talmudic academy and wrote a commentary of his own on the Talmud as well as research on biblical Hebrew. He also composed many poems on predominantly secular subjects, including nature and romance.

Unlike Shmuel ha-Nagid, who migrated to Spain's southernmost coast, or the Maimonides family, who fled all the way to North Africa in the wake of the post-Umayyad turmoil, the broader historical trend led Jews north, away from constantly unstable, frequently hostile, and rapidly shrinking Muslim Spain. Once relocated on the other side of the religious divide, Iberian Jewry initially managed to retain its utility and restore its prominence. Abraham ibn-Daud (c. 1110–1180), for instance, who was descended from a dynasty of senior officials in Spain's Muslim regimes, made a smooth transition to the Christian kingdom of Castile. There he held a senior military position and became well-known for assisting Jews in their flight from the Muslim south to the Christian north.

Ibn-Daud's continued political importance after his dramatic resettlement reflected the accomplishments of many other, less prominent Jews who adjusted economically to Iberia's rapidly changing political circumstances. In their newly reconquered lands, Christian rulers saw in the Jews a useful element for economic revitalization and political consolidation. Consequently, discriminatory laws and norms were sometimes set aside. In various localities Jews were actually encouraged to purchase land, take part in government administration, and manage royal properties. In many places Christian rulers allocated the Jews relatively large, well-located, and highly defensible urban neighborhoods. Sometimes rulers gave their Jewish subjects explicit permission to kill their attackers, and often they personally vouched for their security. However, this benevolence was circumstantial and temporary. Once Christianity consolidated its grip on the reconquered lands, the Jews' status and security began to wane.

The life of Rabbi Moses ben-Nahman, better-known as Nahmanides (c. 1194–1270), illustrates the Iberian dilemma. Born in Girona, Catalonia, just inside Spain's northeastern corner, Nahmanides practiced medicine and headed an academy where he trained some of the greatest-ever Talmudic commentators. His status as the leader of Catalonian Jewry was solid, and King Jaime I often consulted him. However, in 1263,

(ABOVE)

CERVERA BIBLE.

Scribe: Samuel Ben-Abraham Ibn Nathan. Artist: Joseph ha-Zarefati. 1300, Spain. Parchment. Ms. 72, fol. 316v. National Library, Lisbon.

The Cervera Bible is an example of early Castilian Hebrew illuminated manuscripts. Depicted here is the vision of the prophet Zechariah. Olive trees that represent the renewed lineage of King David and of the High Priest provide the oil to light the menorah.

(OPPOSITE)

BIBLE.

Scribe: Moses ibn Zabara. Artist: Joseph ibn Hayyim. 1476, La Corunna. Gouache on vellum, gold and silver leaf. Ms. Kennicott I, fol. 439r. Bodleian Library, Oxford.

La Corunna's Jews prospered until the expulsion itself, benefiting from their city's location on the Atlantic.

that same king forced him to represent Judaism in a public theological debate in Barcelona with Pablo Christiani, a Jew who had converted into Christianity.

Though Nahmanides emerged victorious—the king even awarded him a sum of money—he consequently became anathema to the local Catholic establishment. Two years later monks in Catalonia sought his indictment for blasphemy, thus ignoring the permission the king had given Nahmanides to speak his mind during the great debate.

And so, at seventy-one, after decades of prominence among Catalonian Catholics and Jews, Nahmanides had to flee the region where he had spent his entire life. After crossing the Mediterranean amid considerable tribulations, a dispossessed and disillusioned Nahmanides landed in Acre and then proceeded to Jerusalem. There, he helped rehabilitate the local Jewish community, which had been severely decimated during the Crusades. He established a synagogue in Jerusalem and, scholars believe, a Talmudic academy, before dying in Acre in 1270.

In retrospect, Nahmanides' incredible biography hints at the bleak future that awaited Spain's illustrious Jewish civilization in its remaining two centuries.

Beginning in the second half of the thirteenth century, the Church steadily began to gather power, and Spain's Jews became more vulnerable. Though the process took centuries, the Reconquista's completion was unequivocal and its repercussions swift. The completion came with King Ferdinand and Queen Isabella's conquest in January 1492 of Granada, the region just northeast of Gibraltar and the last non-Christian enclave in Spain.

Inspired by the euphoria that came along with Granada's capture and, more importantly, with the restoration of Christianity's grip on the entire land of Spain, the royal couple now lent an ear to the Jews' sworn enemies. Initially, fifteenth-century Spaniard monarchs had followed in their predecessors' footsteps, appreciating the Jews' economic utility, fearing the repercussions of their mass departure, and dismissing clerical demands to adopt a new and severely anti-Jewish policy.

However, the Spanish Church and its agenda gathered momentum as the reconquest proceeded. In the late 1470s the Spanish Inquisition was established as a tool aimed at treating the country's distinctive "Jewish condition" even more harshly than existing papal norms and tools already allowed. Essentially a religious investigation bureau, this organization searched for people who were Christians outwardly but in fact practiced Judaism. Obsessed with a belief that heretics were contaminating their society while also being in urgent need of salvation, the inquisitors set out to "redeem" nonbelievers.

By the 1480s what had begun as a quest to convert the Jews had transformed into a deep suspicion even of those who did change faiths. Remaining Jews were seen as the culprits behind the *Marranos*' perceived—and often actual—refusal to fully abandon their ancestral faith. Attempts to prevent the newly converted from maintaining their

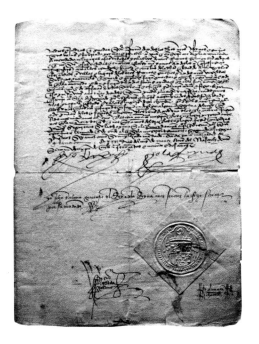

(ABOVE)

THE ROYAL EDICT, SIGNED IN 1492 BY KING FERDINAND AND QUEEN ISABELLA, ORDERING THE EXPULSION OF ALL JEWS FROM SPAIN.
The expulsion came twelve years after pressures from the Church and the burghers led to the establishment of the Inquisition.

(OPPOSITE)

AUTO-DA-FÉ, PRESIDED OVER BY SAINT DOMINIC DE GUSMAN.
OIL ON WOOD. MUSEO DEL PRADO, MADRID, SPAIN.
By the 1480s what began as a quest to convert the Jews transformed into a deep suspicion, even of those who actually converted.

Remembering Jerusalem: Pilgrims and Emissaries

Throughout the centuries when the Jewish settlement in the Holy Land was at its historic lows, two institutions did nonetheless sustain the physical connection between the Jews and their land: pilgrimage and charity.

Regardless of the political situation, tourist traffic from the Jewish Diaspora to the Land of Israel never fully stopped. Even in the worst times, when Jews were legally forbidden to reside in Jerusalem, first by the Byzantines and then by the Crusaders, Jews were allowed to pray at the Western Wall on the Ninth of Av, the annual fast day commemorating the destruction of both Temples. Besides Jerusalem, pilgrims would visit mainly the other three "holy cities," as they came to be known during the Middle Ages: Safed, also known as the city of the Kabbalists; Tiberias, where the Jerusalem Talmud was written (c. 400 C.E); and Hebron, where the Patriarchs are buried.

Following the short-lived Safed renaissance in the sixteenth century, many Diaspora communities financially assisted the Jewish community of the Holy Land. Initially, charity efforts were managed from Istanbul, which became particularly affluent since its conquest by the Muslims. The Istanbul community also benefited from its ability to access to the Ottoman regime. At the turn of the seventeenth century, a special committee, set up in order to raise funds in Greece and Asia Minor, dispatched two shiploads of goods and cash for the Safed community. However, eventually one boat sank and the other was robbed. That failure made the Jews of Venice—where such maritime news arrived quickly—join the effort to help the Jews of the Land of Israel. In fact, the Venetian community went one step beyond the Jews of Istanbul, by imposing an annual tax for the sake of supporting the Jews of the Holy Land. They also urged other communities to funnel their donations to the

Jews of the Holy Land through Venice, which was a major point of origin for ships sailing to the Land of Israel.

As the Venetian state's power began waning in the late seventeenth century—in the aftermath of America's discovery, which shifted the focus of international trade from the Mediterranean to the High Seas—the local Jewish community's leading role in raising funds was lost to the communities of Amsterdam and Leghorn, though those two focused on financing fellow Sephardi communities only.

The effort to aid the Holy Land's Ashkenazi communities was managed from Frankfurt in the west and Poland in the east, where the semi-autonomous Jewish leadership forum—which known as the Council of the Four Lands—earmarked for the Jews of the Holy Land some of the taxes it charged annually. By the eighteenth and nineteenth centuries Diaspora donations became the main source of income for the Land of Israel's Jews.

In some cases the fund-raising effort involved dispatching emissaries from the Holy Land to remote Diaspora communities; in others permanently resident bureaucrats sent to Jerusalem by Diaspora communities managed the charities. Both methods offered rare instruments of communication and expression of solidarity among otherwise disjointed and far-flung communities.

(ABOVE, LEFT)
MOSAIC IN BYZANTINE-ERA SYNAGOGUE, TIBERIAS.
The menorahs, which were depicted by the artist alongside shofars *and four species much like those Jews still utilize during the high holidays, reflect the yearning for the destroyed Temple and Jerusalem, which Jews were forbidden to access at the time.*

(ABOVE, RIGHT)
BAROQUE-STYLED TORAH ARK FROM THE CONEGLIANO VENETO SYNAGOGUE.
1701–1717. U. NAHON MUSEUM OF ITALIAN JEWISH ART, JERUSALEM.
The ark and the rest of the synagogue's interior were moved in the early 1950s to Jerusalem by the city's Italian Jewish community after the city of Conegliano had planned to demolish it.

(OPPOSITE)
JOSEPH'S TOMB OUTSIDE NABLUS.
During the Middle Ages Jews came to the Holy Land mainly in order to make a pilgrimage to Judaism's holy sites.

ties to Jews and Judaism—for instance, by trying to separate them residentially—all failed. Hostility toward those born Jewish, therefore, regardless of their current persuasion, reached new peaks.

The first Inquisition-sponsored public burning at the stake, known as an *auto-da-fé*, was held in Seville in 1481. Two years later the rising anti-Jewish movement managed to get the Jews of Andalusia expelled. In that year, Tomas de Torquemada, the royal couple's personal confessor, was appointed head of the Inquisition. An exceptionally fanatic Dominican priest determined to eradicate the *conversos*' Judaism, Torquemada set out to organize the formidable agency that would ultimately bring Spain's elaborate Jewish history to its abrupt end.

Torquemada and his deputies established a network of local tribunals and torture chambers which it used to extract confessions and encourage people to testify against *conversos*. Informants would name former Jews who had been seen socializing with practicing Jews, buying kosher meat, or refraining from lighting fires on Saturday. In 1488 an associate of Torquemada's published an anti-*Marrano* book, *Alboraique*. This polemic portrayed the *conversos* as sub-humans similar to Mohammed beast (Borak) and besmirched them as inherently disloyal, weak, and unproductive. Such attitudes gradually rendered post-Reconquista Spain's war on its Jews a racist affair, both because it claimed the Jews' "faults" were hereditary and because it suggested—in disagreement with previous Christian dogma—that the Jews were incurable, even by conversion.

The psychosis created by the Inquisition, which started off as an a effort to unveil facts concerning religious faith, soon transformed into an endeavor to invent fiction about political plots. First, in 1490, a group of converted Jews were accused of crucifying a Christian child and attempting to spread disease through witchcraft. (The following year the defendants were all burned at the stake.) Then, in 1491, Torquemada accused the Jews and the *Marranos* of conspiring to take over the country. King Ferdinand and Queen Isabella believed these accusations, and in March 1492 signed an edict ordering all Jews to leave Spain within four months.

In July of that year, in a spectacle that was an inversion of the biblical Exodus, at least 200,000 disenfranchised, dispossessed, and disillusioned Jews forcibly sailed into the unknown, leaving behind them a vast land that Jews had called home for the better part of a millennium.

AFTER THE EXPULSION: A DIASPORA WITHIN THE DIASPORA

The Spanish Expulsion generated a dramatic demographic redistribution. Indeed, during the sixteenth and seventeenth centuries, Spanish and Portuguese Jews spread throughout the broader Mediterranean basin and as far north, east, and west as Germany, Asia Minor, and America. With these people went their rich past and a

מלך

וַיְהִי בִּשְׁנַת תְּמַלְכוֹ אֶת דָּא שֶׁיָּרוֹכֵן
מֶלֶךְ יְהוּדָה הֵמִכִּית כְּלָאוֹ וַיְדַבֵּר
אֶתּוֹ טָבוֹת וַיִּתֵּן אֶת כִּסְאוֹ מֵעַל
כִּסֵּא הַמְּלָכִים אֲשֶׁר אִתּוֹ בְּבָבֶל
וְשִׁנָּא אֶת בִּגְדֵי כִלְאוֹ וְאָכַל לֶחֶם
תָּמִיד לְפָנָיו כָּל יְמֵי חַיָּיו וַאֲרֻחָתוֹ
אֲרֻחַת תָּמִיד נִתְּנָה לוֹ מֵאֵת הַמֶּלֶךְ
דְּבַר יוֹם בְּיוֹמוֹ כָּל יְמֵי חַיָּיו

ויהי אחרי
מות משה
עבד

יהוה ויאמר יהוה אל יהושע בן נון
משרת משה לאמר משה עבדי מת
ועתה קום עבר את הירדן הזה אתה וכל
העם הזה אל הארץ אשר אנכי נתן להם
לבני ישראל כל מקום אשר תדרך כף
רגלכם בו לכם נתתיו כאשר דברתי אל
משה מהמדבר והלבנון הזה ועד הנהר
הגדול נהר פרת כל ארץ החתים ועד
הים הגדול מבוא השמש יהיה גבלכם
לא יתיצב איש לפניך כל ימי חייך כאשר
הייתי עם משה אהיה עמך לא ארפך ולא
אעזבך חזק ואמץ כי אתה תנחיל את העם

ד דמפי
אבא ריגבא
שמשא
מילכא
5
הפטרה
לפרשת
וזאת
הברכה

ב ג
רד
פסו

ב ה
וחס

ו ה
ה

ו ר
פסו
כסף

collective identity as "survivors." This remarkable perseverance is what makes the term *Sephardi* (which in Hebrew means "Spanish") relevant to this very day, particularly in Israel, but also in scores of communities from Western Europe to Latin America. Indeed, during the five centuries since the Expulsion, Sephardic communities have often comprised a diaspora within the Diaspora. Jews of Spanish descent married within their community, maintained their own customs and liturgy, and developed a global network of intercontinental merchants.

Initially, most of those expelled—up to an estimated 120,000 of at least 200,000 Jews, *Marranos,* and New Christians—resettled in nearby Portugal, where the Inquisition's influence had yet to peak. Though in 1496 Lisbon also expelled its Jews, King Manuel I soon changed course. In his quest to both satisfy the church and retain the Jews, he decided to unilaterally impose Christianity on the Jewish community. To accomplish this, he first had thousands of Jewish children kidnapped and baptized, then gathered their parents in public places where they too were baptized en-masse, and finally had them collectively and fully legitimized as Christian subjects of Portugal.

Paradoxically, these Jews were not just allowed to stay in their host country, but in fact were forbidden to leave it. In effect, the regime was pretending its Jews were Christian while the Jews pretended they no longer espoused their ancestral faith. This unwritten deal lasted four decades, until 1536 when Portugal established its own Inquisition. Knowing full well what might be awaiting them, thousands of secret Jews fled Portugal without waiting for events to unfold, even in the face of prohibitions on emigration.

This Portuguese exodus, along with the ongoing trickle of crypto-Jews who continued to leave Spain, eventually created the Sephardi diaspora that settled on four continents. Shrewdly they maneuvered their way through a rapidly changing world, sinking roots in the Ottoman Near East, Christian America, and a host of European commercial hubs where Catholic zeal had either waned or altogether vanished in the wake of the Reformation. As the ironies of Diaspora history go, Christopher Columbus embarked on the journey that ended up in his discovery of the New World just as the last expellees were sailing away from Spain, in August 1492. Thus, a major horizon for Jewish resettlement opened just as another closed and by a person who may have himself been a descendant of *Marranos.*

Coupled with the original expellees of 1492, who had mostly relocated around the Mediterranean basin, from Morocco and Algeria through Italy and Asia Minor to Egypt and the Land of Israel, the Sephardim were now populating a cultural and commercial universe of their own.

Portuguese Jewry's departure from Iberia coincided with Rome's gradual loss of its grip on its own flock, as Protestantism drove a wedge between the pope and much of

central and northern Europe. And so, just when Christian zeal to conquer old lands and new souls brought anti-Jewish abuse to new peaks, Christianity itself—both Western and Eastern—was dealt a severe blow, one from which it never fully recovered, and which inadvertently opened for the expellees new horizons which compensated for those it had lost.

Thus, in the generations immediately after the Portuguese Expulsion, liberal Amsterdam became the beating heart of an exceptionally globalized Spanish-Portuguese Jewry. The community that produced such scholars as Benedict Spinoza (1632–1677) and Manasseh ben-Israel (1604–1657) numbered no more than five thousand Jews in the mid-seventeenth century. Nevertheless, it inspired and provided leadership—spiritually and materially—for dozens of young Spanish-Portuguese communities elsewhere.

In 1492, some fifty thousand Spanish Jews settled in the Ottoman Empire and Italy. As if to continue their ancestors' balancing act between Christian and Muslim lands, the *Marranos* established communities on both sides of the Mediterranean basin's religious divide, whose major poles were the commercial powerhouses of Venice and Constantinople.

Unlike the Italian city-states, whose small size and Christian inspiration limited their ability and willingness to absorb Jews, the Ottoman Empire was now physically vast and economically thirsty for the kind of commercial vigor and political loyalty that Jews in general, and the expellees in particular, could offer.

Sultan Bayezid II (1481–1512), who consolidated the Turkish grip on southeastern Europe and the eastern Mediterranean basin, is believed to have personally ordered local governors throughout the empire to welcome and protect the homeless Jews. His action prompted a massive movement of Iberian Jews to the Balkans, Asia Minor, the Land of Israel, and Egypt. Within one generation of the Expulsion, the Ottoman Empire, which in previous decades had already absorbed Jewish expellees from France and Central Europe, became host to the largest Jewish community in the world.

In Asia Minor, the indigenous Jewish community helped the mostly destitute refugees by raising funds to meet the costs of their absorption. Other refugees, however, retained their former prominence despite being dislocated by the Expulsion. For instance, when Joseph Hamon (d. 1518), a Portuguese physician, arrived in Constantinople, Sultan Beyazid made the refugee his personal doctor and advisor.

In fact, the Iberian influx was so massive that by the end of the sixteenth century the Sephardim, who by then comprised the bulk of Constantinople's and Salonika's communities (each numbered twenty thousand Jews), had grown to dominate Ottoman Jewry, including indigenous Jews (referred to as "Romaniots") who had resided there since antiquity. In later generations, the Sephardim spread out across the Balkans, establishing important communities in places such as Sofia, Belgrade, and Sarajevo.

In North Africa some twenty thousand expellees settled in Morocco, where the Muslim regime greeted them warmly and allowed them to quickly prosper and restore their observance of Judaism. Other expellees went elsewhere in North Africa, including Portuguese-ruled areas where the Inquisition was too weak to confront the regime in its quest to exploit its colonial possessions.

The *Marrano* diaspora also fast embraced its era's newest frontier: America. Jews were interpreters on Columbus's vessels as he landed in Central America the year of the expulsion, and on Pedro Álvares Cabral's fleet when he set out in 1500 for what would later be named Brazil. The colonies that were established in the wake of those journeys included *Marranos*. Soon enough the conflict between the Jews' economic utility and their religious nonconformity that had evolved in Iberia surfaced again in Latin America, as did also the same mechanisms of persecution, denial, and pragmatism. Inquisition trials and torture chambers were set up in various Spanish and Portuguese colonies (in the wake of the two kingdoms' 1580–1640 merger), from Mexico through Brazil all the way down to Peru. And yet New Christians played major roles in pioneering Brazil's raw-material exports, until its reconquest by Portugal in the middle of the seventeenth century, a development that set the Jews sailing hurriedly northwest along the coast to Surinam and Curaçao.

Sephardi Jews found their way to North America as well. Here they benefited from the relative tolerance of the Dutch (notwithstanding the anti-Jewish sentiments of the New Amsterdam governor, Peter Stuyvesant) and the British. The lively and openly Jewish community of Dutch Brazil who arrived in New Amsterdam in 1654 was the first of a dozen predominantly Sephardi-built Jewish communities that sprouted in North America, from New Orleans to Quebec, before the American Revolution. Thus, Iberian Jews sowed the seeds of what would later become the largest and richest Jewish community in history.

In Europe, the Iberian exodus led many *Marranos* north, where they settled in the commercial towns and royal hubs that would be in the forefront of Christendom's transition from feudalism to mercantilism. A rim of such communities straddled Western Europe's seashores, from Bordeaux in the south to Hamburg in the north. In regions torn apart by intra-Christian conflict, a new tolerance for the Jews and their faith gradually evolved and ultimately transformed Diaspora life.

In all, the Spanish-Portuguese effort to erase both Judaism and Jewishness was successful on the local level, but it utterly failed on the global plane. If anything, the expulsions gave Sephardi Jewry both the imperative to spread around the world and the opportunity to become major players in the commercial connection of its continents.

THE DIASPORA
IN THE WEST

P erhaps the most incredible of all Diaspora sagas is the rise of Ashkenazi Jewry. Originally, *Ashkenaz* (the word comes from the medieval Hebrew name for Germany) was but a handful of minuscule, isolated communities in early medieval France and Germany. However, over the centuries their descendants generated monumental Judaic scholars, the Hasidic and Zionist movements, American Jewry, intellectuals on the scale of Sigmund Freud, Karl Marx, and Albert Einstein—and the bulk of the victims of the Holocaust.

That Jews lived in Western Europe before and immediately after the decline and fall of the Roman Empire is undisputed. What is less clear is their number. According to historian Irving Agus, the ten million Yiddish-speakers who lived in the year 1900 practically all descended from some ten thousand Jews who lived in France, Germany, and Italy by the end of the eighth century. Those, in turn, had descended from traders who settled along the Rhine basin during the fourth century and succeeded the Greeks as import-export agents for inner Europe.

SEEDS OF GREATNESS: THE FRANCO-GERMAN SAGA

During the late Roman era, while Europe gradually embraced Christianity, trade across the Mediterranean was dwindling. Consequently, Jewish presence north of the Alps was all but anecdotal. Moreover, initial attempts to convert the Jews in various towns inland led many to move to more worldly Marseilles. However, by the eighth century the Frankish dynasty encouraged the importation of myriad luxuries, and Jewish traders rooted in Mesopotamia were ideal for the role of imperial supplier. Consequently, Jews began settling in the Rhône basin and, without knowing it, laid the foundations for a small but vibrant diaspora that would soon produce some of Judaism's most monumental scholars. It came to be known in rabbinic literature as Ashkenaz, a name first mentioned in the Bible, though not in reference to the Franco-German and Polish-Russian expanses that it came to denote in Jewish history. (It originally referred to a region near the Upper

Euphrates, but by the Crusades Jewish sources used it as a reference to Franco-Germany.)

The Carolingian era's early settlers were soon followed by Jews from Italy and Spain, and the settlement drive that began along the Rhône basin soon proceeded north to the Rhineland and northwest to Paris and its environs. These early French Jews dealt extensively in farming, particularly vineyard cultivation, and enjoyed a status so solid that some of them even served as Frankish diplomats. One of those, a man named Isaac, was a member of a delegation Charles the Great sent in 797 to visit the legendary Harun el-Rashid in Baghdad.

In the Rhineland Jewish merchant families concentrated on the Rhine's west bank, from Speyer in the south to Cologne in the north, and spread also farther east to the Danube basin's Regensburg and beyond there to Prague. These communities, like those to their west, enjoyed the protection of local bishops, princes, and governors who stood up to clerical forces that sought to harass the Jews. This arrangement, which was based on special-privilege contracts that were officially granted to the Jews in lieu of their economic services, worked for early Ashkenazi Jewry repeatedly—until the Crusades.

On the eve of the First Crusade in 1096, Franco-German Jewry had grown to some twenty thousand people who lived in small communities often headed by international traders who specialized in wine exportation. It was in this setting that the monumental Talmudic scholar and Bible commentator Solomon ben-Isaac (c. 1040–1105), better known by his Hebrew acronym Rashi, studied, taught, traded, and died.

Born in Troyes, southeast of Paris, he went northeast to study in the Talmudic academy of Mainz, in the Rhineland, at age twenty. Then he moved south to Worms, finally returning to his hometown, a decade later. Rashi's journeys sliced through the early Ashkenazi sphere of expansion.

(ABOVE)

THE RASHI CHAPEL IN WORMS. *Built in 1034, the chapel was destroyed on Kristallnacht and rededicated in 1982. Franco-German Jewry began to unravel with the launch of the First Crusade, nine years before the great commentator's death in 1105.*

Coincidentally, he returned to the French part of Ashkenaz about twenty-five years before the First Crusade's departure to the Holy Land. Thus Rashi inadvertently avoided the destruction that befell the communities of the Rhine basin in 1096.

Following the collapse of the German centers of Judaic study in the wake of the First Crusade, the Talmudic academy in Troyes became Western Europe's most prominent center of Judaic studies. The blossoming of Judaic scholarship in Ashkenaz before the Crusades benefited from the general renaissance that followed Charlemagne's thirty-year-long conquest of much of Western Europe. According to one legend, the enlightened emperor actually invited a Babylonian scholar, Rabbi Machir, to set up the Talmudic academy of Narbonne in southern France. Though the tale is apparently unfounded, it echoes a vivid, if romanticized, memory of an era of security and tolerance, one that became the backdrop for a steady influx of Jewish immigrants, and which began to wane after the ninth century. From there on, much like Rashi's personal story, medieval Ashkenazi Jewry's became a tale of intellectual excellence amid daunting political circumstances and harsh religious persecution.

The Rhineland massacres were a turning point in Jewish history, since they marked institutionalized Christianity's dramatic transition from theoretical criticism and legal discrimination of the Jews to physical assault. Christianity's ongoing anti-Jewish propaganda spread across Europe and sank into the hearts of its believers. Many Christians became convinced that the Jews in their midst—who unlike most Christians at the time were literate and yet rejected the New Testament—were demons, sub-humans capable of anything and everything, from poisoning wells to slaughtering children.

As they braced for the Crusades' impending doom, the Jews paid hefty sums of money for mercenaries, while seeking—and ultimately obtaining—assorted kings' and bishops' protection from their approaching attackers. Still, when the invaders arrived, all town gates were flung open. In some places local leaders actually defended the Jews, but for the most part the easily inflamed masses were with the Crusaders, and the Crusaders were too mighty to be defied. The Jews, who though utterly ill-equipped and untrained, actually fought in some cases, but in all they were slaughtered by the thousands.

The Crusades had a profound impact on Ashkenazi Jewry. In the short term, entire Jewish communities, including women and children, were slaughtered, including the key communities of Mainz and Worms. In the attacks' aftermath, the quality, frequency, and—above all—legitimacy of anti-Jewish assaults in Europe were dramatically transformed. In the longer term, they formed a watershed between the relative security and tolerance enjoyed by Ashkenazi Jewry in the centuries that preceded the Crusades and the harsh discrimination, persecution, wandering, dispossession, flight, expulsions, and murder that followed them.

The Crusades' violence took place mainly in the Rhineland and the lands to its east. Yet their harsh impact was felt to the west as well. In 1171 some thirty Jews were burned

(ABOVE)

BOOK OF ISAIAH.

FRENCH, IN HEBREW CHARACTERS. THIRTEENTH CENTURY. BIBLIOTHEQUE PUBLIQUE DE L'UNIVERSITÉ DE BASLE.

Medieval French Jews were frequently international traders, and as such were more exposed than other contemporary Jews to the outer world and its culture.

"THE TRIAL OF THE JEWS OF TRENT."
1478-1479. INK, GOUACHE, AND GOLD ON PAPER.
YESHIVA UNIVERSITY MUSEUM, NEW YORK.

*This document records the false
accusation of local Jews for the killing of
a Christian boy. Franciscan friar
Bernardino da Feltre incited the North
Italian city's mob prior to the libel that
resulted in the extinction of the town's
Jewish community.*

DISPUTATION BETWEEN JEWISH
AND CHRISTIAN SCHOLARS.
GERMANY. FIFTEENTH CENTURY. WOODCUT.

*The Jews are recognizable by their
distinctive pointed hats. Due to their
political fragmentation in the German
lands, their treatment was less
consistent than in France.*

alive in Blois, south of Paris, in connection with a blood libel, that is Jews accused of killing Christians for ritual purposes. In 1242 the Talmud was burned in Paris following a public disputation. This dealt a severe blow to Judaic scholarship in the land where some of its greatest luminaries had lived, taught, and written, thus expanding the Catholic Church's war on Judaism to the Jews' bookshelves. During the twelfth century Ashkenazi Jewry was also being severely pressured by kidnappings for ransom, expulsion threats, and occasional killings.

Geographically, the Crusaders' massacres pushed the Jewish settlement eastward and northward, to Munich, Berlin, and Vienna, among other places. At the same time, the French parts of Ashkenaz were gradually depleted of Jews, as expulsions and massacres became increasingly frequent throughout the fourteenth century. At one point pogroms swept through two dozen Jewish communities in Alsace. The expulsion of 1306 (though subsequently rescinded several times), coupled with the turmoil that followed the Black Death of the mid-fourteenth century, eventually left early modern France all but devoid of Jews. A community that according to some estimates numbered one hundred thousand Jews at the turn of the fourteenth century dwindled over the next two hundred years to hardly a few thousand.

Although the German areas originally saw the worst carnage and bloodshed in the wake of the Crusades, Jews ultimately had a more persistent and extensive presence in these lands. German lands were more inconsistent in their treatment of the Jews due to their political fragmentation throughout the Middle Ages. The result was a strange combination of centuries-long hardship, stubborn demographic perseverance, and cultural continuity.

In the thirteenth century German Jews repeatedly faced blood and Host-desecration libels initiated by local clergymen, whose power was growing while an increasingly weak Holy Roman Empire was surrendering much of its authority to regional powers. The consequent lawlessness resulted in frequent attacks on Jewish communities—usually accompanied by blood libels, most notably the 1241 destruction of the Frankfurt community. Toward the end of the century the assaults on Germany's Jews intensified dramatically. In 1285 scores of Jews were burned at the stake in Munich, and in 1298 some 150 communities were destroyed, as thousands of Jews chose death rather than surrender to the mobs' demands that they convert.

That calamity, together with massacres in 1336 that spread over an even larger territory, as well as the wrath that met Ashkenazi Jewry in the wake of the Black Death, and the consequent destruction of three hundred communities should have resulted in the disappearance of Jews from German history. And yet the Jews clung to the German lands, restoring many of the destroyed communities and producing yet more rabbinical luminaries.

(ABOVE)

PLUNDERING OF THE FRANKFURT
GHETTO ON AUGUST 22, 1614.
COPPERPLATE ENGRAVING FROM JOHANN L.
GOTTFRIED'S *Historische Chronica* OF 1657. JEWISH
MUSEUM FRANKFURT.

*The Jews resisted before being herded into
the cemetery while looting continued.
The mayor of Frankfurt intervened so
that the Jews were able to escape, and
even more interestingly Emperor
Matthias intervened and had Fettmilch
and other leaders of the mob arrested and
beheaded. Frankfurt's Jews were allowed
to return, albeit to the ghetto, to which the
emperor affixed his coat of arms.*

In all, German Jewish history's incredible balance between vulnerability and durability reflected a lack of central rule, which in turn meant there was not strong government to defend its subjects (non-Jews too) from rioters, but also no potent authority that could execute a national Jewish policy the way the Spanish royals did. In the German lands, when a Jewish community was expelled from one locality, it could always find nearby another town or principality where the attitude toward the Jews would, at that moment, be better.

Still, the cumulative pressure certainly had its effect and gradually created an eastward migration movement. Initially this trend led to Vienna, where some of the Rhineland's great rabbis resettled. Eventually, the persecution in Germany led a growing number of its Jews farther east: to Poland.

POLAND: THE ILLUSION OF HARMONY AND PROSPERITY

The first Jews who appeared in Poland were apparently traders who passed there as early as the tenth century, but did not settle there. A substantive migration movement, which appears to have first emerged in response to the First Crusade, is echoed in contemporary sources, both Jewish and non-Jewish, as well as coins minted by Jews and bearing Hebrew inscriptions. Still, how the Jews came to Poland has been a subject of much speculation and fantasy over the years.

Suggestions that Polish Jewry may have been the product of the Khazar Empire's elite of Jewish converts have never been substantiated. At the same time, early communities that straddled the Byzantine commercial sphere around the Black Sea, arrived in Poland from the east but were quickly overshadowed by the influx of Franco-German Jews who arrived from beyond the western horizon throughout the thirteenth century. Evidently, whether demographically, geographically, or culturally, Polish Jewry was an extension of the Ashkenazi diaspora. Indeed, one of the first Polish regions to attract a sizable number of Jews was Silesia, which was actually a border region that eventually became heavily German.

(ABOVE)
TYKOCIN SYNAGOGUE, POLAND. *Built in 1642, in the rococo design, the synagogue was restored after World War II. The rise of Polish Jewry began with the eastward migration of Franco-German Jewry. The synagogue now houses a museum.*

The political leaders of Poland and Lithuania felt the Jews (and various other minorities) could be useful for settling newly conquered regions. Here, far from the established urban scenes, Jews specialized in leasing and developing lands owned by nobles, thus inadvertently settling frontiers while escaping the wrath of German royals and Polish townsmen. Jews also quickly became major commercial agents for Poland and Lithuania, linking those vast lands with the Mediterranean basin's Italian and Ottoman ports and goods.

By the time of the Spanish Expulsion there were up to thirty thousand Jews in some sixty areas across greater Poland, from Posnan in the west to Kiev in the east. Within two centuries this Jewish frontier land became the new spinal chord of Ashkenazi Jewry, just when the Diaspora's other pole, Sephardi Jewry, was relocating its own center of gravity.

By sheer coincidence, the plight of Franco-German Jewry in the west during the Black Death coincided with the rise of the tolerant Casimir the Great in the east. King Casimir, who expanded Poland's eastern and western extents into Russian and Western lands, often utilized diplomatic skill rather than military might. He unified the kingdom's government while establishing the self-rule of its towns, built fifty new castles, and opened the country's first university. A mediator by character, Casimir consolidated the Jews' status by confirming their privileges. Tradition claims he had a Jewish mistress

(ABOVE)

WOODEN SYNAGOGUE IN
PREDBORZ, POLAND.

C. 1929.

*Predborz is located about halfway
between Warsaw and Krakow. The
scholars who immigrated to Poland
tended to settle in its western parts, while
the less-developed east often attracted
entrepreneurs and adventurers.*

called Esther with whom he had two daughters. In any event, by the time he died in 1370, after thirty-seven years in power, Poland had become the ultimate haven for Franco-German Jewry.

Within Poland, the westernmost reaches of the Jewish settlement gave rise to new Torah scholars, while the less orderly eastern frontiers attracted a more adventurous and enterprising type of Jew. Having been expelled from many big towns, such Jews found a common cause with the Polish nobility, which had a vested interest in building new townships and developing trade with Western Europe. Poland's nobility, which was at loggerheads with the fiercely anti-Jewish clergy and became increasingly independent-minded in the face of the Reformation's challenge to Catholicism, found its interests served well by the Jews during the sixteenth century.

It was in this geographic setting and against this chaotic backdrop that Ashkenazi Jewry, for the first time since its inception between the Rhône and Rhine basins more

Tav. 25.

Vestire dei Pollacchi

than half a millennium earlier, multiplied dramatically. Economically, the burgeoning Jewish population dominated Poland's retail commerce and wholesale trade. As road safety improved and the nobility moved farther east, their unofficial alliance with the nobility led Ashkenazi Jewry deep into the Ukraine, where the nobles' newly established farms were badly in need of both seed capital and micromanagement, and the Jews were there to deliver them.

Consequently, Ashkenazi Jewry further stretched its geographical reach and economic sway. However, doing so dangerously exposed Polish Jewry's social flank. Much of the rapid development came at the expense of the nobility's other nemesis—the peasantry. In place was a leasing system, whereby Jewish managers sold Polish and Ukrainian peasants most of what they bought, and bought from the peasants most of what they produced. The Jews also commanded the local serfs in their work and, when necessary, punished them. This added up to a kind of friction that was a recipe for disaster.

(ABOVE)

NINETEENTH-CENTURY POLISH JEWS.
As Poland modernized, its Jews, here in attire typical of the time, became a crucial component in its burgeoning middle class.

(ABOVE)

ZHOVKA SYNAGOGUE, ZHOVKA, UKRAINE. *Despite the massacres of 1648–1649, Polish-Ukrainian Jewry continued to multiply and by the middle of the eighteenth century constituted some two-thirds of the Diaspora. The synagogue is an example of monumental masonry synagogues built in Eastern Europe from the late sixteenth through the early nineteenth century. During World War II, German explosives damaged the interior of the synagogue, but the walls were left intact. The Zhovka Synagogue is included on the World Monuments Fund's watch list of one hundred most-endangered sites and has received some funding for restoration.*

(RIGHT)

CHORAL SYNAGOGUE, KIEV, UKRAINE.

(ABOVE)

COSSACKS, LED BY CHEMIELNICKI,
ATTACKING JEWS IN THE FORTRESS
OF TULCHIN
PETER PARR. PAINTING ON CANVAS.
*At Tulchin, Jews defended themselves
together with Polish citizens, who later
betrayed them and abandoned them to
the Cossacks. European Jewry's east-
bound immigration was halted in the
wake of the 1648–1649 massacres.*

Meanwhile, the Jews' sense of security created by the nobles' solid political backing and physical fortification of their communities and synagogues (some were protected with rifles and even cannons) proved illusory. Considering the advances of the Counter-Reformation in the west, and the hostility between Catholic Poles and Orthodox Ukrainians in the east, the Jews' allies were weaker than they seemed.

Eventually, in 1648, the Poles faced a rebellion, led by Ukrainian noble Bogdan Chmielnicki's Cossack army and their Tatar allies. The consequent killing of thousands of Jews, pillaging of numerous synagogues, and torching of entire villages has made Chmielnicki one of the most infamous names in Jewish history. By 1649 Chmielnicki and his Tatar allies all but destroyed Ukrainian Jewry, which on the eve of his assault had already numbered more than 50,000 people. In the town of Nemirov, northwest of the Crimea, 6,000 Jews were butchered in one day. The 1648–1649 Cossack Revolt, which spilled into Poland proper all the way to Lublin in the west, coupled with the growing

GHETTO FIGHTERS SURRENDERING
TO GERMAN SOLDIERS IN
WARSAW, 1943.
*The 3 million Polish Jews who perished
in the Holocaust constituted about
one-tenth of Poland's overall population.
Some believe their absence contributed
to postwar Poland's poor economic
performance.*

Russian pressure on Poland from the east in the wake of its war with Sweden, brought
Ashkenazi Jewry's eastward expansion to an abrupt halt. In fact, its sixteenth-century
movement from west to east was now reversed, leading back from Slavic to
German lands.

Still, devastating though it was, the Cossack Revolt did not annihilate Polish Jewry,
nor did it deprive the Jews of their distinctive role in the Polish economy, where they
continued to constitute much of the middle class for three more centuries. Moreover, a
century after the Cossack massacres, two-thirds of the world's Jews lived in the Polish-
Lithuanian kingdom. By the end of the Napoleonic wars, the 1.25 million Jews in the
lands that once comprised Poland constituted 70 percent of the entire Diaspora.

By the eve of World War II there were 3.25 million Jews in the Republic of Poland.
Of them, 3 million were murdered in the Holocaust. Large and veteran communities
such as those of Warsaw, Lublin, or Cracow, with 352,000, 314,000, and 173,000 Jews

Moses Montefiore: The Gospel of Self-Help

No single individual symbolizes the maturation of modern British Jewry more than legendary philanthropist Sir Moses Montefiore. Born in 1784, while his parents were on a trip to Italy, Montefiore made his fortune in the wholesale tea trade and as one of the city's dozen "Jew brokers." Eventually, he and his partner and brother, Abraham, became sufficiently successful for Moses to marry his client Nathan Meyer Rothschild's sister, Judith.

Then, at the early age of forty, Montefiore abandoned his business activities. This fateful decision would result in an extraordinary, sixty-one-year-long career of donating for Jewish causes, lobbying on behalf of oppressed Jews, and inspiring Jewish self-help and change from within. As he was making his transition from business to philanthropy, Montefiore also began involving himself in Jewish communal affairs, first within the Sephardi community, as he donated thirteen "poor houses," and then in a broader context, as he became president of the Board of Deputies of British Jews, a position he held almost constantly for thirty-six years, and left only as he turned ninety.

In 1838 Montefiore was sheriff of London, and in that capacity hosted Queen Victoria on her first official visit to the capital. It was then that he was knighted. Firmly established within British high society, Montefiore set out to utilize both his formal position and social status in order to better the lot of Jews wherever they might be. His most important breakthrough in this regard was his successful interference with the Ottoman sultan himself in order to refute the 1840 Damascus blood libel and obtain imperial protection for the local Jews. This success earned Montefiore fame throughout the Jewish world. For the first time since the appearance of the false messiah Shabbetai Zevi, the Diaspora seemed to have a leader. In later years Montefiore's lobbying efforts on behalf of oppressed Jews would lead him to countries as far apart as Morocco and Russia.

Though his quasi-diplomacy often failed—most memorably in his effort to dissuade Czar Nicholas I from expelling Jews from western Russia and his failure to convince the Vatican to restore an abducted child to his Jewish parents—its echo was resounding. The city of London awarded Montefiore honorary citizenship after his return from Morocco in 1863, where he secured the sultan's protection for the local Jewish community.

Alongside his extensive activity on behalf of Diaspora Jewry, Montefiore developed a special attachment to the Holy Land, which he visited seven times between 1827 and 1875. Appalled by the conditions in which the local Jewish community lived and by its dependency on donations from abroad, he built Jerusalem's first neighborhood outside the walls of the Old City and equipped it with a windmill. He opened a vocational school for girls, sought to create jobs in the printing and textile industries, and explored the possibility of leasing farming lands for Jewish cultivation.

Despite all these being harbingers of modern Jewish nationalism, Montefiore was nonetheless a product of the traditional era. He threw his weight against the Reform movement, and during the long years when he headed the Board of Deputies, the Reform community was barred from joining it. On a national level he was seen as a hero by many of his contemporary coreligionists mainly because he nurtured Jewish solidarity, and in doing so also won the respect of non-Jewish England. He did not, however, expect the Jews' dispersal to end through any process other than miraculous Redemption, as Jews had believed throughout the Middle Ages.

More than anyone else, Montefiore's life embodied modern England's role in Jewish history as a political bridge between the ages of discrimination and tolerance, a cultural mediator between tradition and modernity, and a geographic way station between the Old World and the New.

(ABOVE)

SIR MOSES MONTEFIORE (1784–1885).
POSTCARD ISSUED IN ST. PETERSBURG, RUSSIA, 1903.
HERZLIYA, ALAIN ROTH COLLECTION.

The British philanthropist was the first Jew who dedicated himself to waging political battles on behalf of oppressed Jews the world over.

respectively, were destroyed to their foundations. So also were more than a thousand years of Jewish efforts to call the lands of Ashkenaz home.

ENGLAND AND HOLLAND: SEEDS OF TOLERANCE

The demise of Iberian Jewry, coupled with the expulsions of the Jews of France (1394), England (1290), and Saxony (1536), all but depleted Western Europe of its Jews. However, just when Spain's and Portugal's imperial designs were being challenged by England's and Holland's, a mental bridge was being haphazardly suspended between Western Europe's xenophobic past and its pluralistic future. That bridge's foundations were in Amsterdam and London. In these places and others, while titanic struggles raged between Protestant and Catholic Dutchmen, Monarchist and Republican Englishmen, Spanish and Dutch soldiers, and Spanish and English sailors, the Jews gradually ceased to be an ideological issue.

Jews initially arrived in the Low Countries while the area was ruled by Spain, since there they could remain in culturally familiar surroundings while socially they could be more anonymous. Politically, too, this Spanish realm was safer since the Inquisition was weaker the farther away one traveled from Spain. Consequently, many New Christians relocated initially to Antwerp, a major commercial hub at the time, where they often practiced medicine or managed international trading firms. Others opted for the French alternatives of Rouen, Nantes, or Bordeaux.

However, north of these cities Calvinism was challenging Catholicism and advancing through what today is Holland. New and better opportunities materialized for the Sephardim, who could emerge from religious hiding. By about 1602, just over a century after the Expulsion, Amsterdam had become the first Christian city to re-legitimize a community of crypto-Jews. Within a few years Amsterdam already had its own rabbi, kosher butcher, ritual bath, Hebrew press, synagogues, and Talmudic academy. Economically, Dutch Jewry thrived on the trade in African precious stones, which they purchased from Portuguese sailors before processing them and shipping them elsewhere.

Thanks to its prosperity, tolerance, and cosmopolitanism Amsterdam soon became a launching pad for other Jewish communities across Western Europe, most notably Hamburg, Copenhagen, and London. In these and other places Jews arrived and behaved as Christians while assuming a leading role in trade with Spain, Portugal, Italy, and the Ottoman Empire. However, from the outset these new immigrants observed their real faith in secret, and increasingly the secret became open, tolerated, and ultimately also superfluous.

The most telling evolution of this nature took place in England, where Portuguese Jews who already had been living in London officially requested permission to settle in England as Jews. Moved in part by millenarian feelings propagated by Dutch-Jewish scholar Manasseh ben-Israel (1604–1657), Oliver Cromwell (1599–1658), then "Lord

(OPPOSITE, TOP)

AMSTERDAM'S JEWS CHEERING THE ARRIVAL OF KING LOUIS NAPOLEON, APRIL 20, 1808.
RIJKSMUSEUM, AMSTERDAM.

(OPPOSITE, BOTTOM)

PORTUGUESE JEWS AT WORSHIP.
BERNARD PICART (1663–1733).

Holland's tolerance toward the Jews stemmed from its cosmopolitanism, but also from the traumas of the wars of religion. The city allowed its Jews, but not its Catholics, to build monumental houses of worship.

(ABOVE)

VIEW FROM THE GALLERY IN
THE CARPENTRAS SYNAGOGUE,
OUTSIDE OF AVIGNON.
EIGHTEENTH CENTURY.

*Originally one of Europe's oldest
synagogues, after the French Revolution
communities like this dwindled, as Jews
found new opportunities in the big cities.*

Protector," or ruler of England, convened a special forum of jurists whom he assigned the
task of looking into the matter of the Jews' return to England. The forum did not emerge
with a verdict, but that inaction tacitly approved the Jews' admission into the country
from which they had been expelled more than three and a half centuries earlier.

EMANCIPATION: THE RETURN OF
FRANCO-GERMAN JEWRY

Just as the mid-seventeenth-century massacres were stemming the Ashkenazi eastward
migration, events elsewhere in Europe were about to altogether reverse this diaspora's
geographic orientation and restore its westward gravitation. In the aftermath of a century
and a half that began with the Thirty Years' War (1618–1648) and culminated with the
French Revolution, ancient anti-Jewish attitudes gave way to a new tolerance that
fundamentally reshaped Jewish-Gentile relations. Consequently, Austria, Germany, and

(ABOVE)
THE GREAT SANHENDRIN OF
THE JEWS OF FRANCE.
LITHOGRAPHY BY VERNIER AFTER E. MOYSE. 1868.
*The need to come to terms with a secular
state was new to Judaism, which until
the French Revolution had only known
religious states, whether Jewish or non-
Jewish. This scene depicts a fictional
session with the members of the
Sanhendrin wearing their official robes.
On the right: Rabbi David Sinzheim,
the first Chief Rabbi of France.*

France, which in previous centuries had repeatedly expelled entire Jewish communities, now restored their roles as major Jewish immigration destinations.

Tolerance arrived in different forms, circumstances, and contexts. In Prussia it was nurtured by a scholarly elite, in Austria by enlightened monarchs, and in France by fiery revolutionaries. In August 1789 the French National Assembly declared that no one would be discriminated against due to his religious faith. This proclamation theoretically emancipated the local Jewish community. However, it took another two years for that abstract statement to specifically and explicitly pertain to the small and disjointed Jewish community that survived France's harsh anti-Jewish policies of previous centuries.

On the eve of the revolution there were some forty thousand Jews in France, more than three-quarters of them poor, strictly religious Yiddish-speakers scattered in villages throughout the region of Alsace-Lorraine. The rest belonged mainly to the tightly knit

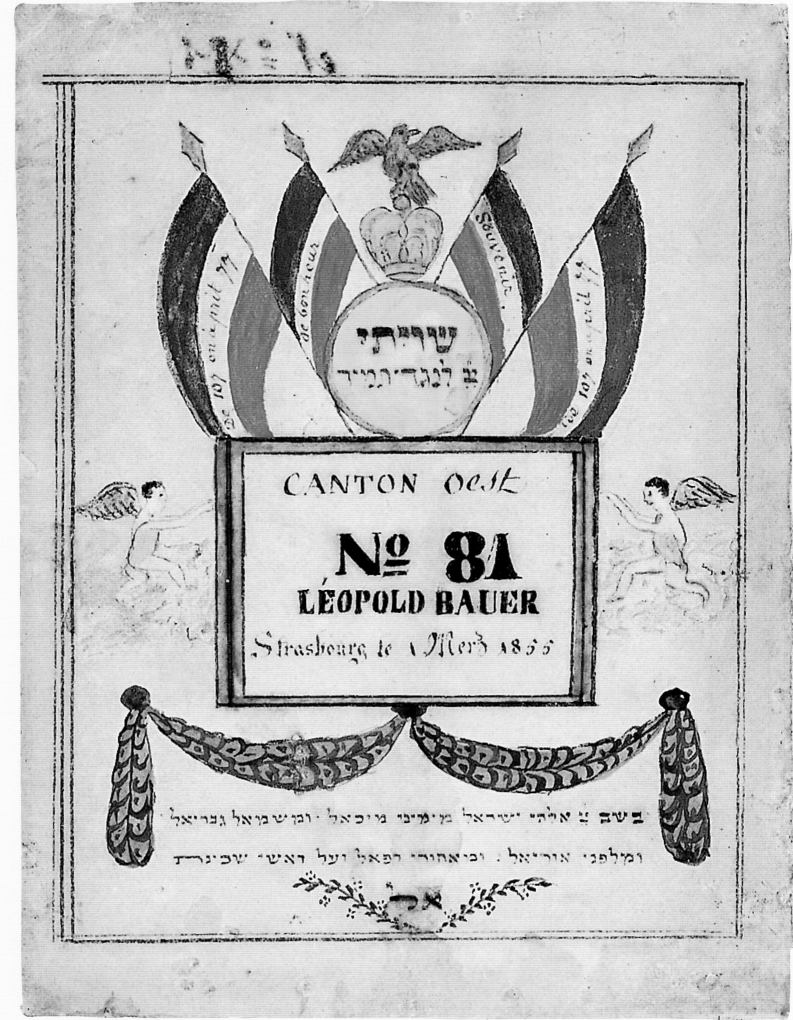

שריתי ני לנגדי תמיד

CANTON Oest

№ 81

LÉOPOLD BAUER

Strasbourg le 1 Merz 1855

בשם יי אלהי ישראל מימיני מיכאל ומשמאל גבריאל

ומלפני אוריאל ומאחורי רפאל ועל ראשי שכינת אל

Marrano community of Bordeaux. Paris itself, the political, commercial, and cultural heart of the kingdom, had but five hundred Jews—a somber monument to the vacuum left in the land once famous for its Talmudic academies and scholars.

Now, with the revolutionaries genuinely prepared to let the Jews join the civil mainstream, most Jews, led by the rabbis of Alsace-Lorraine, initially resisted the trend, fearing change in general, and particularly the demand that the Jews be given "everything as individuals and nothing as a people."

Still, the Alsace-Lorraine community's suspicions notwithstanding, the revolution suddenly opened France's gates to Jewish immigration. Eighty years after the revolution there were already some one hundred thousand Jews in France, nearly half of them in Paris. Commercially vibrant and socially outgoing, the new and improved French diaspora was exceptionally upwardly mobile. Ultimately, French Jewry would become the object of the fierce anti-Semitism that generated the Dreyfus Affair. Still, by the eve of World War II, three hundred thousand Jews, ranging from thoroughly religious immigrants from Eastern Europe to Reform Jews from Germany, lived in France. A third of the community perished in the Holocaust. Today six hundred thousand French Jews, mostly of North African descent, comprise Europe's largest and most traditional diaspora.

(ABOVE)

FRENCH BOARD GAME, INSPIRED BY THE DREYFUS AFFAIR, IN WHICH THE GOAL WAS TO REVEAL "THE TRUTH."

PARIS. 1898. PRINTED BY PHOTOGRAPHIC PROCESS ON POLYCHROME PAPER. MUSÉE D'ART ET D'HISTOIRE DU JUDAÏSME, PARIS. GIFT OF GEORGE ABOUCAYA IN MEMORY OF COLETTE ABOUCAYA-SPIRA.

The anti-Semitic upheaval that came in its wake shocked many who had thought that the Jews' acceptance during the age of emancipation was deep and complete.

(OPPOSITE)

SHIVITI AND SOUVENIR CONSCRIPTION NUMBER.

STRASBOURG. 1855. INK AND GOUACHE ON PAPER. MUSÉE ALSACIEN, STRASBOURG.

This work combines the French flags with the Hebrew text of Psalm 16:8, "I have set God always before me." In the emancipated lands Jews generally identified with their countries.

(ABOVE)
CHARTER OF PRIVILEGES.
1333. SPEYER, GERMANY. SPEYER MUNICIPAL ARCHIVES.
This document declares that "Judges, Council, and citizens of Speyer make a contract with the Jews of Speyer, according to which the Jews' Council and the Jews' 'bishop' will be elected by the Jews without interference from the City Council. The Jewish Council will have twelve members and any of them who are members for ten years will have life tenure. The town puts its sexton at the disposal of the Jews to help them collect any fines above three pounds which they might impose, but the town receives a half of such money collected." A decade after this document was signed, the community of Speyer was destroyed in the wake of the Black Death pogroms.

(OPPOSITE)
THE RESTORED DOME OF THE NEUE SYNAGOGUE ON ORANIENBURGERSTRASSE IN BERLIN.
The German capital's Jewish community mushroomed from 36,000 to 172,000 between 1870 and 1920.

GERMANY: FROM RENAISSANCE TO DISASTER

On the eve of the Emancipation, the Jewish situation in the lands that eventually became modern Germany was unique. Unlike France and Spain, which managed to develop vast, centralized, and solid kingdoms, the German lands were divided into numerous principalities. In addition to this political atomization, the Germans, in contrast with their neighbors, emerged from the Reformation and the Thirty Years' War divided between Protestants and Catholics.

During the Middle Ages, while there were repeated cases of local expulsions, the Germans' political fragmentation prevented wholesale expulsions of the sorts that were carried out by the strong monarchies of Spain, France, or England. In the German lands, when one town would expel its Jews there would be another town that would accept them. That, for instance, is what happened in 1670 to the newly expelled Jews of Vienna. Some of their wealthier families were allowed to settle in Berlin, just when Prussia was beginning to assert itself. And as historical coincidences go, this development was followed a century later by Prussia's sudden absorption of a sizable Jewish population in the wake of Poland's dissolution.

Moisesville: The Limits of Philanthropy

Perhaps the most fascinating thing about the New World's imprint on Jewish history was the way the Jewish masses detached themselves from their traditional leaders and took their destinies in their own hands.

Still, there were in the New World ambitious efforts "from above" to reshape Jewish destiny. While European Orthodox rabbis generally opposed emigration to America, which they saw as a vehicle for secularizing the Jews, secular Jews in Europe sometimes saw in the New World a solution both for removing poor Jews from their anti-Semitic surroundings and for transforming them into the productive laborers that anti-Semites claimed they could never become.

By the time these ideas were conceived, mainly in the wake of the pogroms of the 1880s in southern Russia, North America was already heavily industrialized and absorbing masses of Jewish immigrants. South America, at the same time, remained largely agrarian, relatively unsettled by Jews, and thirsting for immigrants. That is how Argentina—by far the best prospective destination for resettling Jews in terms of its fertility, accessibility, and tolerance—caught the eye of German Jewish philanthropist Baron Maurice de Hirsch.

Born in Munich to a family of bankers who played important roles in developing Bavaria's railways, forests, and factories, Hirsch became an entrepreneur and won fame when he took over and successfully completed the railway project that ended up connecting Europe and Asia through the Balkans. While becoming a leader in developing European railways, Hirsch traveled extensively through areas heavily populated with destitute Jews and sought ways to use his wealth to alleviate his brethren's plight.

Ultimately he despaired of bettering the Jews' condition by creating a network of vocational

schools across the Pale of Settlement. The only solution to the situation, he concluded, would be emigration. Inspired by the creation in 1889 of Moisesville, an agricultural settlement founded by newly arrived Jewish immigrants in Argentina's Santa Fe province, Hirsch decided that the best destination for his resettlement ideas would be Argentina.

To select, ship, settle, train, and equip his project's prospective participants, Hirsch created in Paris in 1891 the Jewish Colonization Association (JCA), which he listed in London with a seed investment of two million pounds. In

Russia, making the most of the czarist government's desire to get rid of its Jews, he obtained permission to solicit Jewish emigrants throughout the Pale of Settlement.

However, by the time Hirsch died half a decade later, the JCA had managed to settle just under seven thousand Jews in five townships, all in northern Argentina. Though eventually more Jewish agricultural settlements were established in Latin America (including several not under JCA's auspices and some beyond Argentina), the number of Jewish farming communities in Argentina peaked in the 1940s at twenty-five,

in which some forty thousand Jews lived, three-quarters of whom were active farmers.

In all, though Hirsch's effort did generate some Jewish farming in South America, it ended up a pale version of his dream, both because Argentina's conditions proved more difficult for settlement than he initially realized, and because the immigrants gravitated toward the great urban centers and nonagricultural vocations. Moreover, Hirsch's endeavor was, at the end of the day, an attempt to manage from above a movement whose hallmark was its spontaneity. The great Jewish emigration from the Old World to the New World was planned by no one, and in fact gathered momentum despite express opposition on the part of the traditional leadership. Just as the rabbis' religious authority failed to stem the emigration movement, Hirsch's money failed to channel and shape it.

(ABOVE)

GAUCHOS IN AN ICA SETTLEMENT, ARGENTINA, 1920S.
All attempts to develop Jewish farming outside the Land of Israel failed.

(OPPOSITE)

POSTER ISSUED FOR THE CELEBRATIONS OF THE FIFTIETH ANNIVERSARY OF THE ICA JEWISH COLONIES IN ARGENTINA.
1939.

Rabbi Aarón Goldman was the spiritual leader of the first immigrant group who arrived in Argentina on the Wesser steamship on August 14, 1889, and founded Moisesville.

HOLESOV SYNAGOGUE, MORAVIA.
Initially, the Hapsburgs restricted Jewish residence in this region to cities only.

(OPPOSITE)
DOME OF THE SZEGED SYNAGOGUE.
The synagogue was built in 1898 following a contest among designers and was a symbol of Austria-Hungary's spirit of tolerance under Emperor Franz Joseph's rule. The dome is laden with symbolism: the twenty-four columns of the drum represent the hours of the day; the flowers represent the vegetation of the earth; the star-strewn blue glass gives a sense of the infinitely expanding heavens. At the very top is a small six-pointed star.

Initially, Prussia tried to limit the number of its Jews but also to expand their sources of livelihood, in line with Friedrich the Great's attempt to reconcile his anti-Jewish feelings and mercantilist inclinations. Much of this tension survived the Napoleonic era, when the formerly occupied German lands became hostile to the revolution's ideas, including emancipation. Still, in the aftermath of the 1848 upheaval and the establishment of the German Empire in 1871, the Jews became full and equal German citizens. By that time, there were just over half-a-million Jews in Germany—the Diaspora's third-largest community—and by the eve of World War I their number had risen to 615,000.

The Jewish population was distributed unevenly within the newly established Germany. The formerly Polish regions of Silesia and Posen had more Jews (46,000 and 62,000 respectively) than regions farther to the west. Still, in 1871, Berlin alone had 36,000 Jews, a number that would grow exponentially, reaching 144,000 in 1910 and 172,000 by the mid-1920s.

(ABOVE)
SUBOTICA SYNAGOGUE.
1902. NORTHERN YUGOSLAVIA.

Throughout the centuries, while the Serbs locked horns with the Ottomans, they were tolerant toward the Jews.

Germany's Jews prospered before and after World War I and usually saw themselves as German patriots of Jewish faith. With the Nazi rise to power, German Jewry's status was systematically dismantled through legislation that first deprived them of their equality, then limited their professional freedom, later discriminated against them racially, robbed them of their property and curtailed their freedom of travel, and finally sent them to their deaths.

Following the Nazis' rise to power Jews began leaving Germany en-masse, to Palestine, Western Europe, and America. By the eve of World war II the interwar community was more than halved, to 230,000. Of those, only 50,000 survived the war.

THE HAPSBURG EMPIRE: THE POWER OF PLURALISM

Despite its repeated expulsions and relocations, the Central European diaspora maintained a critical mass in the Austrian Empire's main cities and along its major trade routes, most notably the Danube River. Still, discrimination was rife and depended on local circumstances. For instance, Jews were altogether forbidden to reside in Croatia and various border areas. Only a small and well-measured number of Jews could live in Vienna, the capital. In Moravia—the eastern part of today's Czech Republic—Jews were forbidden to reside in villages. Yet, as has often happened in European Jewish history, changing geopolitical circumstances played into the Jews' hands, and soon enough turned Austria into a major Jewish center.

In the seventeenth century, Austria began prevailing over the Ottoman Empire, pushing it back south and east after the Turks had already laid siege to Vienna itself. The key country within the vast and newly conquered areas, in terms of its size, fertility, and location, was Hungary. The Austrians' need to urgently settle and develop that flatland made them open it to Jewish settlement. Prospective Jewish immigrants, in turn, were readily available in nearby Galicia and Moravia. Between 1700 and 1790, some fifty-five thousand Jews came from these regions to Hungary, thus laying the foundations for a diaspora that by the eve of the Holocaust would number eight hundred thousand people.

The disintegration of Poland into German, Russian, and Austrian domains turned the heavily Jewish region of Galicia into an Austrian possession overnight. These developments alone sufficed to make Austria a major diaspora, and when Emperor Joseph II issued a series of edicts in the 1780s aimed at improving the Jews' rights, the stage was set for the Hapsburg Empire in general, and Hungary in particular, to become a major magnet for Jews, mainly from East Europe. This image and reality were finally consolidated with the establishment in 1867 of the Austro-Hungarian Empire and its granting of full civilian rights to all its Jews.

By the eve of World War I, Prague, Vienna, and Budapest had become major Jewish centers, with 30,000, 175,000, and 210,000 Jews respectively, while the empire itself was home to more than 2.1 million Jews, three-and-a-half times their number a mere eighty years earlier. Still, Austria-Hungary was increasingly crumbling under the weight of its ethnic problems and failing to live up to its economic potential. Consequently, the rapid growth of its Jewish community peaked soon after the turn of the twentieth century, as many of its Jews joined the great East European emigration movement to Western Europe and the New World.

The dissolution of the Hapsburg Empire in the aftermath of World War I left its Jews scattered in many newly independent countries, such as Poland, Hungary, Czechoslovakia, and Yugoslavia. Though Czechoslovakia and Yugoslavia were tolerant to the Jews, other countries generally abandoned the former empire's pluralistic mind-set, if not formally then mentally. When Nazi Germany conquered Central Europe, its anti-Semitic policies seldom met resistance from the local population. In a sense, the disappearance of the Hapsburgs and their titanic effort to impose tolerance and reconcile conflicting ethnic, nationalist, and religious ambitions foreshadowed the beginning of prewar European Jewry's bitter end.

The Prague Expulsion: The Power of Jewish Solidarity

If the vast Austrian Empire marked the great physical divide between east and west, Empress Maria Theresa's rule marked the transition from medievalism to modernity in Central European rulers' attitudes toward their Jewish minorities.

Though generally remembered as the first woman to inherit the Hapsburg throne, and as a mild reformer and a stubborn ruler who stuck to her guns even when confronted by a Spanish-French-Prussian-Bavarian coalition—when it came to the Jews, Maria Theresa was unabashedly prejudiced, obscurantist, and cruel.

The most recurring theme in her Jewish policies was the expulsions of entire communities, most memorably that of Prague, in 1744, following its reconquest by Hapsburg troops. Maria Theresa's decree was unique in its motivation—a naked, pathological hatred of Jews, which stemmed from the rigid Christian education she received. However, even more peculiar was the very resort to expulsion, a medieval measure whose time had ostensibly passed, and which would sharply contrast with the conciliatory attitude of her son, Joseph II, as it would be expressed in his Toleranzpatent of 1782.

Indeed, while Joseph—who shared power with his mother after she became a widow in 1765—was exposed to the ideas of the Enlightenment movement, Maria Theresa was the product of an era rife with religious zeal and exhausted by the Thirty Years' War (1618–1648). As such, she viewed her subjects with utilitarian eyes, seeking population growth, mercantilist economics, and political loyalty. In other cases, these attitudes, which came as a reaction to the devastation wrought by the religious violence of the Thirty Years' War, meant a more sober, business-oriented attitude toward the Jews. Maria Theresa, however, could scarcely overcome her hatred for the Jews; when she met with them, she stayed behind a

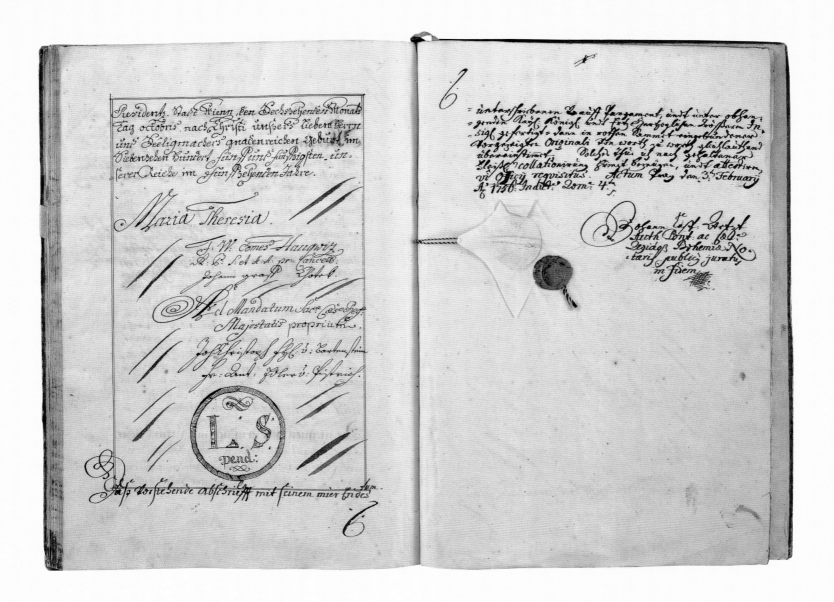

curtain. After ordering the expulsion of Prague's Jews, she did the same with other Jewish communities in today's Romania, Italy, Austria, and Hungary.

In Prague's case, however, she eventually retreated, after a network of Jewish court Jews interfered and managed to leverage international diplomatic pressure that the empress could not ignore. Her face-saving compromise, to allow the Jews' residence in turn for increased taxes, later made her impose broader discriminatory taxes elsewhere, and deepened her dependency on Jewish funding so much that ultimately she banned the spreading of blood libels, lest the monarchy's cash flow would be disrupted.

On the face of it, Maria Theresa's treatment of the Jews, in both its indoctrinated and pragmatic versions, was much like medieval European royalty's. Yet the circumstances in which she operated were markedly different, highlighted by the rise, on one hand, of Jewish string-pullers who could mobilize international pressure, and the presence, on the other, of an heir apparent who was awaiting his turn to allow the Jews greater mobility and equality.

(OPPOSITE)

ALTNEUSCHUL, PRAGUE.
Completed around 1265, this is Europe's oldest extant synagogue. During the two centuries following the 1744 expulsion affair, Jewish Prague flourished, both intellectually and materially. Visible above is the banner of the Prague Jewish Community bestowed by Emperor Karl IV in 1358.

(ABOVE)

ORDINANCES ADDRESSING AUSTRIAN JEWS AND BEARING EMPRESS MARIA THERESA'S SIGNATURE.
1754. BOOK OF PRIVILEGES. AUSTRIA. TERRITORIAL COLLECTION, YIVO ARCHIVES.

The empress, who was the mother of Marie-Anoinette, was so anti-Jewish that in order not to face Jewish visitors she would speak to them only through a partition.

(ABOVE)

KALVARIJA SYNAGOGUE, LITHUANIA.
*The land that was the bastion of
opposition to Hasidism emerged as the
biggest center of Torah studies since
Babylonia.*

(RIGHT)

A JEWISH STREET IN BUSTINO,
CARPATHO-RUSSIA, INTERWAR
CZECHOSLOVAKIA.
*President Tomas Masaryk's gospel of
cultural pluralism and religious tolerance
was crushed in the wake of Germany's
conquest of Prague and its handling of
Slovakia and Carpatho-Russia to Slovak
and Hungarian fascist governments.*

RUSSIA: JEW-HATRED AS OFFICIAL POLICY

The trends of tolerance that first sprang from Holland, England, and France and then crept
into Central Europe were blocked from further advance eastward by a succession of
obscurantist czars. In the sixteenth century, Ivan the Terrible turned down Polish requests
that Jewish merchants be allowed to trade in Russia, suspecting that the Jews would help
Poland expand at his empire's expense. Moreover, in 1563, when he conquered the town of
Polock, Ivan demanded that the local Jewish community convert to Christianity. When
the Jews refused, he had them all drowned in the nearby Dvina River.

As in other affairs, Ivan's legacy concerning the Jews became the Russian norm
for centuries. Jews were formally and practically forbidden to reside, and
theoretically even to trade, in the Russian Empire. Yet all this changed overnight
in the aftermath of the Polish partitions, when Russia suddenly found itself in
charge of a large Jewish population.

(ABOVE)

VICTIMS OF THE KISHINEV POGROM,
(THEN SOUTHERN RUSSIA AND
TODAY MOLDAVA), 1903.
*The massacre, in which forty-nine Jews
were murdered and 2,000 families lost
their homes, shocked the Diaspora and
accelerated Jewish emigration from
czarist Russia.*

The Russian solution to this contradiction between its territorial appetite and anti-Jewish inclinations was to create the Pale of Settlement. Jews were, in effect, shackled to the areas where they had lived before coming under Russian rule. Thus, Jews could move within the area that stretched from Lithuania on the shores of the Baltic to Crimea on the shores of the Black Sea but remained barred from entering Russia proper. Movement from the Russian to the Polish parts of the Pale was also not automatically allowed.

By the end of the nineteenth century Russia had become host to 5 million Jews, or about half the Jewish people. The government's fierce anti-Jewishness led it to tolerate, and in some cases even encourage, anti-Jewish pogroms, which served the regime as a social safety valve. By then, however, Russia's Jews were emigrating massively, mainly to America but also to Palestine and other destinations. The emigration was actually encouraged by the regime, which by the 1880s was contending with popular anti-liberal sentiments and a general reaction to things Western.

Czarist attempts throughout the nineteenth century to forcibly integrate the Jews, for instance through military service and compulsory state education, only intensified the mutual suspicion and consolidated Russia's image in the West as the Jewish people's major enemy. Thus, when Russia was at war with Japan in 1905, American Jewish banker Jacob Schiff led a major bond issuance for the Japanese government in order to help it combat the czarist regime.

The downfall of the Romanov dynasty in 1917, after three centuries of uninterrupted rule, marked a legal, geographic, and cultural watershed in the Diaspora's history. Soon after its rise to power, the provisional Communist government abolished all anti-Jewish discrimination. For the first time since the rise of Christianity, all European Jews, and a vast majority of the entire Jewish nation, were formally emancipated. The Pale of Settlement's abolition also meant that after centuries of expulsions, confinements, and prohibitions on land purchases, there was no corner of the European continent that was out of bounds for any Jew.

However, the prevalence of these freedoms carried the hefty price of cultural oppression and spiritual depletion as the Communists set out to impose atheism on the entire population and eradicate Judaism, along with all other religious practice. Soon the assault on Judaism transformed into attacks on Jewishness, and finally it resulted in attacks on Jewish individuals.

Initially, the Jews were allowed, and eager, to assert and nurture their cultural identity. Hundreds of Jewish schools sprouted throughout Russia, while Jewish literature and journalism, in Yiddish, Russian, and Hebrew, flourished as never before or since. Jewish political parties of all ideological shades, from Zionists to Bundists, engaged in hectic activity and agitation. But this exhilaration lasted hardly eight months before the Bolshevik Revolution nipped a potential renaissance in the bud.

ГЛАВПОЛИТПРОСВЕТ.

Издательство Акционерное общество „ШКОЛА и КНИГА"
Москва, Неглинная ул., 7.

The Bolsheviks at first allowed Jewish groups to retain their independent activities
provided that they engaged in promoting communism. Soon enough, however, even that
minimal measure of autonomy was abandoned, with the disbanding in 1921 of the
Jewish pro-Communist Bund organization. Zionist parties were disbanded, Jewish
publishing houses were shut down, and a Hebrew-language theater, Habima, was
forced to leave Moscow in 1925. (Habima moved to Tel Aviv, where it has remained
active ever since.)

Meanwhile, the former Pale of Settlement became a major arena in the civil war
between Red and White Russians, and in that heavily Jewish area, the Communists made
a special effort to kill any form of private commerce. The result was a fatal blow to the
classical *shtetl*—the Jewish village that was famous for its rich Yiddish culture and
distinctive economic function as a point of contact between town and farm. In fact, the
war on Jewish life was systematic and comprehensive and reached beyond the old shtetl.
As religious education was prohibited, rabbis were arrested, and synagogues shut down,
Russian Judaism suffered blows that it had never been dealt, even by the czars.

Jewishness, however, was not only left untouched but in fact won the Communists'
defense, as Lenin himself personally condemned anti-Semitism and allowed Jews to rise
in the political and administrative hierarchy, especially during the 1920s. Yiddish-
speaking schools, albeit ones where religion was vilified, were tolerated, as were secular
Yiddish theaters and publications. There were even courts that held their sessions in

(ABOVE)

GOLDA MEIR.
RAPHAEL SOYER. 1975.
NATIONAL PORTRAIT GALLERY, SMITHSONIAN
INSTITUTION.
GIFT OF MR. AND MRS. NATHAN CUMMINGS, MR. AND
MRS. MEYER P. POTAMKIN, AND THE CHARLES E. SMTIH
FAMILY FOUNDATION.

*The spontaneous gathering of thousands
of Jews who came to Mosow's Central
Synagogue in 1948 to see the Jewish
state's first ambassador to the Soviet
Union alarmed Stalin, who became even
more suspicious of Jewish conspiracies.*

Yiddish. By the 1930s, however, the use of Yiddish declined sharply. Jewish parents preferred to equip their children with a good command of Russian early on in order to improve their chances of advancement in Soviet society. By the eve of Stalin's great purges of the late 1930s, Soviet Jewry had largely shed its Jewish roots while individual Jews rapidly assumed important positions in the economic and cultural scenes.

Then, in the mid-1930s, what had begun as a war on Judaism transformed into an assault on Jews, specifically leading Jewish Communists.

Initially, following Lenin's death in 1924, the Soviet Union was ruled by a trio in which Joseph Stalin was but an equal to its two other members, who happened to be Jewish: Grigori Zinoviev and Lev Kamenev. In 1935, however, the two were among fourteen people accused in a show trial of killing Communist leader Sergei Kirov. All the defendants were executed, and Stalin set out to consolidate his grip on power by unleashing mass purges across the USSR. Thousands of those killed in the process were Jews, thus signaling to other Jewish Communists that they could only get so far in the country's political hierarchy. Leon Trotsky's murder in Mexico in 1940 sealed the brief but impressive period of Jews' prominence in Soviet history, though one Jew, Lazar Kaganovitch (1893–1991), remained close to Stalin until his death in 1953.

During the war Stalin allowed Jewish identity to be expressed (the same way he allowed Russian patriotism to be mobilized in the effort to rally the people behind the Red Army) through the establishment of a special forum, the Antifascist Committee of notable Jews. In effect, this made its leader and best-known member, Yiddish actor Solomon Mikhoels, the undeclared leader of Soviet Jewry. Mikhoels took his new role seriously, renewing contacts with overseas Jewry during the war and, once it ended, looking after the needs of Jewish refugees. Mikhoels later received both the Stalin Prize and the Lenin Prize as tribute for his artistic accomplishments.

The Soviet Union's wartime tolerance peaked with the Kremlin's recognition of the Jewish state in 1948 and the arrival in Moscow of an Israeli ambassador, Golda Meir. However, those very events generated excitement among Soviet Jews—most memorably a spontaneous gathering of thousands outside the Moscow Synagogue for the Simhat Torah festival in fall 1948 in order to get a glimpse of Meir—that the famously paranoid Stalin would not tolerate. In what would be merely the first shot in a protracted anti-Jewish campaign, Mikhoels was murdered in February 1948, and soon afterward dozens of other leading Jewish literati, artists, and celebrities were jailed, deported, and in some cases murdered, usually accused of being "rootless cosmopolitans"—a euphemism for being Jewish.

In 1952 some of Soviet Jewry's most prominent writers, including Lenin Prize–winner Peretz Markish, were executed for alleged "nationalism." Also that year Czechoslovakia tried and executed its former Communist Party secretary general, Rudolph Slanski, for allegedly conspiring with Zionism, Britain, and the United States to betray his country; and in Bucharest that year, former foreign minister Ana Pauker, by far the most powerful

(LEFT)
BLOWING THE *Shofar*
IN RED SQUARE.
*The fall of communism generated mass
emigration, but also a Jewish renaissance,
though its scope and depth seemed to
remain unclear.*

(BELOW)
RAILING AT THE ST. PETERSBURG
SYNAGOGUE, 1997.
*A Jewish community developed in late-
nineteenth-century St. Petersburg despite
its location outside the Pale of Settlement.*

Jewish woman in the world at the time, was placed under house arrest where she died eight years later.

Finally, in January 1953 the official daily *Pravda* claimed that a group of Jewish doctors conspired to kill Soviet leaders on behalf of the CIA and the Zionist organization. (Researchers, including Stalin's biographer Edvard Radzinski, cite circumstantial evidence that in his last months the Soviet dictator was preparing for a mass deportation of Soviet Jewry to Siberia.) Several weeks later, while Jews were losing their jobs and even being attacked by hoodlums in the streets, Stalin died, and the assault on Jewishness ended abruptly. Yet while Stalin's death ended the physical threat to Soviet Jewry, it could not undo the spiritual damage inflicted on Judaism by two generations of Communist hostility.

In the aftermath of the demise of the Pale of Settlement in the 1920s, Soviet Jews became predominantly urban. The vast majority of Soviet Jews lived in fewer than a dozen metropolises, including Moscow, Leningrad, Kiev, Riga, Odessa, and Tashkent. Within those cities they were often the backbone of the middle class: engineers, doctors, scientists, mid-level managers, and teachers. And though they had hardly any exposure to their national heritage, they were often deeply aware of their national identity—which was also stated explicitly in their passports—and often kept in contact with Jewish relatives abroad. By 1990, as political conditions finally allowed emigration, many Jews swiftly made their way to Israel despite the titanic effort that had been made to detach them and their ancestors from their Jewishness. Within one decade, a million formerly Soviet Jews were residing in the Promised Land.

FUNERAL IN RUDAUTI, ROMANIA,
1975.
*Communist dictator Nikolai Ceausescu
allowed Jewish observance as part of
his effort to distance Romania from
Soviet leadership.*

ROMANIA: A VARIATION ON THE RUSSIAN THEME

Jews had lived in the fertile lands of Moldavia and Walachia, south of the Russian-Ukrainian continuum, since the Middle Ages, but until the nineteenth century their numbers there were small. Tucked between the historic Austrian and Ottoman spheres of dominance, the area that would later be called Romania did not win independence until 1859, and it took an additional two decades until the new state gained international recognition. Even so, these lands began attracting large numbers of Jewish immigrants from the newly disintegrated Poland. By the end of the nineteenth century there already were some 250,000 Jews in Romania, more than ten times their number eight decades earlier.

However, despite this influx, the newly independent country proved exceptionally hostile to its Jews. Inspired, like Russia, by an Orthodox clergy, Romania initially resisted Western pressure to emancipate its Jews, even when that was a condition for recognition

(LEFT)

A COLLECTIVE BAR MITZVAH IN
SZAVAS, HUNGARY.
*The survival of an estimated 100,000
Jews in postwar Hungary turned them
into the former East Bloc's second largest
Jewish community.*

(BELOW)

CELEBRATING PASSOVER IN
BUDAPEST, 1995.
*Most Hungarian Jews remained
reluctant to reassert their Jewishness,
even after the fall of communism.*

of its independence. Economic conditions in Romania also left many of its immigrants disillusioned. Consequently, when the great immigration to the New World began, Romania emerged as a major supplier of Jewish immigrants, sending seventy-five thousand of them to America by World War I. As a result, Romanian Jewry stopped growing, and in fact began shrinking. But then, in the aftermath of World War I, as Austria-Hungary was dismantled and its borders were greatly expanded, Romania suddenly became home to an immense Jewish community—nearly one million people.

In World War II Romania was allied with Nazi Germany. Ultimately, more than half its Jews perished, mainly in areas snatched from the USSR and others that were ceded to Hungary. In Romania proper, however, some 350,000 Romanian Jews survived the fascist nightmare, only to see it succeeded by the Communist eclipse. Eventually, thousands of Jews fled Romania in the years immediately after the war, mostly to Israel, but some 100,000 of them remained in Communist Romania.

Materially, postwar Romanian Jewry's lot was as bad the rest of the country whose Communist leadership was among the most orthodox in the entire East Bloc. Spiritually, however, the Ceausescu regime allowed more religious practice than the USSR, and also a greater deal of emigration, for which Bucharest was being paid by Israel. A decade after the fall of communism Romania's once-vibrant Jewish community is approaching near-extinction, numbering hardly 35,000 people, and still shrinking.

(RIGHT)

SILVER AND GILDED BRASS
TORAH FINIALS.
MYER MYERS. 1766–1776. THE TOURO SYNAGOGUE,
TOURO, RHODE ISLAND.

*Myer Myers, the only Jewish silversmith
of his time for whom any identifiable
work remains, was the leading
silversmith in New York during the late
colonial period. A craftsman whose
commissions came from some of the most
prominent families, he was also a leader
of New York's Shearith Israel
Congregation, which still houses
a pair of his finials.*

AMERICA: A DIASPORA UNLIKE ALL OTHERS

Ironically, the year 1492, which witnessed the traumatic Spanish Expulsion, also saw
the discovery of America, an event that would eventually generate the antithesis to the
classical Diaspora experience of social seclusion, legal discrimination, and psychological
alienation. Although South America took a long time to shed the Old World's anti-Jewish
habits, North America signaled a dramatic break from Diaspora history in that it effectively
embraced the Jews as equals almost from the inception of their settlement there.

Jewish immigration to North America is generally divided into three periods: the
colonial era, the German-dominated influx of the nineteenth century, and the post-1880s
East European immigration. The pre-1776 community was minuscule, no more than a
few thousand by the revolution's outbreak, all of whom lived in the trading centers along
the Atlantic coastline. Some of those merchants arrived from the Spanish-Portuguese
diaspora. Their greater openness to non-Jewish surroundings, coupled with the early-
American settlers' own heritage as religious-persecution refugees and their distance from
the Old World's clerical establishments, produced an atmosphere of tolerance
unparalleled in Diaspora history, at least since the rise of Christianity.

The so-called German immigration was touched off by Central Europe's political
instability toward the middle of the nineteenth century, which culminated in the 1848
revolutions that rocked major urban centers such as Rome, Paris, Budapest, and Vienna,
and unsettled much of what lay beyond them. Pushed to emigrate by the economic

AN OPEN MARKETPLACE AT
THE CORNER OF NORFOLK STREET
AND BOWERY. EARLY 1900S, THE
LOWER EAST SIDE, NEW YORK.
*The Jewish immigrants concentrated in
the big cities, and initially lived in
poverty as unskilled laborers.*

hardship and political upheaval that followed the revolutions' failure, this immigration brought to the United States a more varied population. The descendants of these people became corporate bankers as well as independent-minded clergymen and eventually provided American Judaism with the kind of leadership, orientation, and stature that it sorely lacked during the colonial period.

On the eve of the East European migrations there were some 250,000 Jews in the United States, mostly affiliated with the Reform movement that grew out of the German *haskalah*, or enlightenment movement. Geographically, U.S. Jewry expanded westward during the years of the German emigrations, as did America in general. As a result, the U.S. Reform movement's main center, where it educated its rabbis, emerged in Cincinnati, where it remains until today. Other communities developed farther west, all the way to San Francisco. Economically, the German immigration produced major success stories in wholesale trade, banking, and publishing.

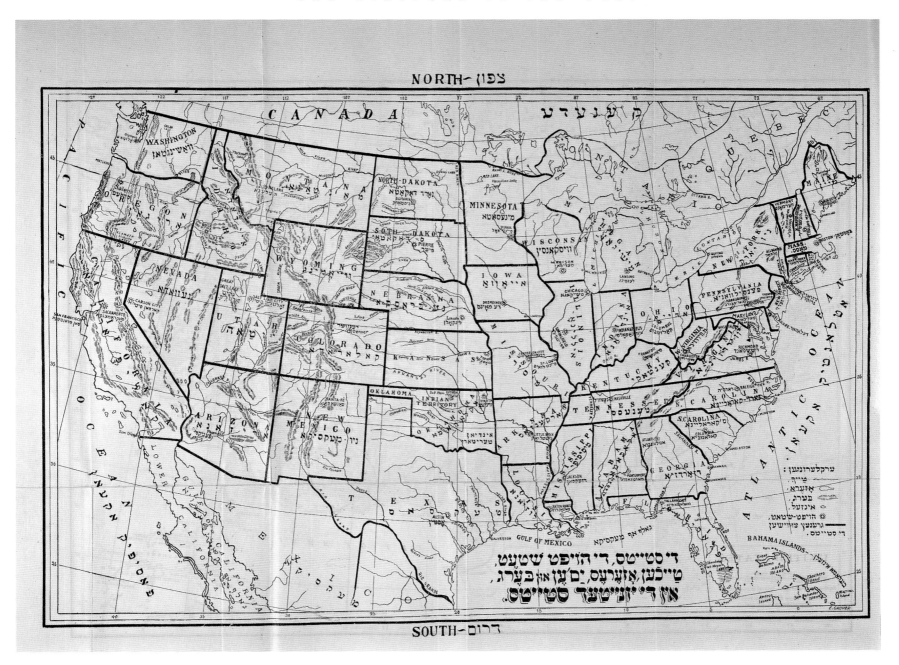

NORTH—צפון

SOUTH—דרום

However, the great watershed in the evolution of American Jewry came after 1880, sparked by pogroms that made Russian Jews seek new horizons, and enabled by cheap steamboat traffic between Hamburg and New York. By the mid-1920s, some 1.5 million Jews, or 30 percent of East European Jewry, had crossed the Atlantic, as the United States became home to 4 million Jews. The United States was, by far, the largest, farthest, and most successful migration movement in the Diaspora's entire history. As of 2003 it still remains such, though the post-Soviet immigration movement to Israel, which has yet to end, might ultimately eclipse it.

In a paradoxical parallel to the social and geographic travails of their brethren who stayed put in Europe and ended up enduring communism, American Jewry's so-called Russian immigrants quickly gravitated to the large cities—New York, Chicago, Boston, Baltimore, and others—where they started off as blue-collar workers and within a few decades became professionals and climbed to the middle and upper-middle classes.

(ABOVE)

YIDDISH MAP OF THE U.S. FROM JOHN FOSTER CARR'S *Guide to the United States for the Jewish Immigrant.* 1912.

JEWISH DIVISION. THE NEW YORK PUBLIC LIBRARY. ASTOR, LENOX, AND TILDEN FOUNDATION.

At first, many among America's veteran Jews saw the influx of East European Jews as a threat and sought ways to direct them elsewhere, including Palestine.

(OPPOSITE)

CHARLES M. STRAUSS AND SON, C. 1880. *Charles Strauss was elected the mayor of Tucson, Arizona, in 1883. Most Jewish immigrants arrived in the United States between 1880 and 1924, and initially settled along the east coast.*

New York, with 1.8 million Jews by the late 1920s, loomed large not only as the beating heart of American Jewry, but in fact as the largest single urban Jewish center that ever came into being in the entire history of the Jews. Though ethnic statistics are difficult to conduct in the United States, it is estimated that by the year 2000 some two million Jews lived in the greater New York area and more than half a million in greater Los Angeles.

Politically, the presence of such a massive community at the heart of what became a major superpower soon translated into power. American Jews not only became pivotal in determining the results of important American political contests, but also gradually learned to pressure other countries in order to achieve goals that were beyond the narrow American interest. Thus, they rallied for Israel's defense in 1967 and for Soviet Jewry in the 1970s, and in both successfully influenced American policy. However, it took long decades to build this power, and when it was needed most—during the Holocaust—American Jewry proved fatefully disorganized, disunited, and impotent. Clearly, American Jewry's post-Holocaust political assertiveness has been, and remains, inspired by this trauma.

Even so, American Jewry's political cohesiveness has been clearer than its cultural common denominator. The Russian immigration nurtured, for a good half century, its native Yiddish tongue, mainly through newspapers and theaters. Religiously, however, American Jewry lacked leadership, having left Europe despite rabbinical rulings (like that of Rabbi Yisrael Meir Ha-Cohen, better-known as the Hafetz Hayim, in 1893) that more or less forbade relocating in a land famously brimming with temptation and sin. Consequently, while America's "Russian" Jews shunned the Reform movement, they ended up supplying masses of members to the newly established Conservative congregations that adapted Orthodox observance to American conditions.

Orthodoxy's great breakthrough in North America came after World War II, as major rabbis such as hasidic luminary Menachem Schneerson, ultra-Orthodox sage Moshe Feinstein, and modern-Orthodox philosopher Joseph Soloveitchik lived in the U.S. and trained a generation of American-born Judaic scholars. Those, in turn, created elaborate educational networks that helped sustain and build hundreds of observant communities from coast to coast. While theologically diverse, ranging for instance from the modern-Orthodox Young Israel movement's staunch Zionism to the ultra-Orthodox Satmar hasidim's fierce anti-Zionism, these communities nonetheless share an ambition to strictly observe Jewish law as it was presented by Rabbi Joseph Karo in his sixteenth-century *Shulḥan Arukh*. Still, by the turn of the twenty-first century, there were merely an estimated one hundred thousand Orthodox Jews in the United States. The rest of U.S. Jewry remained exposed to the fierce centrifugal pressures generated by America's cultural openness and general lack of anti-Semitism.

Socially and economically the success of American Jewry can hardly be overestimated. For instance, a mere two generations after many leading American

(OPPOSITE)
BETH EL CHAPEL, TEMPLE EMANU-EL, NEW YORK, 1929. *The chapel, north of the main sanctuary, is notable for the May Memorial window above the ark. Designed by Louis Comfort Tiffany in 1899 and depicting an idealized Jerusalem landscape, the window was brought from Temple Emanu-el on Fifth Avenue and 43rd Street. The ark was designed by Oscar Bach, a sculptor and metallurgist from New York. The name "Beth-El" meaning "House of God" recalls Congregation Beth-El , which was consolidated with Temple Emanu-el in 1927.*

ROOSEVELT MURAL.

BEN SHAHN. 1937–1938. FRESCO. © ESTATE OF BEN
SHAHN/LICENSED BY VAGA, NEW YORK, 1994.

*Painted for a housing project at the Jersey
Homestead (later renamed Roosevelt),
the mural reflects the artist's social
commentary and distinct style. While
the first section depicts immigration and
the harsh labor conditions the
immigrants endured, the mural continues
with the forces of reform, beginning with
the efforts of the labor union, until, at the
end of the image, the sturggle has been
won with new buildings, homes, and
schools represented by a ground plan of
the Jersey Homestead site itself. Shahn
achieved his reputation as a major voice
of social realism beginning with his
works in the 1930s and was active in
Public Works of Art Projects. From
1935 to 1938 he worked for the Farm
Security Administration (FSA),
traveling to the South and Midwest to
record rural life.*

universities imposed unofficial quotas, these schools are filled with Jewish students and faculty, who often comprise between a quarter and a third of the student body, and an even higher share of the faculty.

Jews have contributed greatly to American literature, film, and theater. In the economy, Jews populate, and frequently lead, major corporate boardrooms, and are famously active and prominent in Wall Street's financial district. In government, Jews are no longer rare in the foreign service, and in the Clinton administration, politicians of Jewish background led at one point simultaneously the Defense, State, Treasury, and Agriculture departments, in addition to the Federal Reserve and the National Security Council.

Yet all this integration both results from and further accelerates American Jewry's intensive acculturation, which in turn results in assimilation. With at least one in two Jews marrying out of the faith, a large question mark looms over the future of the Diaspora's largest-ever community.

BEYOND THE UNITED STATES: OTHER NEW WORLDS

The first Jewish settlements in the New World were not in North America but in Dutch-ruled Brazil's Recife, where Portuguese Jews arrived in 1630 from Amsterdam. The Portuguese ouster of the Dutch in 1654 compelled the Jews to flee Brazil, leading some of them to New Amsterdam and others to Central America.

During the nineteenth century the Inquisition finally disappeared from the face of Latin America, and that region's doors opened to Jewish settlement. Argentina, however, was different from all other immigration destinations since it not only tolerated, but actually encouraged Jewish immigration. In 1881 the government actually appointed a special agent whose task was to attract Jewish newcomers. Toward the end of the nineteenth century Argentina rose as a major Jewish immigration destination. With 30,000 Jews by the turn of the twentieth century, it established itself as Latin America's leading Jewish center, far ahead of Brazil, which had a mere 2,000 Jews at the time. By the end of the twentieth century Argentina was home to some 250,000 Jews; Brazil and Mexico had 120,000 and 35,000 Jews respectively, and all of Latin America had some 400,000 Jews.

Meanwhile, South Africa, Canada, and Australia also attracted sizable Jewish migrations. In 1900 South Africa had 40,000 Jews (mainly from Lithuania), Canada 17,000, and Australia just over 15,000.

Of the three, South African Jewry is the oldest—originating already in the seventeenth century—but its numbers grew mainly during the great emigration from East Europe, which happened to coincide with the discovery of gold and diamonds in the country. More than two in three South African Jews live today, as they have for more than a century, in Johannesburg and Cape Town.

A century later Australia had nearly a hundred thousand Jews due largely to an emigration movement from South Africa, whose Jewish community was declining due to the

JEWISH PIONEERS IN THE
FIRST KIBBUTZ, DGANIA
ON THE EVE OF WORLD WAR I.
*The intensified Jewish immigration to the
Land of Israel after 1880 eventually
reversed a demographic depletion whose
origins dated back to the Crusader and
Byzantine periods.*

(OPPOSITE, TOP)
LITHUANIAN JEWISH IMMIGRANTS
CELEBRATE ROSH HASHANAH EN
ROUTE TO SOUTH AFRICA. 1903.
*Though its origins date back to the
seventeenth century, most of South
African Jewry arrived with the great
East European emigration around the
turn of the twentieth century.*

(OPPOSITE, CENTER)
SOUTH AFRICAN TALMUD TORAH
KINDERGARTEN CLASS
CELEBRATING SHAVUOT, 1931.
*The discovery in South Africa of gold
and diamonds coincided with the great
emigration from East Europe.*

(OPPOSITE, BELOW)
AUSTRALIAN SOLDIERS VISITING
KIBBUTZ GIVAT BRENNER, SOUTH OF
TEL AVIV, DURING WORLD WAR II.
*In the last decades of the twentieth
century Australian Jewry grew
considerably, thanks to a steady
immigration of South African Jews.*

social instability that prevailed there since the 1980s. Nearly nine in ten Australian Jews live today in Melbourne and Sydney, as their forebears have since that community's inception.

In Canada, the Jewish community's center of gravity gradually shifted from Montreal to Toronto as the latter became a major financial center. Today, nearly half of Canada's estimated 280,000 Jews live in greater Toronto, followed by Montreal and Vancouver.

ISRAEL: DIASPORA REVISITED?

The great decline in Jewish presence in the Holy Land that took place during the half millennium between the Byzantine and Crusader eras ended, abruptly and dramatically, in the last two decades of the nineteenth century. In what began as a reflexive response to the massacres of Jews in southern Russia during the early 1880s, some Jews began immigrating to Ottoman Palestine, while much larger numbers were heading toward America.

Historians remain divided about how great a role that immigration to Palestine played in reshaping Jewish history. Clearly, until the turn of the twentieth century, most of the new Jewish immigration to Palestine did not identify with, and in fact often opposed, the social radicalism that was fermenting in Russia. Only the second wave of modern-era immigrants, the one that began arriving after the failed Russian revolution of 1905, introduced the collectivist idea in Palestine. There were obvious social, psychological, and ideological gaps between the two immigrations. The first comprised entire families and was bourgeois, traditional, and conservative, while the second was

(RIGHT)

ASHKENAZI SYNAGOGUE,
ISTANBUL, TURKEY.
INAUGURATED IN 1900.

*The Ottoman's tolerance toward the Jews of
the empire did not prevent them from
treating the Jews of Palestine harshly during
World War I. Note the synagogue façade's
three imposing oriental arches and octagonal
rosette windows. Inside, the floors are of
marble, the lofty dome is painted with stars,
and the elaborately worked ark of dark wood
blends Eastern European and Arabesque
styles.*

(OPPOSITE)

HOLOCAUST SURVIVORS
ARRIVING IN HAIFA, C. 1946.
*Most of the 250,000 survivors who left
Europe came to Israel.*

made up of young, radical, and sometimes promiscuous singles.

Nevertheless, these two immigrations restored the Land of Israel as a viable destination not only for the Jewish pilgrims, scholars, and social misfits that it typically attracted during previous centuries, but also for developers, farmers, scientists, free professionals, and blue-collar workers who found jobs in newly established factories, farms, hospitals, banks, and educational institutions.

In the aftermath of the 1881–1914 immigration, Palestine's roughly 25,000 Jews swelled to 85,000. This marked a watershed in the history of the Diaspora, touching off the process that by the end of the twentieth century would bring the Promised Land to the brink of hosting, for the first time since antiquity, the world's largest Jewish community.

The Jewish settlement in Ottoman Palestine suffered a setback during World War I, when the regional governor, Jamal Peha, while bracing for the British invasion from Egypt, expelled thousands of Jews from the south of the country to its north. A few months later,

in September 1917, when the Turks caught the pro-British underground Nili, many of Palestine's Jews were altogether expelled—to Damascus—while others were arrested. Some were also executed.

Though traumatic, these experiences did not permanently mar modern Palestine's Jewish appeal. The Turks soon lost Palestine along with the rest of the Ottoman Empire, and the British pro-Zionist Balfour Declaration issued in 1917 allowed the renewal of Jewish immigration to the Holy Land.

During the subsequent three decades of British rule, Palestine became a focus of Jewish immigration, despite frequent twists, turns, and ambiguities in the Mandate government's policies toward the Zionist enterprise. The impediments, all involving the Arab opposition to the Zionist endeavor, included three turning points: first, the shrinking of political Palestine, in 1922, in order to create the Hashemite kingdom east of the Jordan River; then, in 1930, the Passfield Paper, which linked the number of Jewish immigrants to Palestine's economic absorption capacity; and finally, the 1939 MacDonald Paper, which altogether halted immigration and land purchases.

Still, other circumstances created counter forces that proved even more potent than British obstruction efforts. First, the near sealing of the United States to new immigrants, through the Johnson Acts of the 1920s, and similar measures taken in other immigration destinations left European Jews with few immigration choices aside from Palestine. Then, the rise of Nazism and the growing disillusionment with social integration in other parts of Europe intensified Jewish emigration. Ultimately, by the end of the World War II, the Jewish community of Palestine had exceeded half a million people, more than seven times the size of the battered community that survived the First World War.

In all, the biggest single immigration during the British period, some 200,000 people, was that of the 1930s, which was largely ignited by Hitler's rise to power (though only half of that wave actually came from Germany and Austria). In the years immediately after World War II, some 250,000 Holocaust survivors left Europe, usually for Israel. By 1950 there already were 1.2 million Jews in Israel, and within two decades that figure more than doubled, to 2.56 million, thanks to a constant inflow of immigrants and a birthrate that was higher than the West's in general and the Diaspora's in particular. Within another two decades the number of Israel's Jews nearly doubled again, to 5.1 million.

Similar to the rest of world Jewry, Israel's Jews are concentrated in dense urban areas, with roughly half of them living in greater Tel Aviv and the coastal plain cities to its north and south. However, unlike most Jewish communities worldwide, Israel's Jews are often sharply divided between traditionalists and secularists. While Diaspora communities (with occasional exceptions, most notably Argentina's) lack the kind of ideological secularism that is common among Israeli Jews, Israel's sizable traditional population usually shuns the Conservative, Liberal, Reform, and Reconstructionist versions of Judaism that are widespread in the affluent parts of the Diaspora.

(ABOVE)
THE TEL AVIV BEACHFRONT
AT NIGHT.
*Israel's Jews are more sharply divided
between traditionalists and secularists
than the Diaspora's.*

However, economically Israel's Jews are not different from their brethren abroad. Israel is a technological powerhouse and a financial island of stability whose annual per capita product is higher than that of several European Union members. Israel's Jews are also no less culturally productive than those in any other part of the Diaspora, supporting some of the world's best universities and research institutions as well as numerous prolific authors, artists and first-class musicians and symphony orchestras.

At the same time, since its inception Israel has been at odds, and often at war, with most of its neighbors. The more than 19,000 soldiers it lost in its first half century of existence were by far the largest number of Jews killed anywhere since the Holocaust.

And so, for the first time since Jeremiah's times, the Land of Israel hosts the world's most vibrant Jewish community, which, at the same time, is also the most embattled. One can only wonder whether the rise of the modern Jewish state heralds the end, within a few generations, of the Diaspora's eternal journey, or whether it merely adds up to yet another place where Jews are vilified, demonized, and in many cases also killed— due to their Jewishness.

The Ten Lost Tribes

The Jews had been exiled, dispersed, and landless for eight centuries when a tall, dark-skinned traveler arrived toward 880 C.E. in Kairouan, North Africa, and claimed to descend from the tribe of Dan. Speaking—according to later accounts—no language other than Hebrew, Eldad Hadani sparked the imaginations of both prominent and simple Jews with incredibly detailed stories concerning their long-lost brethren: the Ten Tribes.

According to Hadani, the tribes of Naphtali, Gad, Asher, and his own tribe, Dan, all lived in East Africa near the biblical land of gold-rich Havilah. Here they formed a kingdom of nomads under the leadership of King Addiel. Constantly on the battlefield, they benefited from the existence in their midst of Samson's and Delilah's descendants, who were particularly able warriors. Only one river, Sambatyon, separated them from "the sons of Moses." The Sambatyon would be impossible to cross on regular days due to its vicious currents, which would calm down on the Sabbath (when travel is forbidden anyway), only to be surrounded by thick fog or immense flames.

Hadani claimed further that the four tribes of his land alternately studied and fought in a three-month rotation system. As for other tribes, Simon and half of Manasseh dwelt in Central Asia and were taxing twenty-five kingdoms, while Zebulun, Issachar, and Reuben lived between today's northern Iran and Turkey, and Ephraim lived in Arabia. As for the Jews living under Christian and Muslim rule, Hadani shared the prevailing view that they were the descendants of Judah and Benjamin.

Some seven centuries later, a man called David Reubeni, probably a black Jew from Ethiopia sold to slavery and redeemed by fellow Jews in Alexandria, appeared in Safed, where he claimed to have been on an official mission on behalf of the king of the Ten Tribes. The king, he said, ordered him to return with a stone from the Western Wall. Reubeni, who did not claim to be the Messiah but insisted that Redemption was imminent, proceeded with his message to Rome, which he entered riding a white horse. Though most local Jews treated him with suspicion, Reubeni, who also claimed to

(ABOVE)

AROER, SOUTHERN TRANSJORDAN.
The tribe of Reuben preferred to settle in this area despite it being outside the Promised Land.

(OPPOSITE)

THE TRIBES OF ISRAEL
ENCAMPED AROUND THE
TABERNACLE IN THE DESERT.
FROM A LATIN IBLE. PRINTED BY
OLIVIA STEPHANI. 1557, GENEVA.
The Jewish people were splintered already before the emergence of the Diaspora.

(OPPOSITE)

THE ARRIVAL OF ELIJAH.

FROM THE WASHINGTON HAGGADAH. ARTIST-SCRIBE: JOEL BEN SIMEON. 1478. NORTHERN ITALY. VELLUM. FOL. 19V, HEBRAIC SECTION. THE LIBRARY OF CONGRESS, WASHINGTON, D.C.

Elijah's career was dominated by his struggle against the Israelite kingdom's embrace of paganism.

command an army, actually met Pope Clement VII in 1524 and urged him to strike an alliance with the Jews against the Ottomans.

Roughly two years later he met with King John III in Lisbon and touched off a messianic euphoria among the local *Marrano* community. Ultimately, after many adventures and journeys, Reubeni and Solomon Molcho, a Portuguese *Marrano* who declared his Jewishness and claimed to be the Messiah, were arrested. Reubeni died in jail and Molcho, whose declaration was seen as a threat to political stability, was burned at the stake.

Just who Hadani and Reubeni really were, why they made their claims, and why no contemporary of theirs set out to actually travel and verify, or disprove, their accounts remain largely unanswered questions. The fact that many of the ritual laws Hadani "cited" were unknown to his generation's rabbis, and that Reubeni's stories about himself were inconsistent (at times he claimed to hail from the tribe of Judah rather than Reuben), not to mention the generally unfounded stories the two told about the Lost Tribes, all make it likely that both men were at least partly charlatans.

Still, their tales' basic assumption—that the Lost Tribes had actually survived intact for centuries away from the Promised Land while preserving their faith—was universally accepted, certainly by Jews, and often by non-Jews, too. In Jewish tradition, the very existence of the River Sambatyon and the notion that the Lost Tribes were trapped beyond it were taken as a given (though Josephus Flavius claimed that the river, which he thought ran north of the Lebanon Mountains, would flow on the Sabbath and dry up on weekdays).

Talmudic sage Rabbi Akiba is said to have mentioned the cessation of the mysterious river's flow on the Sabbath as proof of the Jewish rest day's divinity. Seventeenth-century scholar Manasseh ben-Israel claimed that the Sambatyon's sand would rattle for six days, and rest on the seventh, even when kept in a container outside its place of origin.

Non-Jews also subscribed to the Sambatyon myth. Roman historian and geographer Pliny the Elder reported as fact the Jewish conventional wisdom that the Sambatyon actually existed and ceased to flow every Saturday

MYTH: THE POWER OF LONGING

In 1260, Kabbalist Abraham Abulafya set out to actually seek the Sambatyon (in the Land of Israel), and Benjamin of Tudela cited stories about the tribes of Dan, Asher, Zebulun, and Naphtali residing in a town called Nisaphur, where they were ruled by a Levite prince. The famed traveler added that the tribes of Gad, Reuben, and half of Manasseh lived in the Arabian Peninsula. Some four centuries later Manasseh ben-Israel found attentive ears in Puritan England to his claims that the ingathering of the lost Israelite tribes was feasible, desirable, and even imperative. Two decades later false

Messiah Shabbetai Zevi's followers, who would not accept his death, claimed he had crossed the Sambatyon and would remain with the Ten Tribes until he decided to stage his grand return.

Perhaps more oddly, when the invading Mongols were fast approaching Eastern Europe in the thirteenth century, both Christians and Jews frequently linked the intruders to the Ten Tribes. According to contemporary German and French chronicles, some Jews thought that Genghis Khan's armies were actually the Lost Tribes' descendants and that the great conqueror was out to initially redeem his brethren from Christianity's yoke and then make the Jews rule the world.

The survival of the Lost Tribes was accepted as truth not because of any empirical evidence, but because of sacred scripture. If anything, a factual discovery that would disprove the existence of the Diaspora's ten missing pieces would be perplexing. To contemporary Jews, Hadani's stories were novel mainly in the encounter they suggested with a reality that was only supposed to be unveiled once Redemption actually dawned. Beyond that, the stories also excited Jews in their implicit refutation of Christian dogma, which contended that the Jews' dispersal was part of a humiliating plan whereby they could not be proud, independent, and successful warriors.

Indeed, even more potent than the pervasive belief that the Lost Tribes still existed was the faith that they would play a major role in the Redemption, based on explicit prophecies like this one in Jeremiah (29:13): "And I will turn your captivity, and gather you from all the nations, and from all the places whither I have driven you, says the Lord; and I will bring you back unto the place whence I caused you to be carried away captive."

REALITY: LOST IN SPACE

The facts concerning the Lost Tribes were a bit more prosaic than the many stories that surrounded them for more than 2,500 years. The Assyrian empire, short-lived though it was, left an indelible imprint on the Middle East, due to its policy of relocating the peoples it conquered. That is the context of the Ten Israelite Tribes' expulsion from Samaria and the surrounding regions.

The Bible is quite specific as for the destinations in which the Israelites were resettled: "In the ninth year of Hoshea, the king of Assyria took Samaria, and carried Israel away unto Assyria, and placed them in Halah, and in Habor, on the river of Gozan, and in the cities of the Medes." (Kings II, 17:5) These locations lead to what lies between today's northeastern Syria and northwestern Iran. And while archeology has established that people bearing Israelite names indeed did arrive in those areas, research has failed to find information about the Israelites' fate soon after their forced relocation. Indeed, the disappearance of the Ten Tribes from history's stage apparently had to do with culture more than with geography.

(ABOVE)
MOUNT BAAL HAZOR IN THE LAND
OF BENJAMIN.
*According to the Bible, the tribe that later
produced the first Israelite monarch was
previously nearly erased in the aftermath
of a civil war.*

WELL-DEFINED FIEFDOMS

Despite the poverty of details concerning the Ten Tribes' individual histories during
their roughly five centuries of existence in the Land of Israel, the Bible does describe in
relative detail their respective fiefdoms. According to the book of Joshua, once the
Israelites completed the initial conquest of the Promised Land, God told Joshua to
assign each of the tribes its designated territory, even though much of the land had yet
to be conquered, as the flatlands in the north and along the coastline remained under
Canaanite and Philistine control. Eventually, the tribes were distributed roughly as
follows:

Reuben, following its request from Moses and after having delivered on its
promise to cross the Jordan and join the war for the Promised Land, was granted the
land it coveted on the river's east bank. This area is roughly to the west and south of
today's Aman.

(ABOVE)

SHIVITI PLAQUE (MAP OF THE HOLY
PLACES).

MOSES GANBASH. ISTANBUL, 1838–1839. PAPER, PAINT,
INK, PAPER-CUT SECTIONS. THE JEWISH MUSEUM, NEW
YORK. GIFT OF DR. HARRY G. FRIEDMAN.

Gad, who had joined Reuben's request to Moses, was given the land just north of
Reuben's territory. Thus they reached the southern foothills of the Golan Heights and
the particularly fertile lands southeast of Lake Kinneret.

One half of the tribe of Manasseh, which had joined the request to settle east of the
Jordan, was given the Golan Heights and lands to its east. As such, this part of Manasseh
would eventually represent the northernmost Israelite population, which dwelt not far
from Damascus.

The southern end of the land was to be dominated by Judah, from the central Negev
Desert through the western shore of the Dead Sea and the land to its west that would
become known as the Judean Desert. Its land extended to the mountains that would
become known as the Judean Mountains, including the city of Jebus, which would some

(ABOVE)

MOUNT TABOR.
*Deborah the Prophetess had to
reprimand some of the Israelite tribes for
shunning the battle won here by the
northern tribes, led by Barak ben-
Avinoam.*

(OPPOSITE)

JACOB BLESSING EPHRAIM AND
MANASSAH.
FROM THE GOLDEN HAGGADAH. C. 1320. SPAIN. VELLUM.

ADD. 27210. THE BRITISH LIBRARY, LONDON.

two centuries later become known as Jerusalem, after its conquest by David. Judah, the
largest tribe alongside its archrival Ephraim, was also given the major town of Hebron
south of Jerusalem, and much of the Negev's highlands and mountains. Though
theoretically straddling the Mediterranean coastline, Judah effectively remained
concentrated in the mountains between today's Jerusalem and Hebron.

To its northeast, Judah bordered on Joseph's younger, but preferred son, Ephraim.
Stretching from the outskirts of Jericho in the south to the border of the Jezreel Valley
in the north, this tribe's land included the religiously magnetic town of Shiloh and the
politically powerful city of Shechem, which later became known as Nablus.

The second half of Manasseh was allotted the hills west of Ephraim. Bordering
on the Mediterranean and comprising mainly the hills of western Samaria, this land
lay roughly between the Carmel Mountains and the contemporary coastal resort
town of Netanya.

The lands to Ephraim's south, and just north of today's main Tel Aviv-Jerusalem-Jericho highway, were given to the tribe of Benjamin. Theoretically, Benjamin also received Jerusalem, but the tribe never managed to wrest the city from its Jebusite inhabitants. Otherwise, the best-known towns in this part of the land were Jericho and Bet El. However, Benjamin's most important city would ultimately be Gibeah, just outside the contemporary Jerusalem neighborhood of Pisgat Ze'ev, from where the first Israelite king—Saul—would rule.

In the south, the tribe of Simon was given much of the northern Negev Desert, including the town of Beersheba. However, Simon was from the onset described as both demographically outnumbered and geographically surrounded by the tribe of Judah. (Joshua 19:9)

The tribe of Zebulun, about whom Jacob prophesied (Genesis 49:1) that he "shall dwell at the shore of the sea," was promised most of the fertile lands that stretched to the east of today's Haifa Bay, between the Carmel Mountains in the west and Mount Tabor in the east.

Just north of Zebulun's land, Issachar was promised a fiefdom that went from the Jezreel Valley in the west through the northern foothills of Mount Tabor to the Jordan River in the east, just south of contemporary Tiberias.

Northwest of Zebulun, the tribe of Asher was parceled what today is known as the Western Galilee, stretching from the currently Lebanese cities of Tyre and Sidon in the north to the lands outside Acre in the south.

East of Asher, the tribe of Naphtali was given what today is known as the Finger of Galilee, including the mountains opposite the Golan Heights, where the current biggest town is the Israeli city of Kiryat Shmona. However, during the times of the Israelites its most important city was the Canaanite bastion of Hatzor, which overlooked the fertile Hulleh Valley where the Jordan River feeds into Lake Kinneret.

Lastly, the tribe of Dan was granted the lands between the hills southwest of Jerusalem and the coastline between today's Tel Aviv and Ashkelon. However, several generations after Joshua's conquests, the tribe conceded (Judges 18) its failure to conquer its promised lands from the Philistines, and sent scouts to seek an alternative land. The scouts located the Jordan River's sources between the Golan Heights and the Naphtali Mountains, conquered the local town of Layish and settled the area. That is how the local spring—the largest in the Promised Land—assumed the name by which it is known until today: Dan.

Beyond all these, the tribe of Levi was deliberately given no land. Instead, all other tribes were obliged to allow the Levites to dwell in their midst, so that they

(ABOVE)

LAND OF NAPHTALI, UPPER GALILEE.
The mountainous and distant northern Land of Israel was often difficult to access for the rest of the Israelites, due to the coastal plain's frequent occupation by invading armies from Egypt and Mesopotamia.

could dedicate themselves to religious worship and to the conducting of sacrificial rituals on behalf of all the Israelites.

THE GOLAN HEIGHTS.
The tribe of Manasseh split itself between this region and the hills south of Haifa.

FAMILY FEUDS: THE TRAGEDY OF TRIBALISM

The Lost Tribes' disappearance was preceded, and largely driven, by the Israelites' historic failure to unite. In a sense, theirs was the inversion of the modern American experience, where a bloody civil war was followed by a universal acceptance of common nationhood and the emergence of a geopolitical superpower. The Israelite kingdom that was first established by King Saul lasted for a mere century (1025–928 B.C.E.) before splitting between Judah and Israel.

The tribes' very insistence on dwelling each in its distinct area, and the consequent tendency to marry within the tribe, soon enough generated inter-tribal tension, strife, and bloodshed.

The first expression of tribal envy came early, during the parceling out of the land, as the leaders of Ephraim came to Joshua (who was a member of that tribe) complaining that the land he had designated for them was insufficient considering their numbers and their prospective land's topography. Joshua's rejection of his tribe's demand may have sown the seeds for the civil turmoil that would accompany the Ten Tribes' existence until, and arguably leading to, their disappearance. It should come as no surprise, then, that soon after Joshua's death the disjointed tribal structure's inherent lack of cohesion proved problematic.

When Deborah the Prophetess led the northern tribes to victory over a massive Canaanite army led by King Sisera, she scolded the tribes of Reuben, Gad, Dan, and Asher for not joining their brethren's war. Gideon, the judge who belonged to the tribe of Manasseh and— shortly after Deborah's time—defeated the invading Midianites, was confronted by the people of Ephraim for having failed to formally invite them to participate in the war.

Other tribal leaders, most notably Samson, did not quarrel with fellow Israelites, but their activities were confined to their respective tribal settings. In fact, the Bible generally leaves the impression that the Israelite leaders prior to King Saul were hardly concerned about the other tribes' travails. In Gideon's case the refusal to weld the Israelites into a functioning polity was even ideological. When, following his impressive military victories, the "men of Israel" implored him to become their king he replied: "I will not rule over you, neither shall my son rule over you; the Lord shall rule over you." (Judges 8:23) This attitude led philosopher Martin Buber to portray the tribes' existence prior to the rise of the Israelite kingdom as an idyll. To Buber, theirs was a society of farmers who combined political anarchy with religious piety and industrious husbandry. Either way, behind the passage that appears repeatedly in the Book of Judges—"In those days there was no king in Israel; every man did that which was right in his own eyes"— lurked a failure to confront invasions from without and crime from within.

In one case, a crime committed by one tribe nearly resulted in its annihilation by the rest of the Israelite tribes. Several generations before the establishment of the first Israelite kingdom, a woman from the Judean town of Bethlehem passed through in Gibeah (today a hill within municipal Jerusalem, and then a town in the Land of Benjamin) and was raped and murdered by a local mob, in the presence of her husband, a Levite who resided in the land of Ephraim, just north of Benjamin.

Determined to alert the entire nation to the crime he had witnessed, the traumatized husband butchered the woman's body into twelve pieces, sending a piece to each of the tribes. The tribes, says the Bible, were indeed alarmed and enlisted to the cause: "Then all the children of Israel went out, and the congregation was assembled as one man, from Dan even to Beersheba, with the land of Gilead, unto the Lord." (Judges 20:1) Having gathered "four hundred thousand footmen that drew sword," the tribes handed the tribe

(OPPOSITE, TOP)
BETHEL, IN THE LAND OF BENJAMIN. *Here is where Jacob began his journey back to Mesopotamia, where he ended up finding his four women, before proceeding later in his life to Egypt, where he left his twelve sons.*

(OPPOSITE, BOTTOM)
THE JORDAN VALLEY, NEAR THE YABOK PASS. *Jacob passed here entering the Holy Land with the family he had built in today's Iraq. After the Patriarch wrestled here all night with an unidentified man, God changed Jacob's name to Israel.*

of Benjamin an ultimatum: "Deliver up the men, the base fellows that are in Gibeah, that we may put them to death, and put away evil from Israel. But the children of Benjamin would not hearken to the voice of their brethren the children of Israel."

Considering its weaknesses—Benjamin's population and domain were the smallest among all the tribes of Israel—one might have expected Benjamin to summarily comply with the ultimatum. Instead they turned it down, preferring to touch off a civil war. In what clearly reflected their lack of leadership and organization, the Israelites at first lost several battles to the vastly outnumbered, but highly motivated men of Benjamin, who apparently also benefited from their intimate acquaintance with the landscape. However, the tribes in due course not only won but in fact dealt Benjamin such a severe blow that it nearly lost its entire male population, including twenty-five thousand in one day of fighting.

Just what exactly happened during that first intra-Israelite civil war remains unclear, since there is no other reference to it aside from the largely cryptic story in the Book of Judges. The story does, however, indicate that sectionalism was an intrinsic problem. In fact, within a few generations civil war erupted again.

The tribe of Benjamin recovered from that blow so impressively that when Samuel agreed to crown a king, he chose a member of that tribe, Saul. However, from his castle, curiously located in the same town of Gibeah where Benjamin had previously locked horns with its Israelite brethren, a suspicious Saul lived under the ever-growing shadow of his tribe's elder brother and dominant neighbor from the south—Judah.

Saul was killed in battle up north on Mt. Gilboa, well beyond his own tribe's lands, while providing the kind of intra-tribal solidarity that his monarchy was meant to be all about. However, after his death Saul's successors were engaged in yet another civil war, this time with the followers of David, whom Saul had both admired and hated throughout much of their tragic encounter.

While famously wrapped in the romanticism of the clash between the harpist-turned-warrior's charisma and the aging king's jealousy, Saul's and David's tormented relationship (David also married Saul's daughter, Michal) appears to have been at least inspired by tribal rivalry. Either way, following Saul's death the tribes of trans-Jordan and the mountains north of Judah remained loyal to Benjamin, while Judah seceded and crowned David.

David's warriors ultimately defeated Saul's loyalists in a battle that took place just north of today's Jerusalem. Consequently, Benjamin gradually became part of Judah's orbit, having been both adjacent to and significantly smaller than Judah. Indeed, the tribe that would pose the real challenge to Judah's supremacy would not be its neighbor to the north, but the one just beyond it—Ephraim.

The clash between Judah and Ephraim was at least literarily foretold already in the stories in Genesis where Joseph's dreams of dominating his brothers, and their

(OPPOSITE)

DAVID PLAYING THE HARP.
FROM THE LEIPNICK HAGGADAH.
ARTIST-SCRIBE: JOSEPH BAR DAVID LEIPNICK OF
MORAVIA. BIBLIOTECA ROSENTHALIANA, AMSTERDAM.

*Though David managed to unify the
Israelite tribes, the merger proved
superficial.*

פירוש אברבנאל

אֲשֶׁר בּוֹטֵחַ בָּהֶם יִשְׂרָאֵל בְּטַח בַּיְיָ עֶזְרָם וּמָגִנָּם

הוּא : בֵּית אַהֲרֹן בִּטְחוּ בַּיְיָ עֶזְרָם וּמָגִנָּם

הוּא : יִרְאֵי יְיָ בִּטְחוּ בַּיְיָ עֶזְרָם וּמָגִנָּם הוּא :

יְיָ זְכָרָנוּ יְבָרֵךְ יְבָרֵךְ אֶת בֵּית יִשְׂרָאֵל יְבָרֵךְ

אֶת בֵּית אַהֲרֹן · יְבָרֵךְ יִרְאֵי יְיָ הַקְּטַנִּים

עִם הַגְּדֹלִים · יֹסֵף יְיָ עֲלֵיכֶם עֲלֵיכֶם וְעַל

consequent abandonment of their megalomaniac brother to the devices of slave traders, later culminated in Joseph's astonishing emergence as the omnipotent deputy to a superpower's emperor. When the brothers came to Egypt to buy grain and faced the vengeful deputy emperor—whom they did not recognize and who demanded that they leave their youngest brother with him—it was Judah who faced Joseph and pleaded with him to reverse his decision.

Later, as the tribes sank roots in the Promised Land, Ephraim (which was the dominant tribe that descended from Joseph) showed from the onset signs of a superiority complex: first, when it complained about its designated land, then, when it locked horns with Gideon for not having enlisted them to the war he led on Midian. Worse yet, Ephraim actually fought with the Israelites of the Gilead (apparently members of the tribe of Gad) following the former tribe's complaint to Jephthah the Judge for not having enlisted them to the war that he waged against the kingdom of Ammon. According to Judges 12:6 Ephraim lost forty-two thousand men in that clash, which took place on the banks of the Jordan River. In a further hint at how tribal dynamics worked against Israelite unity, the Bible says that Ephraim's tribesmen were identified according to a distinctive dialect which made them mispronounce the Hebrew word *shibolet* as *sibolet* (and hence the English term "shibboleth").

More importantly, the holiest town in Ephraim, Shiloh, was destroyed by a Philistine invasion in the middle of the eleventh century B.C.E. Consequently, Ephraim's aspirations of leading the Israelites were dealt a severe blow, since the Israelite masses ceased to make pilgrimages to the town whose sanctity they accepted.

When David finally conquered Jerusalem, he designated it the Israelite capital without apportioning it to any of the tribes (much the way that Washington, D.C., was not made part of any state within the United States). That structure was further consolidated when Solomon added to Jerusalem's political centrality a powerful religious dimension by locating his famous temple in it.

However, even during David's and Solomon's days the northern tribes' acceptance of Judah's leadership was superficial. Following his son Absalom's revolt against him, David reformed the military so that it rested mostly on the Judean troops, those whose loyalty to him went back to the days he spent in the Judean Desert when he was hiding from King Saul.

During Solomon's reign, a man called Jeroboam, who belonged to the tribe of Ephraim and was in charge of that tribe's public works, led a failed coup and ended up fleeing to Egypt. Though the tribal package was otherwise kept together thanks to Solomon's personal charisma and governmental efficiency, which relied greatly on heavy taxes, forced labor, and strict conscription, as soon as he died so did the kingdom's unity.

As it were, the northern tribes immediately demanded that the coronation of Solomon's son, Rehoboam, be held not in Jerusalem, but in Ephraim's political center, Shechem (today's Nablus). Meanwhile, Jeroboam returned from Egypt armed with that

superpower's support. An evidently unconfident Rehoboam went the extra mile to Shechem, but once there failed to harmonize with the northern tribes. A messenger, Adoram the tax collector, whom he sent to negotiate a deal with the secessionists, was stoned to death. The glorious Solomonic kingdom was thus split in half between its south and north. The former, Judah, was led by Judah but also included Benjamin and possibly the southern tribe of Simon as well. The north, named Israel, was led by Ephraim, and comprised the northern tribes.

The effects of secession were immediate, and harsh. First, the neighboring kingdoms of Ammon, Moab, and Edom (all on the Jordan River's east bank), which had previously been subjugated by the Israelites, now restored their independence. Then Egypt and the Philistines crippled the fledgling kingdom of Israel with separate attacks. Soon enough Judah, too, attacked Israel and took lands in southern Ephraim, capitalizing on Israel's evident weakness after its crippling by Egypt.

(ABOVE)
THE TEMPLE MOUNT.
David chose this as the site of his capital because it did not clearly belong to any tribe.

(PAGES 184–185)
THE TEMPLE'S MENORAH.
FROM THE DUKE OF SUSSEX SPANISH BIBLE. MID-FOURTEENTH CENTURY. CATALONIA. VELLUM. MS. 15250. FOL. 3V. THE BRITISH LIBRARY, LONDON.
Solomon's attempt to unify the Israelites around the Temple failed.

(ABOVE)
TEL JEZREEL, SITE OF KING
AHAB'S WINTER PALACE.
*The monarch who provoked the
prophets by marrying the idol-
worshipping Isabel lived in harmony
with the Kingdom of Judah.*

Still, Rehoboam gave the northern tribes a religious focus as he built two
alternatives to Jerusalem's temple, one in Bet El, the other in Dan. Yet he failed to
build a durable dynasty, and after his death a general called Baasa, from the tribe of
Issachar, annihilated Rehoboam's heirs and crowned himself king of Israel.
Tragically, during his time the enmity between Judah and Israel intensified,
and the former, under the leadership of King Asa (908–867 B.C.E.), even drew a
foreign power, the northeastern kingdom of Aram, into the conflict between Israel
and Judah.

However, there were also protracted periods of cooperation between Judah and
Israel. During the reign of Judah's King Jehoshaphat, and Israel's Ahab and Omri, the
two kingdoms even joined each other in wars against external enemies, and Judah did
not interfere when Israel built a new capital city—Samaria (outside today's Nablus).
Yet even then the cultural differences between the two kingdoms continued to expand.

The comparatively coastal, commercial, and cosmopolitan Israelite kingdom opened up to foreign cultures in general, and to idolatrous religions in particular.

The alliance with Tyre generated great economic benefits, as that kingdom presided over an elaborate network of commercial outposts around the Mediterranean basin. However, that act of diplomacy also caused Ahab to marry Isabel, whom the prophets scolded for importing her idolatrous culture into Israel.

Judah, at the same time, tried and failed to send sailors into the Red Sea through Etzion Gaver (today's Eilat). Consequently, while Israel was embracing the outer world, Judah was effectively shunning those contacts, or unable to engage them. And while Israel was courting foreign cultures, Judah was on the whole nurturing its ties to its religious heritage.

Moreover, the northern tribes' detachment from Jerusalem and the temple, the embodiment of their faith, ultimately left Israel ill equipped to preserve its heritage under the circumstances of forced exile. Once the Israelite kingdom collapsed and its inhabitants were uprooted, they apparently shed their links to their people, faith, and land. Considering that they never truly integrated with Judah, Benjamin, and Levi (even during the century of Saul, David, and Solomon, when the tribes were politically unified), it is logical that the Lost Tribes never seriously attempted to nurture their embattled heritage, or return to their ancestral land.

Meanwhile, Judah's urge to uphold the national heritage was further boosted by the demise of the Israelite kingdom in 720 B.C.E. Led by King Hezekiah, whose reign (727–698 B.C.E.) began before and ended well after the northern kingdom's destruction, Judah efficiently maneuvered its way among the regional powers, and at the same time embarked on an effort to enhance the Israelite faith. Thus, Hezekiah initially avoided provoking the Mesopotamian superpower, and made sure to ultimately join its enemies only after Assyria's power began to wane. Religiously, Hezekiah accommodated the Israelites' heritage by consolidating its places of worship, though only as part of the Judean system that remained monotheistic and centered at Jerusalem's temple.

The Bible's statement that Hezekiah "sent to all Israel and Judah, and wrote letters also to Ephraim and Manasseh, that they should come to the house of the Lord at Jerusalem, to keep the Passover unto the Lord, the God of Israel," (Chronicles II, 30:1) indicates that after the Israelite kingdom's demise, the Judean king embarked on a policy of national healing based on spiritual restoration, by offering those Israelites who survived their brethren's calamity to make Judah their national home.

In essence, that was the kernel of all subsequent Jewish history. After the Assyrian conquest, there no longer were Israelites, only Judeans, who eventually became knows as Jews. The disappearance of the Ten Tribes troubled both Jeremiah, who ended up in Egypt, and Ezekiel, who was among the Judeans exiled to Babylon.

Jeremiah promised that Lost Tribes "shall come with weeping, and with supplications will I lead them; I will cause them to walk by rivers of waters, in a straight way wherein they shall not stumble; for I am become a father to Israel, and Ephraim is My first-born. Hear the word of the Lord, O ye nations, and declare it in the isles afar off, and say: 'He that scattered Israel doth gather him, and keep him, as a shepherd doth his flock.'" (Jeremiah 31:6–9)

Ezekiel was even more elaborate: "I will take the children of Israel from among the nations, whither they are gone, and will gather them on every side, and bring them into their own land; and I will make them one nation in the land, upon the mountains of Israel, and one king shall be king to them all; and they shall be no more two nations." (Ezekiel 37:21–22)

Still, when Persia's King Cyrus allowed the restoration of Jerusalem's temple, some two generations after Jeremiah's life, the ones who responded to it were "the heads of fathers' houses of Judah and Benjamin, and the priests, and the Levites." (Ezra 1:5) The Israelites, by then, had vanished. Indeed, throughout the Second Temple era there is no indication that the Ten Tribes were actively sought, and in some cases they had even ceased to be passively expected. Mishnaic sage Rabbi Akiba, for instance, said: "The Ten Tribes shall not return again, for it is written (in Deuteronomy 29:28): 'And he cast them into another land like this day.' Like this day goes and does not return, so do they go and not return." (Mishna Sanhedrin, 10, 3.)

Other sages, however, led by Rabbi Eliezer, disagreed: "Just like the day first grows dark and then grows light, so also after darkness falls upon the Ten Tribes light shall eventually shine upon them."

LOST TRIBES FOUND

Originally, the term "Lost Tribes" referred to the Israelites whose kingdom was destroyed by the Assyrians some two generations prior to Judah's surrender to Assyria's own conqueror, Babylon. However, the ebb and flow of Jewish history, where physical relocation and cultural transformation have been a mainstay, ultimately redefined this term so that it encompassed all exotic communities whose origins, or aftermath, were shrouded in mystery.

In modern times the term "Lost Tribes" has come to include Jewish communities whose origins are clearer than those of the many groups seen by some as descending from the Ten Tribes, but who still lost touch with major Jewish centers or observances. Such, for instance, was the fate of many *Marrano* communities that ended up in Latin America during the early imperialist age, when British, Spanish, and Portuguese sailors were storming that continent's shores in search of precious metals.

In Chile, for instance, there still are several communities whose ancestors fled the Inquisition's wrath. For more than four centuries these groups have been partially observing the Sabbath and the holiday of Tabernacles. They live secluded past the Bio-Bio River, which separated them from the Spaniards—a Sambatyon of sorts buffering

(OPPOSITE)

THE BOOK OF LAMENTATIONS. FROM THE FOUR MEGILLOT. MS. 8222, FOL. 9V. LIBRARY OF THE JEWISH THEOLOGICAL SEMINARY OF AMERICA, NEW YORK.

At the time of the first Temple's destruction, the Ten Tribes had already been effectively lost.

אֵיכָה יָשְׁבָה בָדָד הָעִיר רַבָּתִי עָם הָיְתָה
כְּאַלְמָנָה רַבָּתִי בַגּוֹיִם שָׂרָתִי
בַּמְּדִינוֹת הָיְתָה לָמַס : בָּכוֹ תִבְכֶּה בַּלַּיְלָה
וְדִמְעָתָהּ עַל לֶחֱיָהּ אֵין לָהּ מְנַחֵם מִכָּל אֹהֲבֶיהָ כָּל
רֵעֶיהָ בָּגְדוּ בָהּ הָיוּ לָהּ לְאֹיְבִים : גָּלְתָה יְהוּדָה
מֵעֹנִי וּמֵרֹב עֲבֹדָה הִיא יָשְׁבָה בַגּוֹיִם לֹא מָצְאָה
מָנוֹחַ כָּל רֹדְפֶיהָ הִשִּׂיגוּהָ בֵּין הַמְּצָרִים : דַּרְכֵי
צִיּוֹן אֲבֵלוֹת מִבְּלִי בָּאֵי מוֹעֵד כָּל שְׁעָרֶיהָ שׁוֹמֵמִין
כֹּהֲנֶיהָ נֶאֱנָחִים בְּתוּלֹתֶיהָ נּוּגוֹת וְהִיא מַר לָהּ : הָיוּ
צָרֶיהָ לְרֹאשׁ אֹיְבֶיהָ שָׁלוּ כִּי יְיָ הוֹגָהּ עַל רֹב
פְּשָׁעֶיהָ עוֹלָלֶיהָ הָלְכוּ שְׁבִי לִפְנֵי צָר : וַיֵּצֵא מִן

The Karaites: Lost by Choice?

(ABOVE)

IN THE KARAITE SYNAGOGUE OF HASKÖY, TURKEY.
The Karaite synagogue of Hasköy, Turkey, stands behind large stone walls that date to Byzantine times. Their community now numbers fewer than seventy.

While Jewish history lost an assortment of tribes and countless individuals following elaborate geographic journeys and social travails, others were lost to the Jewish mainstream due to spiritual odysseys. Such was the case of the Karaites.

Founded by eighth-century sage Anan ben-David, the Karaites observe the Pentateuch but reject Judaism's oral law. Having been a frustrated leader who lost the appointment of exilarch to his younger brother, ben-David challenged the Babylonian Talmudic academies' religious authority.

Theologically, ben-David's agenda, which he presented in his Book of Commandments, was less about challenging the oral law as such, and more about decentralizing Jewish legal authority. By the tenth century the Karaites had turned their backs to the oral law, and the implications were profound. In a nation where the interpretation of religious law substituted for statehood itself, the Karaite antinomianism meant secession. Worse yet, the Karaites' rejection of the Talmudic divorce laws made Rabbanite Jews refrain from marrying them, lest they inadvertently marry bastards, which is one of Judaism's worst sins.

Still, by the tenth century the Karaites had spread from Egypt to Spain, its leaders were writing prolifically (including David Alfasi's Arabic dictionary of the Pentateuch, the first of its kind), and in some places they also roamed imperial corridors of power as physicians, scribes, and tax collectors.

In Jerusalem the Karaites became during the early decades of the tenth century the dominant Jewish community, boasting an academy that attracted students from across the Diaspora. In Ramla, halfway between Jerusalem and Jaffa, a Karaite community rose a thousand years ago alongside the local Fattimid Muslims' administrative center. Though it declined

with the Fattimids, the Karaite community of that town exists there up until today.

Overall, the Karaites did not escape the medieval Jewish fate, despite their growing distance from mainstream Judaism. The Crusader conquest of Jerusalem abruptly ended their blossoming in Jerusalem. In Muslim lands they paid the *dhimi* taxes, and in the Polish-Lithuanian Kingdom they paid the same communal taxes as the Rabbanite Jews through the same inter-communal roof organization, the Council of the Lands.

Still, czarist Russia distinguished the Crimean Karaites from other Jews, first by exempting them from military service, then (in 1863) by emancipating them. There is also evidence that the Nazis did not deport the Karaites to extermination camps since they did not consider them racially Jewish.

After the Holocaust the Karaites stranded in the USSR all but vanished, and the sect survived mainly in Egypt and Israel.

this lost, but free, Jewish tribe from the calamity that waited had it encountered the nearby Spaniards. In Spain, Portugal, and southern France many non-Jews still carry family traditions and memorabilia linking them to a distant, but clear, Jewish ancestry. Obviously, all these Lost Tribes have nothing to do with the biblical Ten Tribes.

The discovery of America and the astonishing encounter with its native population led to speculation that these people might be descendants of the Ten Tribes. Scholars, however, never found any substance in such claims. If anywhere, it would be plausible to seek the Ten Tribes in Asia and Africa.

MODERN SEARCHES: THE OBSESSION LIVES ON

The dawn of the modern era did not dent the Lost Tribes' mystique. One thing had, however, changed: What in previous centuries was merely a matter of intellectual curiosity concerning the Lost Tribes' whereabouts now became a focus of political action aimed at facilitating the ingathering of the Israelites.

The first such connection was made by Britain's Lord Protector Oliver Cromwell, at the prodding of Dutch-Jewish scholar Manasseh Ben-Israel, who was evidently aware of the Puritan mindset that yearned for a New Jerusalem that could only exist once all the Jews will have been restored to the Holy Land. In *The Hope of Israel*, whose Latin edition he dedicated in 1650 to the British parliament, Ben-Israel wrote about the Ten Tribes' "discovery" in South America.

"A Dutch mariner told me," wrote Ben-Israel, "that not long since he was with his ship in America, seven degrees towards the North between Maragnon and great Para, and he put into an harbour in a pleasant River where he found some Indians who understood Spanish, of whom he bought Meats and Dywood; after he had stayed there six months he understood that that river extended eighteen leagues towards Carybes Indians, as far as the ship could goe; and that the River is divided there into three branches, and they sayling two moths on the left hand, there met them white men, and bearded, well bred, well cloathed, and abounding with gold and silver and many precious stones, Which he having understood sent thither some sea-men; but the Indians dyed by the way, who was their guide, and so they did not proceed, but stayed there two months and trucked with the Indians who were sixty leagues from Sea. That province is called Fisbia, and is subject to Zeland; they have no commerce with the Spaniards and the inhabitants travel securely every way. I heard that story by accident from that Dutch master of the ship; whence some of us guessing them to be Israelites had purposed to send him againe to enquire more fully. But he dyed suddenly the last yeare, whence it seems that God doth not permit that those purposes should take any effect til the end of dayes." (*The Hope of Israel*, London, 1652.)

Ben-Israel's argument was that once readmitted into Britain, the Jews' dispersal will have been complete, in line with the curse in Deuteronomy 28:64: "And the Lord shall scatter thee among all peoples, from the one end of the earth even unto the other end of the earth." Ben-Israel believed that England was that "end of the earth," the last place where Jews had yet to be found, and that once readmitted there, the Jews' dispersal would be complete and their Redemption imminent.

The Dutch-Jewish scholar's lobbying led Cromwell to meet with him in 1655, and ultimately allow the Jews to open a synagogue and cemetery in London. Thus, not only were the Jews effectively allowed to return to England, but for the first time since the Destruction a Gentile ruler treated the Jews favorably not because of economic utilitarianism, but because of a theology of restoration, inspired by the tales of the Lost Tribes and the quest to restore their lost glory.

Such speculation was not unique on both Anglophone sides of the Atlantic in the seventeenth century. In 1650, for instance, Thomas Thorowgood claimed in his *Jews in America, or Probabilities that the Americans are of that Race* that many of the Indian groups descend from the Ten Tribes. While some contemporaries disputed this claim, many others accepted it, including Roger Williams, who established Rhode Island, and John Elliot, who translated the Bible into some native-American languages.

THE SYNAGOGUE IN COCHABAMBA, BOLIVIA.
The discovery of America generated speculation in the sixteenth century that the Indians of South America are descendants of the Ten Tribes.

SHABBETAI ZEVI DEPICTED AS THE COMMANDER OF THE TEN TRIBES.
ENGRAVING. 1666. GERMANY.
The false Messiah's journey to Zion was to begin with the repatriation of the Lost Tribes from beyond the River Sambatyon.

At the same time, Rabbi Nathan Shapira of Jerusalem ventured out to the affluent communities of Italy, Germany, and Holland in order to raise funds, having lost the steady income his community had enjoyed from Poland until the 1648 massacres. In sermons he delivered in Italy, Shapira displayed a letter ostensibly dispatched by the Ten Tribes. The following decade, on the eve of Shabbetai Zevi's messianic "appearance," Shapira told an Italian Jewish audience that the Ten Tribes were dwelling "under no Gentile kingdom's yoke," somewhere under the South Pole, unlike most Jews who were, he believed, under the North Pole. As for Shabbetai Zevi himself, his appearance was laden with references to the Lost Tribes, and initially he was rumored to be actually on his way to gather them from beyond the Sambatyon.

The American linkage to the Ten Tribes continued through the eighteenth and nineteenth centuries, most notably with the foundation of the Mormon faith, which derived much of its inspiration from a tale about an Israelite prophet who leaves Jerusalem before its destruction and ends up in America. Later in the nineteenth century, the English movement British Israel promoted its view that the British were themselves descendants of the Lost Tribes.

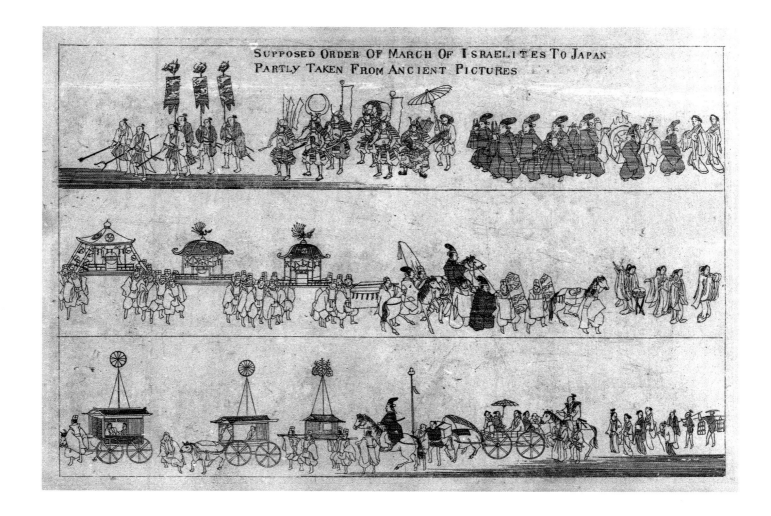

Otherwise, as long as the obsession with the Ten Tribes remained purely religious, they were not actively sought. In the nineteenth century, however, as the British Empire expanded and the science of ethnography developed, the search for the Ten Tribes intensified, albeit with unconvincing results.

ASIA: FROM AFGHANISTAN TO BURMA

In the more recent past, the search for lost Jews has become a vital interest for the State of Israel and an obsession for Christians who see in the ingathering of the Israelites a prerequisite condition for the Second Coming. The sometimes-obsessive search after the lost Israelites has bred theories about assorted tribes and nations—including the British, the Japanese, and the Eskimos—as descending from the ancient Israelites.

However, in terms of biblical references and geographical routes the most historically plausible direction in which the Ten Tribes were sought was Central Asia. The first to suggest that general direction in the context of an actual journey was twelfth-century traveler Rabbi Benjamin of Tudela, who wrote, "There are men of Israel in Persia who say that in the mountains of Nishapur four of the tribes of Israel dwell, namely, the tribe of Dan, the tribe of Zebulun, the tribe of Asher, and the tribe of Naphtali, who were included in the first captivity of Shlamaneser King of Assyria, as it is written (Kings II 18:11): 'And he put them in Halah and in Habor by the River of Gozan and in the cities of the Medes.' The extent of their land is twenty days' journey, and they have cities and large villages in the mountains; the River Gozan forms the boundary on the one side. They are not under the rule of the Gentiles, but they have a prince of their own, whose name is Rabbi Joseph Amarkala the Levite. There are scholars among them. And they sow and reap and go forth to war as far as the land of Cush by way of the desert."

Rabbi Benjamin of Tudela did not himself visit these places and makes it plain he is only passing on things he had heard from others. In modern times, however, scholars, adventurers, and men of faith, both Jewish and Christian, did venture out to seek the Lost Tribes, mainly in Asia and Africa.

In Central Asia assorted tribes have been suggested as offspring of the Ten Tribes. Names such as Gadoon, Ephtalite, and Amnasa—in which some detect echoes of the Lost-Tribe names Gad, Naphtali, and Manasseh—or the clinging onto the monotheistic Islam in a setting otherwise dominated by non-monotheistic faiths, led some to see in assorted local tribes offspring of the Ten Tribes. Tribe-seekers have speculated that the Jews of Bukhara, in today's Uzbekistan, are descendants of the tribe of Issachar because the name Issachcaroff is common among them.

The several million Afghan Pathans, who control the famous Khayber Pass from Pakistan to India, have been traced this way to the tribe of Gad. A local river, Gazni, resembles the name Gozan that the Bible cites as the exiled tribes' original destination.

(OPPOSITE, TOP)
JAPANESE ILLUSTRATION DEPICTING THE ALLEGED MARCH OF THE ISRAELITES TO JAPAN.
FROM "ILLUSTRATIONS TO THE EPITOME OF THE ANCIENT HISTORY OF JAPAN" BY N. MCKEOD, KYOTO, 1877.
Jews are not known to have arrived in Japan before the nineteenth century.

(OPPOSITE, BOTTOM)
THE JAPANESE CALLIGRAPHER MASTER KAMPO HARADA, IN FRONT OF THE HOLY ARK IN HIS HOME, KYOTO, JAPAN, 1987.
The Master believes himself to be of the Zebulon tribe.

(ABOVE)

MEMBERS OF THE DURANI TRIBE OF THE PATHAN TRIBAL GROUP IN AFGHANISTAN.
EIGHTEENTH-CENTURY DRAWING.

A Persian chronicle from 1612 traced their origins to the Ten Tribes.

According to local oral traditions that were put in writing already in the Persian chronicle of 1612, *Makhsan I-Afghani*, the Durani and Yosofzai tribes are descendants of the Ten Tribes. Members of a large tribe nearby, Afridi—whose name reminds some of Ephraim—light candles on Saturday and wear a garment decorated with black stripes that can remind one of a Jewish prayer shawl.

The largest Afghan tribe, Pashtun, has an ancient tradition tracing its origins to King Saul. According to local oral traditions the Afghans' forefathers were two of Saul's sons who after his death served King David. Local tales demonstrate an awareness of the existence of Solomon's Temple, as well as its destruction by the Babylonians and the exiling that followed it. The trek to Afghanistan, according to these traditions, followed a revolt against the Babylonians that compelled its perpetrators to seek hiding in a remote and difficult to access area, which the Afghan mountains clearly are.

In 1891 H. W. Bellew, a senior British colonial official in Afghanistan, presented a paper in London where he described the Pashtuns' belief that they descend from the Ten Tribes, though he stressed that as devout Muslims it is for them but an explanation of their pre-Muslim roots. This was possibly the first secular, public discussion of the Lost Tribes based on relatively impartial and firsthand observation. At the same time, Jewish scholar Adolf Neubauer argued that the Samaritans—of which a small community survives outside today's Nablus—descended from the Ten Tribes.

In the twentieth century this trend of secular curiosity expanded. Biblical scholar Allen Godbey's *The Lost Tribes: A Myth* argued that the more worldly northern tribes knowingly went with their faith to various parts of Africa and Asia, where some of them later joined the rising monotheistic religions that competed with Judaism.

Recent research, based among other things on Assyrian inscriptions, concludes that the Israelites' deportations were incomplete, and left behind at least some of them, in the northern parts of the Land of Israel. As for the expellees' destinations that the Bible mentions, which are generally between Iran's Zagros Mountains in the east and the sources of the Euphrates River in the west, archeology has indeed unearthed in these locations Assyrian-era documents containing Israelite names.

At any rate, the search for the Lost Tribes remained focused on central and southern Asia. Beyond Afghanistan, on the Indian-Burmese border, there are tribes that have been suggested to descend from the lost tribe of Manasseh. In recent years, some of their members have officially converted to Judaism and moved to Israel. Some Burmese tribes, who eventually became Christian, preserved ancient sacrificial rituals—which the surrounding Confucian and Buddhist faiths reject—as well as tales of the deliverance from slavery in ancient Egypt; some see these as proof of their Israelite ancestry. Though they eat pork and even use it in their rituals, they are said to do so in order to commemorate and atone for the original for which they were originally exiled.

LIAN TUAL, SECRETARY OF THE "BEITH SHALOM" COMMUNITY WITH HIS FAMILY. TIDDIM, BURMA, 1987.

Israeli author Hillel Halkin, generally a skeptic about the searches for the Ten Tribes, recently followed Israeli rabbi Eliahu Avichail, who has dedicated his career to tracking down the Ten Tribes, on a journey to alleged Lost Tribe communities in China, Thailand, and the Indian-Burmese border. In his book, *Across the Sabbath River*, Halkin tells of an ancient local song about the crossing of the Red Sea; a local tradition that says

(LEFT)
THE OHEL RACHEL SYNAGOGUE,
SHANGHAI.
*The local Jewish presence, begun by
merchants from Iraq, India, and Egypt,
followed Shanghai's opening for
international commerce in 1843.
A Sephardic synagogue, Ohel Rachel was
built by Jacob Sassoon in 1920.*

(OPPOSITE, TOP)
MEMBERS OF THE AI FAMILY IN
FRONT OF THEIR HOME, KAIFENG,
CHINA, APRIL 2002.
*The Jewish community of China was
started by merchants who arrived from
Persia by traveling the historic silk road.
The man in the picture is the grandfather,
the head of the small community who in
1952 went to Beijing to seek for the
community recognition as a Jewish
minority but was rejected.*

(OPPOSITE, BOTTOM)
CHINESE JEWISH CHILDREN OF
KAIFENG WITH MATZAH.

the local Mizos' ancestors worshiped a god named Yah; that centuries ago their ancestors
used to circumcise their boys; that old local texts mention the Israelite patriarchs; and
that during a local holiday celebrated in the spring, the locals eat unleavened bread,
much like the Jews do on Passover. Based on these and other findings, Halkin concluded
that in the provinces of Mizoram and Manipur there is a population whose claim to
have descended from the tribe of Manasseh is valid, despite its modern-era conversion to
Christianity by European missionaries.

CHINA: THE ODD STORY OF KAIFENG JEWRY

Though Judaism failed to last there, the easternmost extent of the medieval Diaspora
was China. Documents written in Hebrew characters and found in Sinkiang, on the
western fringes of the Takla Makan Desert, indicate that Persian-Jewish merchants
passed through China in the eighth century. Traveling merchants also passed through
the southern port of Canton, near today's Hong Kong, and some were apparently among
thousands of foreigners who were killed there in the wake of a local conflict in 878.

BEGINNING OF THE BOOK
OF GENESIS.
FIFTEENTH CENTURY. KAIFENG, CHINA. KLAU
LIBRARY, HEBREW UNION COLLEGE-JEWISH INSTITUTE
OF RELIGION, CINCINNATI, OHIO.

*The evaporation of Kaifeng's Jewish
community apparently stemmed from its
distance from the Diaspora's main
centers, and from the lack of antagonism
on the part of its Chinese neighbors.*

TORAH CASE.
EIGHTEENTH CENTURY. KAIFENG, CHINA.
HEBREW UNION COLLEGE SKIRBALL MUSEUM
COLLECTION, SKIRBALL CULTURAL CENTER, LOS
ANGELES.

*There is no indication that Kaifeng's
Jews had the Talmud.*

Half-a-millennium later, a sizable Jewish presence was also reported in Peking by
Marco Polo in his accounts from China, and Mongol legislation also mentioned
various prohibitions pertaining to Jews (and Muslims).

However, a substantive Jewish community appeared in pre-modern China only in
Kaifeng, toward the turn of the tenth century, when several hundred families settled in
the Sung dynasty's imperial capital. Apparently having originated in Persia, whose
access to China through the historic Silk Road had improved, these Jews were cotton
dyers. European travelers' reports clearly indicate that they observed Jewish law for
generations, while adapting to local norms and appearance, from the architecture of
their pagoda-shaped synagogue, to their confusion of R and L in pronouncing Hebrew
words while praying. Several steles from the fifteenth, sixteenth, and seventeenth
centuries suggest Jews arrived in China already during the Roman era, a claim
researchers dismiss as legend.

Otherwise, until the rise in the 1840s of a lively community in Hong Kong
following its conquest by Britain, no new Jewish communities emerged in China.
On the whole, Jewish existence east of Central Asia failed to last. The Jews of
Kaifeng soon began to intermarry and ultimately disappeared from the face of
Jewish history.

Why the Diaspora failed to sink roots in China remains an open question. Was it
the geographic barriers that made mass migration there too difficult? Or was it a local

景教流行中國碑頌并序

大秦寺僧景淨述

粵若常然真寂先先而無元窅然靈虛後後而妙有揔玄樞而造化妙衆聖以元尊者其唯我三一妙身無元真主阿羅訶歟判十字以定四方鼓元風而生二氣暗空易而天地開日月運而晝夜作匠成萬物然立初人別賜良和令鎮化海渾元之性虛而不盈素蕩之心本無希嗜洎乎娑殫施妄鈿飾純精閒平大於此是之中隟冥同於彼非之內是以三百六十五種肩隨結轍競織法羅或指物以託宗或空有以淪二或禱祀以邀福或伐善以驕人智慮營營恩情役役茫然無得煎迫轉燒積昧亡途久迷休復於是我三一分身景尊彌施訶戢隱真威同人出代神天宣慶室女誕聖於大秦景宿告祥波斯睹耀以來貢圓廿四聖有說之舊法理家國於大猷設三一淨風無言之新教陶良用於正信制八境之度鍊塵成真啟三常之門開生滅死懸景日以破暗府魔妄於是乎悉摧棹慈航以登明宮含靈於是乎既濟能事斯畢亭午昇真經留廿七部張元化以發靈關法浴水風滌浮華而潔虛白印持十字融四照以合無拘擊木震仁惠之音東禮趣生榮之路存鬚所以有外行削頂所以無內情不畜臧獲均貴賤於人不聚貨財示罄遺於我齋以伏識而成戒以靜慎為固七時禮讚大庇存亡七日一薦洗心反素真常之道妙而難名功用昭彰強稱景教惟道非聖不弘聖非道不大道聖符契天下文明

太宗文皇帝光華啟運明聖臨人大秦國有上德曰阿羅本占青雲而載真經望風律以馳艱險貞觀九祀至於長安帝使宰臣房公玄齡揔仗西郊賓迎入內翻經書殿問道禁闈深知正真特令傳授貞觀十有二年秋七月詔曰道無常名聖無常體隨方設教密濟群生大秦國大德阿羅本遠將經像來獻上京詳其教旨玄妙無為觀其元宗生成立要詞無繁說理有忘筌濟物利人宜行天下所司即於京義寧坊造大秦寺一所度僧廿一人宗周德喪青駕西昇巨唐道光景風東扇旋令有司將帝寫真轉摸寺壁天姿汎彩英朗景門聖迹騰祥永輝法界案西域圖記及漢魏史策大秦國南統珊瑚之海北極衆寶之山西望仙境花林東接長風弱水其土出火綄布返魂香明月珠夜光璧俗無寇盜人有樂康法非景不行主非德不立土宇廣闊文物昌明

高宗大帝克恭纘祖潤色真宗而於諸州各置景寺仍崇阿羅本為鎮國大法主法流十道國富元休寺滿百城家殷景福聖曆年釋子用壯騰口於東周先天末下士大笑訕謗於西鎬有若僧首羅含大德及烈並金方貴緒物外高僧共振玄網俱維絕紐玄宗至道皇帝令寧國等五王親臨福宇建立壇場法棟暫橈而更崇道石時傾而復正天寶初令大將軍高力士送五聖寫真寺內安置賜絹百疋奉慶睿圖龍髯雖遠弓劍可攀日角舒光天顏咫尺三載大秦國有僧佶和瞻星向化望日朝尊詔僧羅含僧普論等一七人與大德佶和於興慶宮修功德於是天題寺牓額戴龍書寶裝璀翠灼爍丹霞睿扎宏空騰凌激日寵賚比南山峻極沛澤與東海齊深道無不可所可可名聖無不作所作可述

肅宗文明皇帝於靈武等五郡重立景寺元善資而福祚開大慶臨而皇業建

代宗文武皇帝恢張聖運從事無為每於降誕之辰錫天香以告成功頒御饌以光景衆且乾以美利故能廣生聖以體元故能亭毒

我建中聖神文武皇帝披八政以黜陟幽明闡九疇以惟新景命化通玄理祝無愧心至於方大而虛專靜而恕廣慈救衆苦善貸被群生者我修行之大猷汲引之階漸也若使風雨時天下靜人能理物能清存能昌歿能樂念生響應情發目誠者我景力能事之功用也

大施主金紫光祿大夫同朔方節度副使試殿中監賜紫袈裟僧伊斯和而好惠聞道勤行遠自王舍之城聿來中夏術高三代藝博十全始效節於丹庭乃策名於王帳中書令汾陽郡王郭公子儀初揔戎於朔方也肅宗俾之從邁雖見親於臥內不自異於行間為公爪牙作軍耳目能散祿賜不積於家獻臨恩之頗黎布辭憩之金罽或仍其舊寺或重廣法堂崇飾廊宇如翬斯飛更效景門依仁施利每歲集四寺僧徒虔事精供備諸五旬餧者來而飯之寒者來而衣之病者療而起之死者葬而安之清節達娑未聞斯美白衣景士今見其人願刻洪碑以揚休烈詞曰

真主無元湛寂常然權輿匠化起地立天分身出代救度無邊日昇暗滅咸證真玄

赫赫文皇道冠前王乘時撥亂乾廓坤張明明景教言歸我唐翻經建寺存歿舟航百福偕作萬邦之康

高宗纂祖更築精宇和宮敞朗遍滿中土真道宣明式封法主人有樂康物無災苦

玄宗啟聖克修真正御牓揚輝天書蔚映皇圖璀璨率土高敬庶績咸熙人賴其慶

肅宗來復天威引駕聖日舒晶祥風掃夜祚歸皇室祅氛永謝止沸定塵造我區夏

代宗孝義德合天地開貸生成物資美利香以報功仁以作施暘谷來威月窟畢萃

建中統極聿修明德武肅四溟文清萬域燭臨人隱鏡觀物色六合昭蘇百蠻取則

道惟廣兮應惟密強名言兮演三一主能作兮臣能述建豐碑兮頌元吉

大唐建中二年歲在作噩太蔟月七日大耀森文日建立

時法主僧寧恕知東方之景衆也

朝議郎前行台州司士參軍呂秀巖書

助檢校試太常卿賜紫袈裟寺主僧業利

檢校建立碑僧行通

僧靈寶

בָּרֽוּךֽ שְׁמוֹ, כְּ-יֽוֹפֽֽי אֱלֹהֵנוּ אֲהֽי

צֽוּרוֹ, שֽׁ מֵ, מַ רֽ הֽוֹףֽ רֽֽעֽרֽם, וֽעֽד

*Juif de Caifum lisant la Bible à la
chaire de Moyse, avec deux souffleurs.*

(LEFT)

READING THE TORAH IN KAIFENG.

1722. DRAWING BY FATHER DOMENGE. CHANTILLY.
ARCHIVES DES JESUITES DE PARIS.

*The Jew on the left holds a printed
Pentateuch with vowels to help the
Torah reader.*

(OPPOSITE)

A RECORD OF THE REBUILDING OF THE SYNAGOGUE, KAIFENG.

1489. INK RUBBING ON PAPER OF AN INSCRIPTION
CARVED ON A STELE AND PLACED IN THE COURTYARD
OF THE SYNAGOGUE. COURTESY HEBREW UNION
COLLEGE SKIRBALL MUSEUM COLLECTION, SKIRBALL
CULTURAL CENTER, LOS ANGELES.

*This rubbing gives the ancestry of the
community, a description of their
religious practices, and the eight clan
names that were given to the community
by the Ming emperor of China.*

disparagement of the non-Chinese world that nipped Jewish immigration in the bud, the same way it curtailed Chinese travel overseas? Or perhaps there was a Jewish reluctance to venture out to the Far East, since the arduous journey it necessitated entailed excessive challenges to observance?

Curiously enough, the latest of the Jewish steles found in Kaifeng (etched in 1663) traces Chinese Jewry's origins to Pan Ku, the Chinese Adam. Indeed, historians concluded that the Jews of Kaifeng, detached from the big Jewish world that lay far beyond their western horizon and constantly exposed to a powerful Chinese civilization, gradually assimilated, as the stele's Confucian echoes attest.

India: In the Footsteps of Elijah

The other place beyond the monotheistic sphere where Jews sank roots, albeit in small numbers, was the Indian Subcontinent. For centuries, prior to the British era, there were two communities on the coastal plain south of Bombay: the Bene Israel, who lived in the Konkan Plain which is closer to Bombay, and the Cochins, who lived on the Malabar Plain, just south of Calcutta.

The Bene Israel, who were the larger group, believed their ancestors arrived in India as refugees fleeing the forced Helenizing of King Antiochus in the second century B.C.E. Historians have established that Jews lived here at least since 1000 C.E. Tradition claims the Jews of Cochin, who are dark skinned, followed the trade routes of King Solomon's sprawling empire of commercial interests.

Malabar was indeed well positioned on a major international trade route, and as such attracted Jewish merchants from Babylonia during the early Middle Ages, and refugees

(ABOVE)
THE PARDESI SYNAGOGUE.
COCHIN, INDIA.
Built in 1568 by descendants of European Jews, the synagogue is still in use today, the sole functioning synagogue in the area.

(OPPOSITE, ABOVE)
A SEPHARDIC COMMUNITY CELEBRATING THE FESTIVAL OF PURIM IN THE SUBURB OF THANE OUTSIDE BOMBAY, INDIA.

(OPPOSITE, BOTTOM)
BAKING MATZAH, 1992, BOMBAY, INDIA.
The local community of Bene Israel believe their ancestors arrived in India from Jerusalem in the second century B.C.E., after fleeing Antiochus's decrees against the practice of Judaism.

from Spain, Germany, Yemen, and the Land of Israel, about a millennium later. By then, the veteran Jews had become so identified with the region that they kept the newcomers at arms length, labeling them Paradesi, or "foreigners."

However, when the Portuguese conquered the region and sought to impose on it their anti-Jewish persecution by allowing the Inquisition to operate in Goa, Jews flocked to the town of Cochin where the local Rajah allowed complete freedom of worship. That freedom was further developed with the Dutch rule, and consolidated under the British.

Unlike the Jews of Cochin, who encountered Jews from the large communities of the Middle East and Europe, the Bene Israel were more secluded and their origins were shrouded in greater mystery. Discovered by missionaries only in 1750, these Jews had a special cult of Elijah the Prophet, himself a member of the Ten Tribes, who hailed from Transjordan and was active mainly in the regions of Samaria, Carmel, and Jezreel, where the tribes of Ephraim, Manasseh, and Zebulun resided.

During the British era the Bene Israel migrated to Bombay, where many of them climbed to the middle and upper-middle classes. When the State of Israel was established most of them—more than 20,000—immigrated to the Jewish state, as did most of the Cochin Jews.

KHAZARIA: THE CONVERSION VOID

Few tales in Jewish history have been as enigmatic, bewildering, and intriguing as the rise and fall of Khazaria, the medieval Eurasian kingdom whose elite adopted the Jewish faith in 740 C.E.

A Turkic nation of nomads that made its way westward from deeper Asia, the Khazars left no original historical sources to testify about their origins, travails, and aftermath. However, varied Byzantine, Arabic, Armenian, Persian, Jewish, and other sources attest that Khazaria lasted for centuries, during which it dominated much of the planes between the Don and Dnieper rivers. Among medieval Jews the stories about this Jewish kingdom's presence on the Europe's doorstep was sometimes confused with the legends about the Ten Tribes.

Located at different times in varying sizes between the Aral Sea in the east and the Crimean Peninsula in the west, Khazaria's efficient cavalry loomed ominously as the impregnable barrier that in a sequence of seventh- and eighth-century battles blocked the Arab armies' advance into Europe from its eastern flank, much the way the Franks did in the continent's western end. However, the Khazars' most formidable enemy proved to be the Russians, whose southward approach, down the Volga basin, culminated in the destruction in 965 of Atil, the Khazar capital that was situated at the mouth of the Volga. Having depended for its existence on the peaceful commercial traffic from Eastern Europe into Byzantium, Khazaria never recovered from that blow, although Atil itself was initially rebuilt. By the Mongol invasions of the thirteenth century, the area known as Khazaria was no longer ruled by the Khazars.

(ABOVE)

TORAH CROWN.

PARDESI SYNAGOGUE, COCHIN, INDIA.

The elaborate crown was presented to the Jewish community in 1808 by the Maharajah of Tirvajer in honor of the festival of Hanukkah. Unlike Bene Israel, the Jews of Cochin were exposed throughout the centuries to Jews from other countries.

While all these facts emerge rather clearly from the disjointed historical evidence left by Khazaria's neighbors, its embrace of Judaism remains enigmatic, though it is generally agreed that it actually happened, some time in the middle of the eighth century. One tradition, later monumentalized in Judah Halevi's *The Kuzari* (a philosophical defense of Judaism written in twelfth-century Spain), contends that the conversion followed a debate among three scholars, a Christian, a Moslem, and a Jew, organized by, and held in the presence of, an unnamed Khazar king. Halevi's book is an imaginary reconstruction of the debate in which the Khazar king presents theological questions to the three scholars, until he decides to adopt the Jew's faith.

Medieval Muslim historians attribute the conversion to the influence of Jewish immigrants from Byzantium into Khazaraia. A letter ostensibly written to tenth-century Spanish-Jewish notable Hisdai ibn Shaprut by Khazaria's King Joseph, who had inquired about the kingdom's origins, physique, and faith, indicates the conversion took place in the middle of the eighth century, under King Bulan, and was later perfected by the Khazars' great religious reformer King Obadiah.

According to the letter, that king introduced rabbinical Judaism, including the Talmud, to the Khazars. However, the lack of contacts between the Khazars and the great communities and rabbinical authorities of Mesopotamia, who were geographically accessible to them, raises doubts concerning the quality of their Jewish observance. The authenticity of the letter by King Bullan, whose oldest extant copy dates from six centuries after the event, has also been challenged, though the existence of a correspondence has been mentioned by other sources in the eleventh and twelfth centuries.

The mysteriousness of the Khazars stems not only from the peculiarity of their adoption of a persecuted faith, but also from their total disappearance from the stage of history, much like the Ten Tribes. Their reported custom of burying their kings under water, their largely nomadic way of life, and the inaccessibility of their main city's ruins (apparently drowned in the shifting waters of the Volga delta) have all made it difficult for archaeologists to discover anything substantive about the Khazar kingdom.

Digs in the Khazar town of Sarkil, in today's southern Russia on the lower Don, have generated no hints of Jewish religious practice. However, the Khazars are often mentioned in passing by medieval sources, like Benjamin of Tudela, who tells of Khazars in Constantinople and Alexandria in the twelfth century, and a Hungarian assembly of bishops that issued in 1309 a prohibition on marrying Khazars. Generally, Khazar footprints are hinted throughout the Middle Ages between the Caucasus Mountains in the east and the Black Sea basin in the west. The frequent presence of Karaite communities in these areas, as well as evidence of some ties between them and the Khazars, support assumptions that the Khazars' observance was less of the oral and more of the written Jewish law.

One largely dismissed theory, presented in Arthur Koestler's *The Thirteenth Tribe* (1976), argued that after the fall of their kingdom the Khazar Jews migrated westward, eventually forming the seed of European Jewry.

(ABOVE)

THE FIRST EPISTLE BY HISDAI IBN-SHAPRUT TO JOSEPH, KING OF THE KHAZARS.
TENTH CENTURY. OXFORD.
CHRIST CHURCH COLLEGE LIBRARY.

In this letter, the Spanish Jewish leader ostensibly inquires about the kingdom's Israelite roots. The Khazars, whose elite is believed to have converted to Judaism in the eighth century C.E., welcomed Jews who fled the Caucasus after its conquest by the Arabs.

What can be said with fair certainty concerning the Khazars is that they and their kingdom existed, that there was some kind of relationship between them and Judaism, and that whatever that commitment may have constituted, it was chosen by the Khazars themselves. If anything, this episode merely highlights the most fundamental political difference between Judaism and the other two monotheistic faiths, namely that Judaism did not encourage proselytizing. One wonders what course Jewish history would have taken if it had.

AFRICA: WHO IS A LOST TRIBE?

Two-and-a-half millennia after their disappearance, the Ten Tribes' myth and reality reached a dramatic turning point, as the State of Israel faced practical dilemmas that stemmed from the ideological demand and logistical opportunity to import en-masse questionably Jewish communities. Since the early 1950s Israeli decision makers, scholars, and advisers secretly debated what to do about "exotic" Jewish communities from numerous regions worldwide, from South America to the Far East.

The Law of Return, which upholds the right of born-Jews to be automatically eligible for Israeli citizenship, made it imperative to establish the Jewishness of newly arrived immigrants. In some cases, such as that of the Bene Israel, there were doubts concerning the communities' actual Jewish roots. In other cases, such as the Karaites, the community's Jewish origins were clear, but doubts arose concerning its ability to marry "mainstream" Jews, after centuries of conducting marriage and divorce in a way that did not conform with Jewish law. "Doubtful" Jews, those from Burma and Peru, for instance, simply underwent Orthodox conversion soon after their immigration to Israel, so as to remove any doubt concerning their Jewishness.

Clearly, the one community whose story best encapsulated the mystery, dilemmas, and drama of the Lost Tribes was Ethiopia's. The Beta Israel (House of Israel) communities, who lived in various locations across this East African country for centuries, were pejoratively called by their neighbors *Falashas*, or foreigners, and were indeed discriminated against accordingly. According to some traditions, the Beta Israel, whose complexion resembles their black neighbors', originated with King Solomon's entourage to the Queen of Sheba. Others attributed their roots to the Lost Israelites. Scholars tend to dismiss that possibility, however, since the Assyrian exiles are believed to have led the Israelites north rather than south. The more accepted theory locates the Beta Israel's ancestry in Yemen, which is relatively close and whose Jews are also dark skinned.

Yet unlike the Jews of Yemen, who maintained throughout the generations close ties to the established communities of Egypt and Babylonia, and thus observed the teachings of the Mishna, the Talmud, and medieval sages like Maimonides, the Ethiopian community remained on the whole unexposed to, and apparently unaware of, Judaism's oral law. Still, as Ethiopia's Christian regimes isolated them (particularly following the

(ABOVE)
YEMENITE CHILDREN.

(OPPOSITE)
YEMENITE BOYS DANCING.
The Jews of Yemen refrained from playing musical instruments other than drums, as an expression of mourning for the Temple's destruction.

A JEWISH FAMILY IN SAN'A YEMEN, 1930S.
Unlike the Yemenites, who kept close contact with the community of Egypt and were familiar with the major rabbincal texts, the Jews of Ethiopia remained secluded until 1790, when the world learned of them through Scottish traveler James Bruce's Travels to Discover the Sources of the Nile.

early fifteenth-century prohibition on land ownership by non-Christians) the Beta Israel's Jewish distinctiveness intensified, as they lived a life of seclusion and destitution, usually in the northern region of Gondar.

In 1790, Scottish traveler James Bruce's *Travels to Discover the Sources of the Nile* brought the Beta Israel's existence to Western attention, thus paving the way for their steadily growing exposure to mainstream Judaism. In the 1860s thousands of Beta Israel embarked on an ill-fated trek to the Promised Land, in the course of which thousands of them died. Not one made it to the Land of Israel. By the turn of the twentieth century, representatives of the Alliance Israelite Universelle first visited the Beta Israel, and within several years a Jewish school was opened for the first time in Ethiopia.

(ABOVE)

IN THE BETA ISRAEL COMPOUND IN
ADDIS ABABA.
*The decision to bring Ethiopian Jewry to
Israel followed decades of indecision.*

(LEFT)

AVEVA BARON, 1984, WALAKA,
ETHIOPIA.
*The origins of Ethiopia's Jews remain a
subject of debate and legend.*

ETHIOPIANS CARRYING A TORAH.
In Israel, the Ethiopian community is gradually splitting between Orthodoxy and secularism.

After the establishment of the State of Israel, officials debated for years, though never publicly, what to do about the estimated 30,000 Beta Israel. Some doubted their Jewishness, others feared they would suffer a traumatic encounter with modernity. Others yet, led by Israel's second president, Yitzhak Ben-Zvi (1884–1963)—who was a consummate student of Jewish ethnography in his own right—contended that the Beta Israel belonged in the Jewish state along with the rest of the Jewish nation.

Initially, only a select few of the Beta Israel diaspora, all young and educated, were brought to Israel where they were trained as teachers, so as to return to Ethiopia and help further nurture their community's Jewishness. Eventually, a ruling by Chief Rabbis Ovadya Yosef and Shlomo Goren in 1973, that the Beta Israel were descendants of the Tribe of Dan and as such were Israelites, paved the way to their official embrace by the State of Israel. Then, in two dramatic military operations in 1985 and 1991, 30,000 Beta Israel were airlifted to Israel.

(ABOVE)

ABAYUDAYA JEWS IN FRONT OF A
HADASSAH SCHOOL IN UGANDA.
*The local community of converts survived
the Idi Amin years of persecution.*

IN THE GENES

In southern Africa, the Lemba tribe of Zimbabwe has been for centuries circumcising
newborn baby boys and observing a set of dietary laws that largely resemble Judaism's
slaughter restrictions. While scholars dismiss as anecdotal and unscientific most
"evidence" of Israelite origins elsewhere, research has indeed found genetic evidence to
the Lemba's oral tradition that traces their origins to the First Temple's Levite priests.

In eastern Africa, on the foothills of Mt. Elgon some 150 miles outside the
Ugandan capital, Kampala, a community of several hundred Africans known as the
Abayudaya have been observing Judaism for nearly a century. Founded by a warrior
named Semei Kakungulu, who converted to Judaism in the aftermath of a troubled
history with British colonialists and missionaries, the Abayudaya survived the Idi
Amin years, when they were forbidden to practice their faith and their synagogues
were destroyed. Today the community maintains warm ties with American Jewry

(ABOVE)

A SYNAGOGUE IN WINDHOEK, NAMIBIA.
This synagogue serves the country's roughly 100 Jews.

(ABOVE, RIGHT)

LEMBA TRIBESMAN BLOWING A HORN, REMINISCENT OF THE SHOFAR, 1980S.
The Zimbabwean tribe observes rituals of circumcision and animal slaughter similar to Judaism's.

and has become famous for its unique blending of Jewish liturgy with African melodies.

DJERBA: A KINGDOM OF PRIESTS

One of the rare tangible locations possibly connected with the Ten Lost Tribes is Djerba, a 510-square-kilometer island off the Tunisian mainland. Blessed with fishing fields, rich with date and olive orchards, and located between European and African markets, the island was a trading center for the Phoenicians, and has been home to a solid Jewish community at least since the tenth century C.E.

A local legend contends that the Jews in the Hara al-Kabira neighborhood, near the island's southern seaport, descended from the seafaring tribe of Zebulun, who laid anchor at

Djerba already in the times of King Solomon. More peculiarly, the Hara al-Saghira quarter's Jews are all *kohanim*, or priests. However, these people do not trace their ancestors' odyssey to the First Temple's destruction, but to the second's. According to their tradition, one of the Herodian Temple's doors is built into their opulent al-Ghariba synagogue, which over the centuries has been a pilgrimage target for Jews from across the Maghreb. According to local legend, the Levites who once lived on the island all died after they refused to heed Ezra the Scribe's request that they return to help rebuild Judah, following the Cyrus Declaration. There is no clear explanation, however, as to why the community remained exclusive to *kohanim*.

(ABOVE)
AL-GHIRBA SYNAGOGUE, DJERBA.
The Tunisian island community is the only one in the entire Diaspora's history to consist exclusively of priests ("kohanim").

Europe

GALUT: THE PRICE OF DISPERSAL

B
ut it shall come to pass, if thou wilt not harken unto the voice of the Lord
thy God, to observe to do all His commandments and His statutes which I
command thee this day. . . . And the Lord shall scatter thee among all
peoples, from the one end of the earth even unto the other end of the earth;
and there thou shalt serve other gods, which thou hast not known, thou nor
thy fathers, even wood and stone. And among these nations shalt thou have no repose, and
there shall be no rest for the sole of thy foot; but the Lord shall give thee there a trembling
heart, and failing of eyes, and languishing of soul. And thy life shall hang in doubt
before thee; and thou shalt fear night and day, and shalt have no assurance of thy life.
(Deuteronomy 28:15, 64–66)

For nearly two millennia the Diaspora experience was an ongoing trauma,
astonishingly close to the prophetic "will" Moses bequeathed to the Israelites shortly
before his death. Indeed, the great legislator's inability to enter the Holy Land was
symbolic of his people's subsequent fate: For centuries upon centuries and throughout
dozens upon dozens of lands, the reality of landlessness and its interpretation as a divine
punishment were the hallmark of Diaspora life. In the Jewish psyche and lexicon, this
combination became known as *galut*, which literally means "exile," and figuratively
became synonymous with all the legal discrimination, social humiliation, material
hardship, and mental near-despair that characterized Diaspora life throughout
most of its history.

Despite its remarkable continuity, the persecution of the Jews by a succession of
states, regimes, and religions, from the Byzantines to the Communists, was seen by
many—both Jews and Gentiles—as a historical anomaly. Yes, Jewish existence after
the loss of sovereignty was not an uninterrupted continuum of persecution, exclusion,
disharmony, and hopelessness. Both in Muslim and Christian lands there were
protracted periods of stability, tolerance, prosperity, and engagement. Yet even those
who idealized the Diaspora experience, from Simon Dubnow to Salo Baron, conceded

(OPPOSITE)
EUROPE I (DETAIL).
LARRY RIVERS. OIL ON CANVAS. THE MINNEAPOLIS
INSTITUTE OF ARTS. ANONYMOUS GIFT. © ESTATE OF
LARRY RIVERS/LICENSED BY VAGA, NEW YORK, NY.
*This powerful painting records a painful
history of rejection and attraction, love
and hate, creation and destruction.*

(ABOVE)

EMPEROR CONSTANTINE THE GREAT
(306–337 C.E.).
MARBLE HEAD, FRAGMENT OF A COLOSSAL STATUE
FROM THE BASILICA OF CONSTANTINE IN ROME.
PALAZZO DEI CONSERVATORI, ROME.

Constantine's baptizing signaled a
fateful turning point in the history
of the Diaspora.

(ABOVE, RIGHT)

MOSES PROVIDING WATER FOR THE
TRIBES OF ISRAEL IN THE DESERT.
WALL PAINTING FROM THE DURA EUROPOS
SYNAGOGUE. THIRD CENTURY.

Roman Christianity sought not merely to
compete with, but to succeed, Judaism.

that until the dawn of modernity the Jews were, on the ideological level, tolerated at best, while on the political plain they were subject to the whims of unpredictable rulers and clerics.

THE LAW: SETTING THE JEWS APART

Special legislation—whether in the form of privilege or discrimination—was a fixture of medieval life across the monotheistic world, regardless of the Jews' particular case. In fact, it was the eradication of this kind of anti-Jewish enactments in the aftermath of the French Revolution that largely made the difference between the modern and medieval ages.

For the Jews, the loss of equality before the law dramatically aggravated the already harsh challenges created by the destruction of the Temple. What began in the first century C.E. as the mere passing away of a physical religious center turned gradually after the fourth century into a demise of status, security, and legitimacy. This dramatic transformation of the Jewish fate came in three phases: first, when Christianity sought not merely to compete with Judaism, but to succeed it; then, when the new monotheistic faith set out not only to market its own convictions but also to de-legitimize Judaism's; and finally, when Christianity set out to deprive the Jews of rights enjoyed by non-Jews.

(ABOVE)

JEWISH OCCUPATIONS IN
HELLENISTIC ALEXANDRIA, EGYPT.
FRAGMENT OF WALL PAINTING. SECOND– THIRD
CENTURY. BETH HATEFUTSOTH, TEL AVIV.

*Most Jews were engaged as manual
workers such as farmers, shepherds,
craftsmen, or weavers.*

This combined theological, political, and legal assault ultimately became a permanent condition of social confinement, economic discrimination, cultural siege, and physical vulnerability.

The crux of the tragedy of galut, therefore, lay less in the original loss of the Temple, Jerusalem, and Judea, and more in Christianity's conquest of the Roman Empire, just when the rapidly expanding faith's targeting of Judaism grew ever more sharp, bold, and immoral. The turning point was Constantine the Great's personal baptism as a Christian, and his recognition in 313 C.E. of Christianity as a legitimate religion. This event, along with the massive proselytizing effort that was afoot across

scripta quaxdi litteai que in thesaunia nia

the empire during his reign, ultimately resulted in Christianity becoming Rome's official
faith, the brief exception of the pro-Jewish Julian the Hellene notwithstanding.

Though increasingly hostile toward Jews, early medieval Christian theologians did not
seek the disappearance of the Jews or Judaism. Rather, they wanted the Jews visibly
humiliated as proof of Christianity's theological truth, political prowess, and historic victory.
By 438, when Emperor Theodosius II completed the imperial codex, the Jews had been
formally forbidden to celebrate the holiday of Purim or own slaves. Jews had also ceased to
be hired by the government and military, and were prohibited from marrying Christians,
treating them as doctors, or being their superiors in practically any context or circumstance.

Thus began an elaborate history of discrimination and dislocation that lasted for
centuries, traveled across continents, crossed the gap between medieval religiosity and
modern secularism, and ultimately culminated in the Holocaust. The inclusion of anti-
Jewish laws in Rome's imperial legal codex etched in stone the fingering of the Jews as
Christ's killers and consolidated the Church's determination to punish any Jew in any
place at any time for a crime attributed to other Jews in another place at a distant time.
From here on the Jews were vilified in a way that no other nation or religion were in
mankind's history, before or since the rise of Christianity, until the rise of Nazism (when
such attitudes were also aimed at Slavs, Gypsies, and others).

(ABOVE)

PERSECUTION OF THE JEWS.
C. FOURTEENTH CENTURY. ILLUSTRATION FROM A
PAGE OF TEXT. COTT. NERO. D. II. FOLIO No. 181v
THE BRITISH LIBRARY, LONDON.

*The man on the right is beating the other
three, who are Jews, made identifiable by
the white patches on their clothes.*

(OPPOSITE)

ST. PAUL PREACHING TO THE JEWS IN
THE SYNAGOGUE AT DAMASCUS.
BYZANTINE MOSAIC. LATE TWELFTH CENTURY.
DUOMO, MONREALE, ITALY.

*In the first centuries of the Diaspora's
existence there was no sign that Judaism
would become another faith's obsession.*

By the fifth century, what began with legal discrimination evolved into forced conversions and the burning of synagogues. By the seventh century Jews were already being expelled from towns across Europe. Still, during its first millennium the Diaspora had yet to become the target of wholesale violence. That first happened only in the wake of the Crusades, when Christian clerics had the upper hand over secular rulers who had a vested economic interest in retaining "their" Jews and sought to protect them. A particularly symbolic anti-Jewish twist came with the Crusader conquest of the Holy Land, as the Christian conquerors restored the Byzantine prohibition on Jewish residence in Jerusalem.

Back in Europe, another deeply symbolic turn for the worse accompanied the 1215 Lateran Council, when some four hundred bishops and eight hundred envoys of European kings decided to force the Jews to wear distinctive dress. The Dominican order, which sought at the time to protect the Church from heresy, began to censor Jewish religious books and to summon Jews to public disputations.

By then, Jews were being routinely accused of killing Christian children and desecrating the Host (the wafer used in the Mass to represent the body and blood of Christ). The first such incident was recorded in Norwich, England, in 1144, where the local Jewish community was accused of murdering an apparently epileptic child named William as part of a religious ritual. The accusations impressed the ignorant mob, which consequently assaulted the Jews and their property. From England, the blood libel phenomenon spread into the continent.

Several popes throughout the centuries, beginning with Innocentius IV in 1247, openly conceded that the Jews did not use blood in their rituals. In 1343 an illegitimate child was offered to the Jews of Brunn, who in turn brought the case to a local court, which ordered the woman who made the offer buried alive. However, blood libels became a vehicle for releasing local pressures and for gathering a popular following as part of local power struggles. They persisted for centuries and in fact crossed the border into Muslim lands, thus reflecting the extent to which the Jews had become vulnerable after centuries of stereotyping and demonization.

VIOLENCE: THE INEVITABLE RESULT OF DEMONIZATION

The combination of triumphalist theology, legal discrimination, and populist incitement ultimately created, in the course of half a millennium, a triangle of Jewish tragedy that was also the essence of medieval galut. In Germany, the Crusades washed in blood a previously flourishing Diaspora of exceptional scholars and prosperous businessmen; in Spain, the 1492 Expulsion shook to the foundation a community famous for its longevity, confidence, and acculturation; and in mid-seventeenth-century Ukraine, the mass murders of entire Jewish communities by Cossack troops exposed the vulnerability

BURNING OF A JEW AND HIS FAMILY
AT THE STAKE FOR ALLEGEDLY
DESECRATING THE HOST.

PAOLO UCCELLO. FROM A SERIES OF SIX PAINTINGS FOR
A PREDELLA, 1465–1469. GALLERIA NAZIONALE DELLA
MARCHE, URBINO.

*Blood libels against Jews became common
following the one in Norwich, England,
in 1144.*

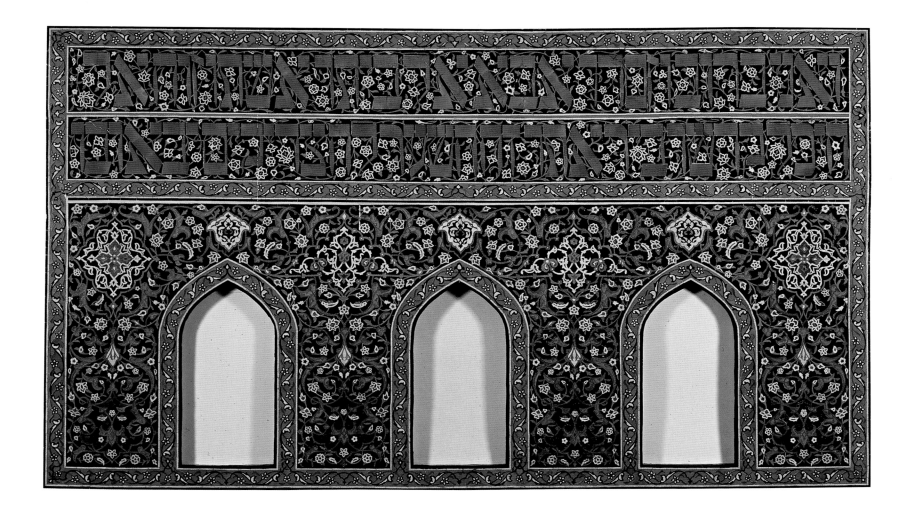

(LEFT)

ANTI-SEMITIC CARTOON
ON A RECEIPT ROLL.
THIRTEENTH CENTURY. PUBLIC RECORD
OFFICE, LONDON.

The only significant religious and racial minority in England, Jews were protected by King John and his successors, who saw them as a source of wealth and taxed them heavily. However, in 1290 Edward I withdrew that protection and expelled the Jews from England.

(OPPOSITE, TOP)

MAP OF THE CRUSADES
IN THE HOLY LAND.
1096–1270. MUSÉE DES ARTS D'AFRIQUE ET
D'OCEANIE, PARIS.

The religiously inspired transcontinental campaigns produced the first massive physical assault of entire Jewish communities in the Diaspora's history.

(OPPOSITE, BOTTOM)

PORTION OF A SYNAGOGUE WALL.
SIXTEENTH CENTURY. ISFAHAN (?) PERSIA. FAIENCE
TILE MOSAIC. GIFT OF ADELE AND HARRY G. FRIEDMAN,
LUCY AND HENRY MOSES, MIRIAM SCHAAR
SCHLOESSINGER, FLORENCE SUTRO ANSPACHER, LUCILLE
AND SAMUEL LEMBERG, JOHN S. LAWRENCE AND
FLORENCE LAWRENCE, LOUIS A. ORESMAN, AND KHALILI
RABENOUS. THE JEWISH MUSEUM, NEW YORK.

The rich arabesque of the synagogue wall reflects the influence of Islamic design, as does the inclusion of a biblical verse modeled on the use of quotes from the Koran in Arabic integrated into mosque decoration. The two quotes in Hebrew here are from the Psalms: "But I through your abundant love, enter your house; I bow down in awe at your holy temple" (Psalm 5:8) and "This is the gateway to the Lord, the righteous shall enter through it." (Psalm 118:20)

of Jewish existence even when it was founded on a solid dependence between Jewish entrepreneurs and landed nobles.

These calamities, which took place in three very different times and places, also mobilized different sources of anti-Jewish energy: mobs, clerics, and chauvinists. The Crusades deployed thousands of ignorant peasants who burned synagogues and slaughtered Jews on an unprecedented scale. The Spanish Inquisition was a state-sanctioned bureaucracy inspired, masterminded, and micromanaged by a fanatic clergy that no longer made do with the Church's traditional stance that the Jews should be humiliated rather than eradicated; and the Cossacks' assault on Ukrainian Jewry targeted the Jews as allies of a foreign nation and an upper class.

However, attacks on Jews were far from limited to such collective dramas. Most frequently they were localized, but continual and often devastating. In southern Italy, for instance, prominent rabbis were faced with an ultimatum to convert in 930 (and committed suicide instead), and the Jews of Mainz, Germany, were expelled as early as 1012. In the fifteenth century, beginning in 1417, the Franciscan priest John of Capistrano traveled across Italy, inciting mobs and lobbying with rulers in order to libel and displace Jewish communities. His subsequent anti-Jewish journeys to Germany and Poland resulted in a blood libel against the community of Breslau. In the aftermath, those Jews who were not burned at the stake were expelled (in 1453). Capistrano's disciple, Bernardino de Feltre, blamed the Jews of Trent in northern Italy for the

(ABOVE)

ON THE TRAIN TRACKS
BEFORE AUSCHWITZ.
C. 1945.

*Snow-covered personal effects of those
deported to the Auschwitz concentration
camp in Poland litter the train tracks
leading to the camp's entrance.*

disappearance of a child named Simon. Consequently, the entire community were arrested and tortured. Ultimately some were executed and the rest were expelled.

In 1614 a mob stormed the Frankfurt ghetto, pillaging, killing passersby, and ultimately chasing the entire Jewish community from the town. Responding to the riot, Emperor Matthias tried and hanged some of the attackers. Nevertheless, the persistent possibility of such disasters made a Jew's life in medieval Europe fragile, uncertain, and vulnerable.

In the Muslim sphere the Jews were far more secure. Religiously, Islam lacked Christianity's theological obsession and Oedipal complex with its parent faith, Judaism. Politically, major Muslim powers like the Ummayid dynasty or the Ottoman Empire were relatively tolerant, and had no qualms about allowing Jews to amass

The Black Death: A Jubilee of Horror

Most of the persecution, discrimination, and hardship that characterized galut were products of local circumstances. In line with the generally narrow horizons of medieval life, hostile acts against Jews were ordinarily also limited in their geographic scope. Yet there were exceptions, when calamity swept entire regions, crossing successive rivers and leaping above mountains as immense as the Alps and the Pyrenees. The first such crisis came in the eleventh century, when Franco-German Jewry was decimated as the Crusaders marched from Europe to the Holy Land. Yet even that devastation paled in comparison with what the Jews suffered during the fourteenth-century outbreak of the of the Black Death.

The bubonic plague that was carried by rats from Asia and spread north and west from the Black Sea through Italy ultimately killed at least one in four Europeans between 1347 and 1350. At a loss to explain the disaster that had befallen them, the ignorant masses were set to finger the Jews. Initially, others besides the Jews—from invalids to clergymen—were also blamed for the plague, but ultimately the belief that the Jews had conspired to kill all non-Jews captured the masses. Both Church and state dismissed this accusation. Pope Clement IV officially wrote in 1348 that the plague was the devil's doing, that the Jews were suffering from it just like everyone else, and that the plague had struck even in places where there were no Jews at all. Holy Roman Emperor Charles the IV concurred with a statement in a similar spirit. The mob, however, wanted a scapegoat. In the castle of Chillon on Lake Geneva, for instance, the Jews were forced to "confess" in 1348 to having fulfilled the orders of a certain John of Savoy to poison the wells of Venice. The rumor quickly spread and led to more such forced confessions, from Spain to Austria, and a consequent wave of severe terror against Jews across Europe. In Strasbourg, two thousand Jewish men and women were burned in one big fire at the local

(ABOVE)

THE TRIUMPH OF DEATH.
PIETER BRUEGHEL THE ELDER. 1562–1563. OIL ON
WOOD. MUSEO DEL PRADO, MADRID.

Jewish cemetery. In Frankfurt some six thousand Jews died in the flames that they had themselves kindled in their own neighborhood, after having concluded they could not defend themselves.

In all, some three hundred Jewish communities were destroyed in the wake of the plague. In Germany, the Black Death massacres followed half a century of incessant anti-Jewish violence, the result of successive blood libels. Combined, the years 1298–1348 are remembered by Jews as the Jubilee of Horror.

The Black Death's anti-Jewish sentiment was so fierce that many German towns vowed to never again allow Jews to reside in their midst. Although the oath was quickly violated, many of the restored communities initially consisted mainly of orphans and widows. More lastingly, the Black Death set the precedent for blaming major calamities on the Jews, a reflex that would repeatedly play a role in European history, most memorably in the Nazi claim that the Jews caused Germany's defeat in World War I and its punishment in the war's aftermath.

(ABOVE)
VISITORS PAYING TRIBUTE AT
THERESIENSTADT, 1989.
*The anti-religious Nazis borrowed from
medieval Christianity a wealth of anti-
Jewish weapons, from book burnings
and yellow badges to the ghetto and the
blood libel.*

wealth as merchants and hold high public office as bureaucrats. Still, anti-Jewish violence was not limited to Christendom.

In 1066 in Grenada, Spain, a Muslim mob killed Jewish leader Joseph ha-Nagid and chased the entire Jewish community from town. During the messianic fervor of the mid-1660s, which made thousands of Jews prepare for immigration to the Land of Israel, Yemeni Jews were attacked in the streets and Egyptian Jewish leaders were lynched.

Muslim regimes could also be occasionally extremely hostile to the Jews on a grander scale. Egypt's eleventh-century Fatimid caliph al-Hakim, for instance, ordered the Jews to wear calves' images as necklaces, "as they did in the desert," and banned them from riding horses. However, al-Hakim's was a generally capricious regime that targeted Jews and Christians alike, and particularly singled out women (who were forbidden to enter public baths, and if found there were locked within brick walls until they died). When al-Hakim died in 1021, so did his decrees.

(ABOVE)

MARCH OF THE LIVING AT
AUSCHWITZ, POLAND, JULY 1994.
*Although the March of the Living
experience is greatly touted in the
United States, some Israeli educators
question the value of the pilgrimages
to the death camps.*

Still, overall, there can be no comparison between the galut experience under Christianity and Islam. The Muslim world discriminated against the Jews, but it usually did so mildly and in measures no different from those reserved for other minorities. Theologically, while Islam also believed that it succeeded Judaism, it never developed Christianity's kinds of anti-Jewish obsessions, dogmas, and bloodletting. Indeed, throughout the Middle Ages most of the Diaspora did not live under Christian rule.

Can it be, then, that modern Jewish historiography, which was pioneered by Europeans, over-emphasized medieval European events which, while admittedly more dramatic, ultimately affected only a fraction of the Diaspora? The answer is negative. Geographically, as the modern era approached, Europe's share of world Jewry rose steadily. Culturally, as the tragedies of modern anti-Semitism proved, medieval Christianity's anti-Jewish indoctrination not only survived the dawn of secularism, enlightenment, and emancipation, but in fact generated the greatest crime in human history.

That crime, the Holocaust, which was accompanied by centuries-old European-bred anti-Jewish weapons like the yellow badge, the ghetto, the canard, the burning of books, the torching of synagogues, and of course the murder of innocent men, women, and children—resulted from, epitomized, and monumentalized what galut was all about.

FAITH: IN GOD'S HAND

Throughout their unending hardship, persecution, and despair, medieval Jews accepted their lot almost fatalistically. Surely there were thousands who could not resist the pressure, converted to Christianity—or, in fewer cases, to Islam—and fell by Jewish history's wayside. The most notable and largest group among these were the New Christians of Iberian Jewry. In inner Europe, however, conversion was much less widespread and martyrdom more common during the Middle Ages.

Neither martyrdom nor conversion was a matter of fate: Both were choices, and the frequent demand to choose between the two—perhaps the harshest epitome of the galut experience—was imposed on numerous Jews regardless of their class, profession, or location. The martyrs included simple and learned people alike, while some of the converts were actually pillars of the community.

During the 1096 riots in Germany, some Jews killed with their own hands their entire families before committing suicide, rather than allow, let alone see, any of their relations baptized. By contrast, four centuries later, Abraham Seneor, one of Spanish Jewry's most prominent leaders at the time of the Expulsion, became a Christian along with his son-in-law, Meir Melamed, in a public ceremony in which the two were baptized by King Ferdinand personally. At eighty, after having been a royal tax farmer and the president of a Jewish court, Seneor abandoned his heritage and threw his lot with his homeland, rather than be expelled from it.

To be sure, galut also offered choices other than these two, and dramatic moments such as those of 1096 in Germany, 1492 in Spain, or 1648 in the Ukraine, while deeply traumatic and exceptionally lasting in their impact, were brief and rare. Even in those moments of trial there were compromise options. Seneor's peer Don Isaac Abravanel, for instance, chose emigration. Many Jews in fifteenth-century Spain, sixteenth-century Portugal, and nineteenth-century Meshed, Iran, opted for secret observance.

Yet galut weighed on Jews even during uneventful times. In the day-to-day routines of most communities, legal discrimination, social humiliation, and economic strangulation served as frequent reminders that the Jews were merely guests in someone else's land, and negative heroes in another religion's spectacle.

At the same time, the same religious observance that antagonized their neighbors also unified the Jews, even while they lacked a mutual land and even a common tongue. Throughout the Middle Ages, Jews anywhere and everywhere from Spain to Afghanistan

(ABOVE)

SHECHITA LICENSE.
1774. VENICE MANUSCRIPT (NS) E96, LIBRARY OF THE JEWISH THEOLOGICAL SEMINARY OF AMERICA, NEW YORK.
The Jews' observance of the dietary laws meant Jews and Christians seldom shared a meal.

(OPPOSITE)

A JEWISH WEDDING.
J. ISRAELS. 1903. RIJKSMUSEUM, AMSTERDAM.
Until the nineteenth century, marriages between Jews and Christians were nearly unthinkable. The Dutch artist, who was influenced by Rembrandt, tenderly captured the moment when the groom clasps the bride's hand to place the ring on her finger. The whiteness of the tallit *that envelops the couple sets them apart and contributes to the intimacy of the moment.*

and from Yemen to Lithuania sanctified the Sabbath, married under canopies, built ritual baths, circumcised their baby boys, prayed three times a day facing Jerusalem, sat for seven days in tabernacles in the fall, and ate Passover's unleavened bread on the same seven days in the spring, to mention but a few of hundreds of facets of Jewish observance that were ordinarily practiced by any pre-modern Jew. In fact, observance, with the thousands of commandments, rulings, customs, responsa, and traditions that shape it, was as integral a part of galut as were the quest for Redemption in the other world and the stubborn resistance of persecution in this one.

This deeply religious outlook also lent Jews the explanations they sought for their torment in galut. Just as the loss of the Land of Israel and the consequent rise of the Diaspora were attributed to "our sins," as Orthodox Jews say even today on the holidays that once focused on pilgrimage to the Temple, so the Jews who went through galut's calamities had no doubt that their own tragic fate was God's doing.

(ABOVE)
KOSHER CAFÉ IN THE
GHETTO VECCHIO.
The Jews' segregated residence during the Middle Ages reflected not only non-Jewish decrees, but also Jewish religious constraints.

(OPPOSITE)
LAWS FOR THE RITUAL SLAUGHTER OF FOWL AND ANIMALS.
FROM THE *Shulhan Arukh* LEGAL CODEX.
SCRIBE: JACOB BEN ASHER. CODEX ROSSIANA,
MS. 555, FOL.127/128. BIBLIOTECA APOSTOLICA
VATICANA, VATICAN CITY.

(ABOVE)

WARSAW, POLAND, IN RUINS AFTER
THE END OF WORLD WAR II, C. 1945.
*After the war, Polish citizens still
attacked, and occasionally killed,
Holocaust survivors who were returning
to their homes.*

(OPPOSITE)

RESTORATION OF A BUILDING,
PART OF THE JEWISH GHETTO IN
ROME, C. 1955.
*The emancipation of West European
Jewry in the nineteenth century meant
the removal of physical ghettos, but not
mental ones.*

GHETTO: FACETS OF DISTINCTIVENESS

Due to a mutual Jewish-Christian interest in keeping themselves distinct, the Jews
maintained their own courts, schools, relief organizations, and charity societies. They
dressed differently, ate according to their own special laws, spoke languages of their own,
and practiced trades that set them apart from their neighbors.

The Christian permission, and the Jewish desire, to run separate courts—ones which
conducted their proceedings in a host of Jewish jargons and leaned on a voluminous
literature that hailed from Asia and was written either in Hebrew or Aramaic—was a
matter-of-fact statement, on the part of Jew and Gentile alike, that the Jews did not truly
belong in the countries where they resided.

Even more debilitating for their sense of belonging was the effect of the Christian
prohibition on Jewish land ownership and its cultivation, and the simultaneous
maneuvering of European Jews into money lending. The combination of being detached
from the soil while collecting debts from non-Jews was a sure recipe for the demonizing
of an already absurdly mystified image of the Jew.

Another major cause of alienation was the residential situation, whereby Gentile
and Jew seldom shared the same street, let alone house. Unlike most other facets of
galut, this one stemmed from Jewish constraints no less than from Christian malice.
First, there was the instinct of communities constantly on the defensive to huddle
together. Beyond that, the medieval Jewish community's determination to observe

(ABOVE)

AFTER THE POGROM.
MINKOWSKI, MAURYCY. C. 1910. OIL ON CANVAS
LAID ON BOARD. GIFT OF LESTER KLEIN, 1860–80.
THE JEWISH MUSEUM, NEW YORK.

*Minkowski gained renown for the
dramatic realism of his works, which
portray Jewish life in Poland before the
Russian Revolution. Here, recording the
flight of refugees after the pogrom, he
faithfully chronicled the sheer weariness
and utter dislocation of a group of
women and children who have
stopped to rest.*

Jewish law to its letter, including praying in a quorum three times day, bathing frequently in ritual baths, buying meat from a kosher butcher, and maintaining a communal cemetery, all entailed living together, separately from the majority. In Spain, some of the Jewish settlements were actually cities in their own right, replete with their own wall and gates.

This haphazard self-segregation was common for centuries in both Christian and Muslim settings, but it was voluntary, and occasionally also incomplete, with non-Jews sometimes dwelling in the Jewish neighborhoods, and Jews sometimes living in the non-Jewish sections of their towns. However, in twelfth-century Europe, the Catholic Church set out to explicitly outlaw Jewish-Christian neighborliness as part of its effort to isolate and humiliate the Jews. The Third Lateran Council's prohibition in 1179 on such mutual dwellings was the first step toward the creation of the ghetto, arguably the most symbolic and effective of galut's many fixtures.

Unlike the Muslim world, where the Jews and other minorities lived separately but not according to any regulator's scheme and in no way under deliberately humiliating circumstances, the European ghetto was intended as an act of social aggression and a spiritual affront.

In subsequent centuries the ghetto was instituted throughout Italy as well as many places in Central Europe, including Frankfurt, Prague, and Worms, and various places in Eastern Europe, too. Once built, the Jews were forbidden to settle anywhere beyond its walls. In Rome, the well-established Jewish community was forced out of its houses in 1555 and relocated in a newly designated area, which was duly surrounded by a wall of its own. Thus, the already socially marginalized Jew was now also physically confined in a fenced quarter, whose heavy gates would be locked every day from dusk to dawn, and for entire days (sometimes more than one) during Christian holidays. The inability to build, rent, or develop real estate beyond the walls lent to the development of exceptionally dense streets and multistory buildings, at times in disregard of elementary safety standards.

The ghetto walls became symbols of medieval clericalism and inequality, and as such were torn down by French soldiers when they conquered Italy—only to be restored with Napoleon's downfall. However, Rome's ghetto walls were not torn down until 1848, and the Jews' official obligation to live in special quarters was not formally lifted until 1870.

In the Muslim world, variations on the ghetto theme—where it was often called the *mellah*—was frequently emulated in Shi'ite regions in greater Persia, but also in Morocco, Bukhara, Afghanistan, and Yemen. In these places Jews were also often confined within special walled neighborhoods that were locked at night.

Galut's most severe form of confinement was imposed by czarist Russia. There, following Moscow's takeover of vast Polish territories with large Jewish populations, special legislation forbade the Jews to reside beyond the frontier regions of the expanded empire. Thus the "Pale of Settlement," which stretched between the Baltic and Black Seas, came into being. Though vast, this confining territory was carved out as part of a traditional, religiously inspired anti-Jewish attitude, and offered its many Jewish inhabitants little opportunity for social mobility and economic fulfillment. Though established well after the Middle Ages, it involved what then was the world's largest diaspora, and loomed ominously as proof that galut's ugly face would not disappear even after the dawn of the modern era.

Economically, the European Jews were frequently set apart from their Christian neighbors by the Church, which chased them away from agriculture. The European guilds, too, often blocked Jews from industry and artisanship, inspired and supported by Christian clergy. For its part, the Church wanted the Jews confined to an occupation that Christianity forbade and which could further embarrass Judaism, according to contemporary mentality—money lending. Thus French Jews, for instance, had ceased by the thirteenth century to cultivate vineyards the way they had in Rashi's times three centuries earlier, and dealt instead exclusively in money lending.

However, the maneuvering of European Jews into finance did not take place in a void, since they had been disproportionately involved in commercial banking, wholesale trade, and international commerce in the Muslim world as well. The *jahabdiyya* bankers, for instance, prospered in ninth- and tenth-century Baghdad, and wielded power in the caliph's court, while the Rhadanite intercontinental merchants on the caravans that connected the Abbasid Empire were present from Afghanistan to Morocco.

Apparently, this excessive involvement in trade and finance was natural for a nation that was frequently on the move and extensively spread out. Like the Greeks and the Armenians, who also developed extensive diasporas, the Jews could more easily establish international networks and help each other by sending and receiving merchandise over large distances. Even more importantly, a Jewish businessman on the road could always count on being aided on his way by a string of Jewish communities along his route, even if he didn't personally know people there. Thus, while galut meant that the Jews were nowhere fully at home, it also meant that they could always be partly at home anywhere.

LANGUAGE: ONE NATION, MANY TONGUES

One of the first symptoms of dispersal was the decline of Hebrew as the Jewish *lingua franca*. Toward the end of the Second Temple period, when the Diaspora was already larger than the Jewish settlement in the Land of Israel, Greek quickly became the major tongue of the Jewish people. That early discrepancy between the Diaspora's day-to-day realities and the Jewish people's age-old literature, heritage, and liturgy was a harbinger of things to come. Apparently, during centuries in which they traveled through, fled from, and settled in scores upon scores of countries, Jews spoke collectively more languages and developed more varied dialects than has any other nation.

Even before the destruction of the Temple, the decline of Hebrew was already apparent in the translation of the Bible into Greek, known as the Septuagint. According to the Talmudic tradition, that dramatic deviation from a national to a universal mindset came in response to a request by the third-century B.C.E. Egyptian king Ptolemy II, who had seventy sages work on the translation simultaneously but separately, in order to compare their results. In reality, however, while a circumstance of such a royal initiative may have actually happened, the translation apparently reflected a Jewish quest to reconcile cultural worldliness and tribal distinctiveness, the way Egyptian philosopher Philo wrote his timeless Judaic works in Greek, leaving no proof he even knew Hebrew.

This linguistic condition changed dramatically, however, in the aftermath of the Destruction, as liturgy became part of the effort to substitute for the lost Temple and

GREEK LANGUAGE SIGN ON THE OUTER WALL OF JERUSALEM'S TEMPLE INDICATING THE LIMIT BEYOND WHICH NON-JEWS WERE PROHIBITED.

THIRD CENTURY B.C.E.–FIRST CENTURY C.E. PLASTER CAST. MUSEO DELLA CIVILITA ROMANA, ROME.

Unlike Christianity and Islam, Judaism never saw a value in converting nonbelievers, and seldom engaged in it systematically.

Martin Luther: The Persistence of Hatred

The European Middle Ages ended with the decline of the papacy's grip on the continent's spiritual life, which in turn was ignited by the Reformation movement begun by Martin Luther (1483–1546). However, the man who could have changed Christianity's attitude toward the Jews and their faith not only failed to do so but in fact ended up writing a chapter of his own in galut's book of tears.

Initially, Luther's attitude to the Jews was relatively positive. The dissenting theologian who dealt Catholicism the blow from which it never fully recovered scolded the Christian tendency to blow out of proportion what he saw as the Jews' failures. He also condemned the militantly anti-Jewish apostate Johann Pfefferkorn's (c. 1469–1524) demand that Judaic literature, including the Talmud itself, be confiscated. Luther even

portrayed himself as the disciple of the great humanist Johann Reuchlin (1455–1522), who battled Pfefferkorn in his effort to enlist the Vatican to his cause. In a 1523 article Luther actually justified the Jews' initial rejection of Christianity, since the version they had been offered was, as he saw it, pagan. If he had been a Jew at the time, he wrote, he would rather become a pig than adopt that type of Christianity.

However, while apparently genuinely revolted by the Church's traditional anti-Jewishness, Luther had high, and unrealistic, hopes that the Jews would abandon their faith and follow his lead. Luther's attitude was merely a variation on a thousand-year-old Christian quest to convert the Jews, and his response to his failure to win over the Jews was characterized by the same vehemence for which his Catholic nemeses were notorious. In the 1530s a frustrated Luther already described the Jews as "stiff-necked" and "stubborn as the devil" for their refusal to reconsider their understanding of the Bible, and in the 1540s he called the Jews "thieves" and described then as "venomous vermin." After initially calling for an expansion of the Jews' occupations, Luther ultimately scolded them as usurers.

The charismatic Luther's growing following among German leaders made the vitriol he spewed in *Concerning the Jews and Their Lies* fall on attentive ears. In 1543, his anti-Jewish passion—which now led to a recommendation that the Jews be condemned to forced labor—inspired the Jews' expulsion from Saxony.

Still, in the long run, the Reformation did help assuage Europe's anti-Jewish wrath. The Thirty Years' War in the seventeenth century, a result of the Reformation, left much of the continent religiously exhausted. Thus Europe was ripe for the age of tolerance that transformed the relationship between medieval Christianity and Judaism.

(ABOVE, LEFT)
MARTIN LUTHER.
LUCAS CRANACH THE ELDER. MUSEO POLDI PEZZOLI, MILAN.
The founder of the Reformation movement harbored unrealistic hopes to win the Jews' following.

(ABOVE, RIGHT)
MARTIN LUTHER POSTING HIS NINETY-FIVE THESES ON THE CASTLE CHURCH DOOR AT WITTENBERG.
ENGRAVING.

ach dem Tode Mosches, des Knechtes Jehovas, sprach Jehovah zu Jehoschua, dem Sohne Nuns, dem Diener Mosches, also: ²Mein Knecht Mosche ist tot. So mache dich nun auf und ziehe über diesen Jarden, du und dieses ganze Volk, in das Land, das ich ihnen gebe, den Kindern Jiszrael. ³Jeder Ort, auf den eures Fußes Sohle tritt, — euch habe ich ihn gegeben, wie ich zu Mosche geredet. ⁴Von der Wüste und diesem Lebanon bis zum großen Strome, dem Strome Perath, das ganze Chittimland bis zum großen Meere, dem Sonnenniedergange, soll euer Gebiet sein. ⁵Kein Mensch soll dir Stand halten alle Tage deines Lebens; wie ich mit Mosche gewesen, werde ich mit dir sein, ich laß dich nicht fahren und verlasse dich nicht. ⁶Sei stark und fest, denn du sollst diesem Volke das Land vererbteilen, das ihnen zu geben, ich ihren Vätern geschworen. ⁷Nur stark sei und überaus fest, zu beobachten und ganz nach der Lehre zu tun, die mein Knecht Mosche dir geboten; nicht rechts weiche davon noch links, damit du Glück habest, wo du überall gehest. ⁸Nicht weiche dieses Buch der Lehre aus deinem Munde, Tag und Nacht sinne darüber, damit du all das zu tun beobachtest, was darin geschrieben; ja, dann sollen deine Wege dir gelingen, dann sollst du Glück haben. ⁹Hab' ich dir doch geboten: sei stark und fest! Erschrick nicht und sei nicht zag, denn dein Gott Jehovah ist mit dir, wo du überall gehest. ¶¹⁰Hierauf gebot Jehoschua den Amtleuten des Volkes also: ¹¹Ziehet durch das Lager und gebietet also dem Volke: Bereitet euch Zehrung vor, denn nach drei Tagen werdet ihr über diesen Jarden ziehen, um das Land zu besitznehmen zu kommen, das euer Gott Jehovah euch zur Besitznahme gibt. ¶¹²Zu den Reubeniten aber, den Gaditen und dem halben Stamme Menasche sprach Jehoschua also: ¹³Gedenket der Worte, die euch Mosche, der Knecht Jehovas, also geboten: Euer Gott Jehovah ge-

währt euch Ruhe und gibt euch dieses Land. ¹⁴Eure Weiber, eure Kindchen und eure Herden sollen im Lande bleiben, das euch Mosche jenseits des Jarden gegeben, ihr aber, alle Kriegstüchtigen, ziehet gerüstet vor euren Brüdern und leistet ihnen Hilfe, ¹⁵bis Jehovah auch euren Brüdern Ruhe gewährt, wie euch, und auch sie das Land in Besitz nehmen, das euer Gott Jehovah ihnen gibt; dann kehret zurück nach eurem Besitzlande, das euch Mosche, der Knecht Jehovas, jenseits des Jarden, gegen Sonnenaufgang, gegeben, und besitzet es. ¹⁶Da antworteten sie Jehoschua also: Was alles du uns gebietest, wollen wir tun, gehen, wohin du uns sendest. ¹⁷Ganz wie wir Mosche gehorcht, gehorchen wir dir, daß nur dein Gott Jehovah mit dir sei, wie er mit Mosche war. ¹⁸Jeder, der sich deinem Munde widersetzt, auf deine Worte nicht hört, was alles du ihm gebietest, werde getötet; nur sei stark und fest.

ierauf sandte Jehoschua, Sohn Nuns, aus Schittim heimlich zwei Kundschafter, indem er sprach: Gehet, besehet das Land und Jericho. Sie gingen fort und begaben sich in das Haus eines Buhlweibes, Rachab ihr Name, und legten sich da schlafen. ²Dem Könige von Jericho aber ward also berichtet: Siehe, Männer von den Kindern Jiszrael sind diese Nacht hierher gekommen, das Land zu erkunden. ³Da sandte der König von Jericho zu Rachab also: Gib die Männer heraus, die zu dir gekommen, die in deinem Hause eingekehrt, denn das Land zu erkunden, sind sie gekommen. ⁴Das Weib aber nahm die beiden Männer und verbarg sie, dann sprach sie: Freilich kamen die Männer zu mir, ich wußte nicht, woher sie waren, ⁵aber als bei Dunkelheit das Tor geschlossen werden sollte, gingen die Männer fort. Ich weiß nicht, wohin die Männer gegangen; setzet ihnen eilends nach, und ihr holt sie ein. ⁶Sie hatte sie auf das Dach hinaufgeführt und unter die Flachsstaengel versteckt, die (ihr) auf dem Dache geschichtet waren. ⁷Da setzten ihnen die Männer nach über den Weg des Jarden an den Furten, und nachdem die Männer, die ihnen nachsetzten, hinaus waren,

carry Judaism wherever the Jews would go. Consequently—and paradoxically—Hebrew achieved a status it lacked previously in the Diaspora, when the weekly portion was apparently read in many places in Greek. Now Hebrew became the sole language of Jewish ritual, a status it would retain until the nineteenth-century Reform movement opted for German and English.

For all mundane purposes, however, as most Jews migrated from the Greco-Roman sphere to the Mesopotamian basin, their main language changed from Greek to Aramaic in the generations following the Temple's destruction. Indeed, the Babylonian Talmud itself was studied and written in Aramaic. Then, as Islam dawned and Arabic swept over the Middle East, where most of the world's Jews resided at the time, Jewish-Arabic dialects emerged; ultimately, some of Judaism's most monumental writings—including the works of Sa'adia Gaon and Maimonides—were written in Arabic, with Hebrew characters.

An even greater proliferation of Jewish languages took place in later centuries, as the Jews sank roots in Europe. There, about six Latin-Jewish dialects developed in Italy, France, and Spain, though none was nearly as famous and widely spoken as Ladino. The Jewish migration into inner Europe gave rise to the most famous of all Jewish tongues—Yiddish. That language, which mixed medieval German, Slavic, Hebrew, and Aramaic elements, was ultimately spoken by some 12 million Jews before that figure was halved, in one fell swoop, by the Holocaust.

(ABOVE, LEFT)
A PRINTER IN LONDON'S EAST END PRINTING POSTERS FOR THE YIDDISH THEATER, APRIL 12, 1952.
Jews across the Diaspora spoke numerous languages and dialects, many of them distinctly Jewish, but never abandoned Hebrew as the language of liturgy, until the rise of the Reform movement in the nineteenth century.

(ABOVE, RIGHT)
YIDDISH LOVE LETTER.
1786. FROM KOSMAN BEN AARON SEGAL TO RANCHE, CLEVE. BIBLIOTECA ROSENTHALIANA, AMSTERDAM.
The language that on the eve of the Holocaust was the most commonly spoken among the world's Jews, became all but extinct soon after the war.

(OPPOSITE)
GOLDSCHMIDT BIBLE.
BOOK OF JOSHUA.
This Bible, with its design harkening back to the Gutenberg Bible, is the first Jewish Bible that was printed in post-World War I Germany.

לִימוֹת הַמָּשִׁיחַ לּרֹה הָרַחֲמָן הוּא יְחַדֵּשׁ
עָלֵינוּ אֶת הַחֹרֶשׁ הַזֶּה:
וּלְחַיֵּי הָעוֹלָם לְטוֹבָה וְלִבְרָכָה
הַבָּא • מַגְדִּיל מִי"ט הָרַחֲמָן הוּא יַנְחִילֵנוּ
בַּשַּׁבָּת חוּמ' (מִגְדּוֹל) לְיוֹם שֶׁכֻּלּוֹ טוֹב
יְשׁוּעוֹת מַלְכּוֹ יְקִימֵנוּ אֶת סֻכַּת דָּוִד
הַנֹּפֶלֶת:
וְעוֹשֶׂה חֶסֶד
לִמְשִׁיחוֹ לְדָוִד וּלְזַרְעוֹ עַד עוֹלָם
עוֹשֶׂה שָׁלוֹם בִּמְרוֹמָיו • הוּא
יַעֲשֶׂה שָׁלוֹם עָלֵינוּ וְעַל כָּל
יִשְׂרָאֵל וְאִמְרוּ אָמֵן •
יְראוּ אֶת יְיָ קְדשָׁיו כִּי אֵין
מַחְסוֹר לִירֵאָיו

כְּפִירִים רָשׁוּ וְרָעֵבוּ וְדֹרְשֵׁי יְיָ לֹא
יַחְסְרוּ כָל טוֹב • הֹלֵכֶט כֹּלֵהַ
בָּרוּךְ אַתָּה יְיָ אֱמָהּ בּוֹרֵא פְּרִי
הַגָּפֶן •

וֹאֹן וֹנֹד וֹוֹיֹן גֹטרֹוֹנֹקֹן הֹט וֹחֹגֹעֹ וֹנֹד יֹח מֹאֹך בֹרֹכֹה:

בָּרוּךְ אַתָּה יְיָ אֱלֹהֵינוּ מֶלֶךְ הָעוֹלָם
עַל הַגֶּפֶן וְעַל פְּרִי הַגָּפֶן •

(ABOVE)

THE BLESSING AFTER THE MEAL.

1724. VIENNA. MS. 8232, FOLS. 7V-8R. LIBRARY OF THE
JEWISH SEMINARY OF AMERICA, NEW YORK.

*The text, which observant Jews say after
every meal that includes bread, invokes a
plea that "the Merciful will break the
burden from over our neck," alluding
to galut's yoke.*

(OPPOSITE)

A JEW AND HIS PASCAL LAMB.

NICHOLAS OF VERDUN. 1181. ENAMEL. BERDUN ALTER.
SAMMLUNGEN DES STIFES, KLOSTERNEUBURG ABBEY,
OUTSIDE VIENNA, AUSTRIA.

*The Jew is recognized by the pointed hat
worn by late-twelfth-century Jews. The
altarpiece's fifty-one plaques are divided
into three eras: Before Moses, between
Moses and Jesus, and since Jesus.*

In all, part of the galut experience was a Jew's mastery of a dialect that was unique to Jews, but one that was never intelligible to all Jews, and often not even to most Jews, elsewhere in the world. (Outside the European sphere there were many other distinctive Jewish languages, for instance in Persia, Bukhara, and the Caucasus.) Linguistically, what bound together Jews from far-flung lands was Hebrew, which was used in rabbinical responsa, and sometimes also in nonreligious contexts. Most Jews, however, hardly knew any Hebrew and could not converse with fellow Jews who dwelled in other lands. The languages of galut, therefore, while binding together Jews within an individual region, otherwise demonstrated the atomization of the Jewish people in the Diaspora.

APPEARANCE: THE CLOTHING OF GALUT

Throughout the lands and continents they crossed over the centuries, Jews often wore clothes that set them apart from their neighbors. Some of these dissimilarities arose from

·XPI· MACTANDVS· INFORMAM· CLAVDITVR· AGN̅VS

AGNVS· PASCALIS

(RIGHT)

A Passover Seder in Bohemia.

FROM THE "SISTER OF THE VAN GELDERN HAGGADAH."
MOSES LIEB WOLF OF TREBITSCH. 1716–1717. MS. 4441.
KLAU LIBRARY, HEBREW UNION COLLEGE–JEWISH
INSTITUTE OF RELIGION, CINCINNATI, OHIO.

Jews were particularly distinguishable on Saturdays and holidays, when they wore their best clothing while non-Jews wore ordinary clothes. In this particular rococo scene with elegant déco, the obviously affluent husband and wife are in silks and lace, food is plentiful, and each of the adults holds a large silver goblet. In the background a young man fills the fifth cup. The decorations in the room, the view to the lush garden, and even the dog and birdcage are evidence of this family's high status, a few decades before the Jews of Prague were expelled by Maria Theresa.

(OPPOSITE)

The Revelation at Sinai, from the German Prayer Book for the Holidays.

C. 1320. SOUTH GERMANY. VELLUM. ADD. 22413,
FOL. 3R. THE BRITISH LIBRARY, LONDON.

The pointed hat was commonly imposed on medieval Jews in various parts of Europe.

religious observance; others, eventually, were imposed as part of an effort to assure that the Jew remained "other."

A list of an ordinary man's eighteen items of daily clothing that appears in the Talmud conspicuously refrains from mentioning anything unique to a Jew's appearance. In actuality, however, these bits and pieces were obviously "Jewish." Jewish men wore *tzitzit*, the fringes that the Torah commands Jews to wear on the four corners of their main article of clothing. Jews obeyed the prohibition to wear any cloth made by mixing wool and flax. On the Sabbath and holidays, Jews were also easily distinguishable, since they wore their finest clothes on days that for the rest of the population were ordinary

אריך ויריעו קי יהיה התורה הק
יומינו וזהיה ריולו יומון ד
פירוצג סרסתכמיסר יסיר היזווין יותהדינך
יולתיה וסמר קודם שנבריה העולם יייניעו ד
יירבו שכנע היית שוכנתיעלו עד עבטין
ועתה ליורם הקנכי ליוטו וליקבי לפנטריה
ב גין מערט וטטוטן הק טין העולם פי
שן יורטו כה ה ה ועתיייגן ט עובר העולם
כדסת וטב עיני ' פבטועטוטי מדבר יוב היית
וושת על פרט טל הק ' ושטטעבו והה היה
רושית וטר שו הקבה טוטי לתליו
והתריעון עטר ביותשנש לת יובל חברו
גירת כותלי כבל הק ' ב שנמער עליו וכל גושטוין
סלי היו שלהק ' לו זה היב חו ' כי יטטליר קוח
שנטעל ועשה העולם ד תותי עולם וקוב וקיבה
עליה ובשבין יותרותוט ' תורה שמנתכן
ותוריה שנבעולפה ' רטב כלחפנים ליי יטוון כה
רוד ליהועולם ' לדורם ליוונהכי ישר ליהועולם
טיינע מדיעה טול פהנם טל ליוירך וליורד' היוטשל
רעת ה העולם טרד לרעת תרי תרה שוביד ני
נטטלויים מווז רעולם ה ' בבן ליירוט
טנטריון קורם טתעטיי העל ד הקנב פ קטין

אָ	מֵנַנִי	א יְנְלוּ שְׁבַנְנִי	
		וַל הְקנָנִי "	א רָם הֵקנַנֵנִי '
	בַּזוּבָעַרְטֵי	ב וְעֵץ זְרַבְוּ	
בָ	שַׁעֲשׁוּעֵי בְּרַטֵּי	רֵאשִׁיתְ דַּרְכּ"	
	שָׁתֵּי לִרְגְלֵי	ג רַתְּי בִּיגַלֵי	
גָ	עוּזְעֵי עָלַי	קֶדֶם מְפַעֲלֵי "	
	תֵּתֵי עֵילַם	ד וְרֵי לְהוֹעֵילַם	
דָ	עַתְּהַנַּעֲלָם	מֵאֲזָ מֵעוֹלָם "	
הָ	גֵּיגֵּי לְאָרִישׁ	ה מֵזֵּקְלַפְרֹשׁ	
	נָפְלָא לְדָרוֹשׁ	נָסַכְתִּי מֵרֹאשׁ "	
	אֶהֱיֶה בְּעֵרִיזְ	וָ שַׁעֲשׁוּעֵי רֵיזָ	
וָ	קַדְמֵנֵי בְּמֶחֶדְ	מֵקֶדְמֵי אָרֶץ "	

ה מֵי גֵּיה שֵׁיוֹרֵם יִשׁלוֹ טוֹב יִשׁ הְוֵוֹעֲדֵיוֹ כָּפָה טוֹבֵי חַיִּים הֵם והוֹיֹעֲדוֹהֶם ' לֵיהֹבֵיהֶם כָּפֵה טוֹלִיוֹ יִטְטוּתְכוֹ טְרִיוֹ כְמֵיוֹכִי '
ובָי לֵיאָרִישׁ כַּמ מַ אִרְטוּתְ טוֹטְטוּ וְטוֹ רְטוֹ הַיְחַזֵּק רָבֵּם הַמֵּחְזֵקֹות כְּבֹאַף ' כַּרְעַת מַיֵּזֵּק לִפְבֹוֹן יֹוֹוֹתֵם בְּטֵיוֹט ' מֵטְלֵי רַמֵּם וְטְטוֹ '
וְנַפְלֵיִים לֵדֵיוֹטוּ יֹוֹתֵם נָסַכְתֵּי מֵיִיֹטְ בְּטֵוֹהֵה הַיְתֵי עַם הַק ' יֵרֹיוֹטֹ ' קֹדֵשׁ טְנַטְרֵי הָעֹולֵם נַסַכְתֵּי לֹטֹ שׁוֹרֵה ' יֹוֹדֵה כֵּטֵין כָטֵיוֹנֵי '
חֵזֵקִים וְטֵטַּשׁוּעֵי יֵירֵץ יֵירֵעֵה בֵּם וְהָק רוֹפֵה מֵירֵן קֹולֵיוֹ בֵּידֵוֹטְיֵה ' אֵילֵבֵי טוֹטֹה טֹונֵה הָעֹולֵם וְקֹורֵיב לֹדֵורֵים
טְנַטְרֵיון קֹורֵם טֹוֹעֲטֵיוֹ לֹוֹרֵים

workdays. Married women's Jewishness was also apparent, since they were compelled by Jewish law to adhere to a set of rigid rules aimed to ensure the modesty of their appearance, which included covering their hair. Beyond these, there were assorted Talmudic directives expressly aimed at differentiating Jews from their non-Jewish neighbors. While Judaic scholars were expected—at least according to one school of thought mentioned in the Talmud—to dress elegantly, the general rabbinic expectation from a Jew was to avoid extravagance.

Still, for centuries Diaspora Jews' distinctive dress was their religious leaders' choice rather than their non-Jewish rulers' whims. Though there were many exceptions, beginning with the ninth-century Egyptian caliph al-Muatawaqil's order that all Jews wear yellow coats and belts, or a more common and lasting decree in Morocco that Jews dress in black, those were not part of a systematic attack on the Jewish faith; Christians were also ordered to dress differently than Muslims in most times and places that Jews were. Throughout the Muslim lands there was a distinctive dress code for every faith. In the Ottoman Empire Jews wore distinctive hats—first yellow, then violet—and slippers; in North Africa they wore black gowns and skullcaps, and in India the Bene Israel community wore sideburns.

None of these restrictions compared with the situation in Christendom. There, the demand that the Jews dress differently, which spread steadily following the 1215 Lateran Council, was not part of a system aimed at distinguishing between faiths while respecting them, but part of the Church's ongoing effort to humiliate the Jews, in this case by making them carry with them a tool for their own discrimination wherever they went.

By 1227 the Jews in the French provinces of Normandy, Provence, and Languedoc had been ordered to wear distinctive dress. Then the decree proceeded to England, Italy, Spain, Germany, and Austria. The special sign was not immediately designed as the famous yellow badge, but as a circle, and then also a T shape. Though the imposition of a distinctive badge was occasionally relaxed in certain localities following some successful lobbying, all Jews in later medieval Europe were compelled to wear this mark. Women occasionally were ordered to wear different signs, such as blue ribbons in their hair or bells attached to their dresses so that they could be heard from afar.

In the last centuries before the Expulsion, Spanish Jewry's males were forbidden to shave their beards and were compelled to wear the Jewish badge. Elsewhere in Western Europe, the *Judenhut*—a pointed hat that was originally part of the Jews' voluntary attire—joined the badge as part of the dress code imposed on the Jews from without. In thirteenth-century Poland a succession of Church councils ruled first that Jews wear a distinctive hat, then also a red badge. In Italy a distinctive yellow hat remained part of the Jews' obligatory dress until the Napoleonic conquests, when anti-Jewish legislation was abolished.

ובהמתיה ובמישריה אחזתו לא ימכר ולא יגאל כל חרם קדשים הוא ליהוה כל חרם אשר
יחרם מן האדם לא יפדה מות יומת וכל מעשר הארץ מזרע הארץ מפרי העץ ליהוה
הוא קדש ליהוה ואם גאל יגאל איש ממעשרו חמישתו יסף עליו וכל מעשר בקר
וצאן כל אשר יעבר תחת השבט העשירי יהיה קדש ליהוה לא יבקר בין טוב לרע ולא
ימירנו ואם המר ימירנו והיה הוא ותמורתו יהיה קדש לא יגאל אלה המצות אשר
צוה יהוה את משה אל בני ישראל בהר סיני ׀

חזק

סימן סכום פסוקי דספרא בטו

LITERACY AND SOLIDARITY: THE SECRET WEAPONS

Even more than his distinctive dress, language, residency, and occupations, literacy distinguished the galut Jew from the gentile masses. In a feudal setting where only clergy and nobility had either access to or appreciation for education, the Jews not only sought to teach every child how to read and write, but also nurtured scholarship in a way that could be found nowhere else in Europe during the Middle Ages.

Inspired by a Second Temple–era decree that all children should attend school, Jews effectively made compulsory education part of the galut experience. Though not legally coerced, the communal norm was to make elementary education available to all. Moreover, the parental ambition was that a boy would excel intellectually, both because that was a supreme religious value and because academic accomplishment offered a sure ticket to social mobility: Wealthy Jews gladly married off their daughters to a poor family's prodigy-son.

The curriculum itself was mainly religious, beginning with the Hebrew alphabet, which was indispensable for praying and for following the Torah reading in the synagogue, and then proceeding to Bible, Mishna, and Talmud studies. Women, too, usually learned how to read and write, though they were not allowed to study Talmud.

So pervasive was the Jewish fixation on education that the poor also, on the whole, sent their children to the primary school, known as the *cheder*, and even those who lived in remote and secluded places too distant from the nearest cheder hired private tutors for their children.

With the rise of the synagogue, sage, and community that replaced the lost Temple, its rituals, and spirituality, the full-time scholar enjoyed a special social status as well as communal authority and national sway. The second-century sages of the Mishna in the Land of Israel; the early medieval rabbis of the Talmud in Babylonia; their successors in Spain, France, Germany, and North Africa before and after the Crusades; the late-medieval scholars of mysticism in the Ottoman Empire; and the early modern Talmudists of Poland and Lithuania—all these added up to a unique, tri-continental spiritual superstructure that served as galut's intellectual foundation. By corresponding among themselves throughout the generations, and by passing on their writing to future generations, the rabbis kept Jewish ritual practice basically consistent, even if they could not avert the development of disparate local traditions. Galut's Jews, while always politically ruled by a Gentile power, were at the same time governed spiritually by rabbis, who in turn were governed by Torah.

Another "secret weapon" that kept the Diaspora from unraveling was Jewish solidarity. Despite their lack of commonalities such as language, Jews from distant corners of the Diaspora did care for each other, and at times even went out of their way to aid fellow Jews in far-flung corners of the world.

THE HEDER.

MORITZ DANIEL OPPENHEIM. 1878. OIL ON CANVAS.
GIFT OF THE OSCAR AND REGINA GRUSS CHARITABLE
AND EDUCATIONAL FOUNDATION, INC. THE JEWISH
MUSEUM, NEW YORK.

*Scholarship was a means for social
mobility no less than money.*

Perhaps the most telling manifestation of this inclination was the redemption of prisoners. A value hailed already by early rabbinical literature, paying ransom to free a Jew who was captured or enslaved was considered by the Talmud "a great obligation," and Maimonides said this value was even more important than feeding the poor. Apparently, large numbers of Jewish prisoners were released in the wake of the Temple's destruction thanks to the efforts of Rome's Jewish community. The Talmud mentions communal prisoner-redemption funds, and the sages permitted the reallocation to such redemption funds monies originally earmarked for other purposes (though Jewish law also forbade to pay for such redemption more than the person's "market value").

As European persecution intensified, its Jewish victims were increasingly aided by fellow Jews from afar. Thus, Jews from Jerusalem captured by the Crusaders ended up redeemed by Syrian Jews in Antioch. Egyptian Jews in Cairo helped the Jews of Ashkelon set loose their coreligionists who were brought to the coastal city in order to be sold to slavery.

Alongside the smaller-scale cases, whereby travelers would be taken captive by highway robbers, there were more significant cases that reflected major historical situations, and in turn gave rise to a special kind of pan-Jewish solidarity. One such ongoing circumstance was the intrinsic Christian-Muslim friction across the Mediterranean Sea. Muslim pirates frequently brought cargoes of Jewish prisoners from Byzantium to Alexandria's main slave market, and the local rabbinical courts in turn raised funds on both sides of the Mediterranean in order to redeem the prisoners. There were times when such efforts were accompanied by mass prayers and fast days in order to create an atmosphere of emergency and convince the public to stretch its contributions as much as possible. Prisoner-redemption action was perfected by Don Isaac Abravanel (1437–1508), who created a system of regional fund-raising so as to redeem 250 Jews caught by Portuguese invaders in Morocco.

The fall of Byzantium and the rise of the Ottoman Empire in the fifteenth century turned Constantinople into an international slavery hub, and its Jewish community into the junction of the ongoing Jewish redemption efforts. Here thousands of Jews originally from the thick of Christian Europe ended up shipped to slave markets in Muslim countries, most notably in the aftermath of the 1648–1649 massacres in the Ukraine. Many were redeemed by fellow Jews with whom, for lack of a common language, they usually could not even conduct a basic conversation.

The prisoner-redemption mechanisms lasted until the nineteenth century, when marine piracy and highway robbery declined dramatically. Still, the seventeenth-century prisoner-redemption effort encapsulated galut's paradoxical combination of sharp local vulnerability with that distinctive grassroots transcontinental sway that practically no other nation at the time could display.

Hope: The Elusive Energy of Yearning

Beyond their sometimes imposed and sometimes self-imposed exclusiveness, galut's Jews shared a deep sense of yearning for divine Redemption. Across the Diaspora, from simple silversmiths in Ottoman Yemen and destitute peddlers in Polish Lithuania to affluent merchants in Umayyad Baghdad and powerful court Jews in Hapsburg Vienna, all Jews shared the belief that ultimately God would bring galut to an abrupt end. They shared an idyllic view of a distant past, when the Jews and Israelites fulfilled God's commandments and were rewarded with mental peace, political stability, and even imperial grandeur. Such was also their view of the future: They had no doubt Redemption would be heralded miraculously with the arrival of the Messiah, the re-conquest of the Land of Israel, the rebuilding of the Temple, and the ingathering of the exiles. These notions, that the very state of dispersal was temporary and that living among the nations was an aberration, were the most solid facets of galut, shared equally by rich and poor, simpleton and scholar, Ashkenazi and Sephardi.

However, that basic faith also underwent dramatic transformation when the scholars of Kabbala developed a theology that linked personal observance and salvation. The belief that Redemption's arrival could be hastened by individual action—including vigorous study of Judaism's rational and mystical disciplines coupled with near-ascetic personal

(ABOVE)

STATUE OF RABBI LOEW (JUDAH LOEW BEN BEZALEL (D. 1609), BETTER KNOWN AS THE MAHARAL OF PRAGUE. NEW TOWN HALL, PRAGUE.

The Diaspora was led by scholars much more than by statesmen or plutocrats.

conduct, extremely devout prayer, and a rigorous observance of every detail in Jewish law—was revolutionary.

Following the Expulsion this new thinking also became more relevant, since the expellees, and other Jews, sought explanations for the calamity that had befallen the Diaspora's largest community. Thus, "practical Kabbala"—that version of Jewish mysticism that demanded extreme personal piety in addition to rigorous study of secret texts—became widespread throughout the sixteenth century.

In the next century, aided by the invention of the printing press and improvements in marine traffic, and fueled by the Cossack massacres of 1648, the entire Diaspora was mentally ripe and relatively accessible for news about the Messiah's arrival. In 1665 rumor broke out in Jerusalem, and quickly traveled across the Diaspora from Yemen to Germany and from Holland to Persia, that the Messiah had actually arrived. His name, people said, was Shabbetai Zevi.

Born in 1626 in Smyrna, Turkey, to a food merchant, Shabbetai Zevi studied Judaism with local rabbis, and already as a teenager showed symptoms of manic-depression. When news of the Cossack massacres arrived in Smyrna—a cosmopolitan port city bustling with foreign merchants, some of whom were his father's business partners—he fell into a severe depression. Shabbetai Zevi started publicly uttering God's full name, in blunt violation of Jewish law, and claiming he was the Messiah.

SHABBETAI ZEVI.
The false Messiah's appearance in 1666 came at a time when the Diaspora was mentally ripe and physically accessible for such news to spread and take root.

Initially seen as a lunatic, he was ultimately expelled from Smyrna by its rabbis. After wandering for several years through the southern Balkans and being expelled also from Salonika and Istanbul—where he actually declared the abolition of Judaism's commandments—he proceeded to Cairo before arriving in Jerusalem in 1662. During the next three years he led a relatively quiet life, during which he married a prostitute who had survived the Cossack massacres. However, his manic attacks persisted, and he sought the help of other Kabbalists in treating him.

One of those, a gifted scholar named Nathan, was reputed to be able to correct anyone's troubled soul. Shabbetai Zevi went to meet him in Gaza, but instead of curing him, Nathan actually convinced him that he indeed was the Messiah. Unlike ShabbetaiZevi, Nathan was a balanced man and a respected intellectual. His conclusion that Shabbatai Zevi was the Messiah was based on his comparison between the Jewish mysticism he had studied and what Shabbetai Zevi was telling him of his visions, as well as on his own visions. In the spring of 1665 Nathan announced Shabbetai Zevi as the Messiah, and Shabbetai Zevi, now convinced of his destiny, began parading through Gaza riding a white horse, followed by a growing crowd of supporters, twelve of whom he appointed as his emissaries to the Twelve Tribes of Israel.

Shabbetai Zevi and Nathan then proceeded to Jerusalem, where they were snubbed by most of its rabbis, but Shabbetai Zevi, riding his horse, circled the city's walls seven times, and his following only grew.

The stories about the Messiah began reaching far, fueled by a letter sent out by
Nathan to the Diaspora and by Shabbetai Zevi's trip back to Smyrna and Istanbul. In his
letters Nathan said the Messiah was not supposed to prove his authenticity by performing
miracles, and he claimed that Shabbetai Zevi had the power to punish his opponents and
reward his followers. Within a few years, Nathan promised, Shabbetai Zevi would unseat
the sultan, and then proceed to redeem the Lost Tribes and marry the biblical Moses's
thirteen-year-old daughter, Rebecca. The redemption process would be completed with
the full repentance of the entire Diaspora.

As news of the Messiah's arrival traveled worldwide, rumors also proliferated, some
claiming that the Lost Tribes had been found, or that Shabbetai Zevi had conquered
Mecca and was proceeding to Persia. In Aleppo, Syria, where Shabbetai Zevi passed on his
way back north, rumor claimed that Elijah the Prophet had appeared. Across the
Diaspora people began selling their property, fasting several days a week, frequenting
ritual baths, and raising funds in order to finance the journey to the Promised Land
for the needy.

From Kurdistan to Holland, Jews wrote poetry in praise of Shabbetai Zevi. In Poland and Lithuania Jews caused disturbances while parading with his picture. Back in Smyrna, Shabbetai Zevi's presence caused general hysteria, highlighted by massive dancing and parading in the streets that at times brought commerce to a standstill. At one point he made a big audience utter God's full name, while abolishing fast days that commemorate the Temple's destruction and deleting from services the prayer for the sultan's safety.

Then, as Shabbetai Zevi set sail from Smyrna to Istanbul, he was arrested at sea. Though initially he was treated with a kind of respect the Ottomans seldom accorded rebels, and even continued to receive delegations from all over the Diaspora, Shabbetai Zevi was eventually brought to the sultan's inner council. On September 15, 1665, Shabbetai Zevi was given a choice: convert or die. Shabbetai Zevi converted, thus shocking numerous prominent rabbis and established communities, who now realized they remained as deep in galut's throes as they ever had been.

According to Jewish-mysticism scholar Gerschom Scholem (1897–1982), the Shabbetai Zevi messianic fervor's compromising of Jewish law and challenge to rabbinical rationalism shook the ghetto walls from within, and thus helped lead the Jewish majority to the secularism it embraced in later generations. While this thesis is debatable, the Shabbetai Zevi affair clearly demonstrated the Diaspora's impatience with galut's unending misery, and its eagerness to follow a leadership that would show it the way to Redemption.

As it were, the sole available value system for accomplishing this goal was religion, albeit in a revolutionized version. That would change only when modern thinkers would reevaluate the concepts of both Diaspora and Redemption. By the end of the eighteenth century, as the Jewish Enlightenment's ideas began taking root, the traditional view that the Diaspora was an anomaly began changing. That transformation, whereby Gentile and Jew not only tolerated one another as transient guests and benevolent hosts, but actually accepted each other as fellow citizens with equal rights, marked the end of galut. This was not because it ended discrimination against the Jews or their murder, but because these would now happen in secular rather than religious contexts. Similarly, as nationalism swept Europe, Jewish thinkers concluded that Redemption was less about otherworldly repentance and more about earthly power.

MODERNITY: THE PROMISE AND PERILS OF FREEDOM

A major facet of the Diaspora since the fall of communism is that, for the first time since antiquity practically the entire Jewish people is politically free (the only exception that adds up to a community is Iranian Jewry). This is the culmination of a two-hundred-year-long process that began with the French Revolution's emancipation of the Jews, and eventually signaled a marked change in the Diaspora's formal status and in its collective psyche.

Historian Simon Dubnow (1860–1941) saw Emancipation as the watershed event that altered medieval Europe's anti-Jewish discrimination. In its aftermath, Jews would be

(ABOVE)
THE GRAND SANHEDRIN.
EDOUARD MOYSE. 1867. MUSÉE DU JUDAISME, PARIS.
Civil rights came at the expense of communal autonomy.

allowed to own land, earn higher education, join the civil service, and reside and build houses of worship wherever anyone else could. In return fort this entry ticket to the social contract, the Jews were to abolish their separate judicial system. The way Dubnow saw it, these changes heralded the Jewish Modern Ages, because the legal discriminations that emancipation undid were what the previous era, galut, was all about.

Other historians saw the demise of galut differently. Heinrich Graetz (1817–1981), often viewed as the founding patriarch of modern Jewish historiography, thought the arrival in Berlin in 1750 of the philosopher Moses Mendelssohn was the end of the Jewish Middle Ages, since it symbolized the dawn of cultural reconciliation between Gentile and Jew. To him, the crux of galut was not in the Jews' legal condition but in the mentalities, both Jewish and Gentile, that produced it. The ghetto, in other words, was more than merely a physical structure, and by no means the non-Jews' exclusive creation. Rather, the ghetto was a state of mind, paradoxically shared alike by those within and beyond its walls, all of whom contended that the Jews did not really belong in their surrounding cultures. As the Enlightenment movement began breaching these mental walls, the age of galut began to wane.

Lastly, historian Benzion Dinur (1884–1973) saw in the rise of Zionism the end of galut. Himself an ardent Zionist who at one point served as Israel's minister of education, he believed

TITLE PAGE IN HONOR OF THE
CORONATION OF THE PRUSSIAN
KING FRIEDRICH I.
1701. BERLIN. WATERCOLOR. BERLIN, GEHEIMES
STAATSARCHIV PREUSSISCHER KULTURBESITZ.

*Jewish existence until the emancipation
depended on constant nurturing of
the power-that-be's protection. On
January 18, 1701, in Königsberg, the
elector Friedrich III was crowned
Friedrich I, King of Prussia. This
document was written by the Schutzjude
(Protected Jew) Simon Wolff Brandes in
honor of the coronation. Using Psalm 21,
he composed "A Divine Secret Revealed"
in which, on behalf of the Jewish
community, he expressed the hope that
the new king be granted power, glory,
and a long life.*

the medieval Diaspora's subjugation could be treated neither by legal nor by cultural rapprochement, but only by the Jews' restoration of their ancestral land. In other words, even in its more benign forms the Diaspora was the cause, the result, and the epitome of galut, all at once.

With the benefit of some 250 years' hindsight, it seems the truth lies in a combination of these three theses. The second half of the eighteenth century saw the rise of a new tolerance toward Jews and Judaism among Central European scholars who figured prominently in the Enlightenment movement. This dramatic transition, whose ultimate Jewish symbol was Moses Mendelssohn, preceded and inspired the legal changes that came with the French Revolution, which formally declared the Jews equal citizens, provided they confined their religious practice to the private domain. The Jews' transition from a near-pariah class to fully-fledged citizens not only revolutionized their status but also challenged the Diaspora's very survival genes as they had been engineered seventeen hundred years earlier by Rabbi Johanan ben-Zakkai. For the first time in the history of the Diaspora, the power that that visionary had bestowed on the nuclear community as a substitute for what had been lost with the Temple's destruction was being challenged.

In a setting where Gentiles were prepared to accept the Jews' faith as a private affair while considering them not only full citizens but even part and parcel of their country, society, and history, Jews no longer had to choose between their heritage and their surrounding "host" societies; suddenly the two could be reconciled. Back in the Middle Ages, a Jew could join the social majority provided he adopted the ruling faith. Now, theoretically at least, a Jew could belong without abandoning his faith. The Diaspora, in turn, could now cease to be seen as a mere way station en route to Redemption; if anything, it could be reinterpreted as a Jew's final destination, even if he was religious.

The rising secular state's commitment to egalitarianism and its consequent emancipation of formerly oppressed groups such as women, serfs, or slaves threatened other groups that stood to lose their inherited privileges. In revolutionary France, the problem for many Jews in this regard was the new insistence that the rabbinate cease to settle civil suits among Jews, as they had for centuries. Many were reluctant to lose this autonomy. For the relatively assimilated Portuguese Jews of Bordeaux the loss of juridical freedom was not much of an issue. However, to the thoroughly religious Jews of eastern France, Stanislas de Clermont Tonnerre's memorable call to grant the Jews everything as individuals, which effectively meant the end of Jewish legal autonomy, was a menace. In the heady days of the French Revolution, radicals even had the Jewish community of Carpentras "voluntarily" hand over its synagogue to the state. In various localities prayers actually had to be conducted in hiding. Moreover, with the twists and turns of the revolution's advance, places such as Switzerland and Westphalia, where Napoleon had initially emancipated the Jews, later rescinded that legislation after France's defeats.

Still, in the long term the French Revolution's clear-cut statement concerning the Jews' moral right to count as full citizens, and the state's legal duty to accept them as such sank

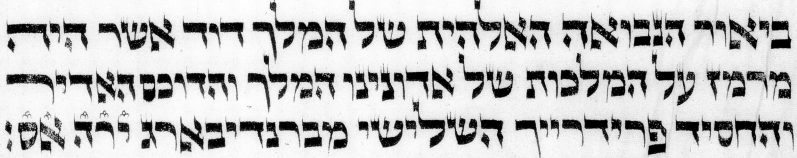

ביאור הנבואה האלהית של המלך דוד אשר היה
מרמז על המלכות של אדוגינו המלך והדוכס האדיר
והחסיד פרידרייך השלישי מברנדיבארג ירה אס:

כתב לך הדברים האלה על לוח ועל ספר חקה חקה לזכרן :

דוד בעזך ישמח מלך ובישועתך מה יגיל מאד :
תאות לבו נתת לו וארשת שפתיו בל מנעת סלה :
כי תקדמנו ברכות טוב תשית לראשו
עטרת פז : חיים שאל ממך
נתת לו ארך ימים עולם ועד : גדול כבודו
בישועתך הוד והדר תשוה עליו : כי תשיתהו ברכות
לעד תחדהו בשמחה את פניך : כי המלך בוטח בלל
ובחסד עליון בל ימוט : תמצא ידך לכל איביך
ימינך תמצא שנאיך : תשיתמו כתנור אש לעת פניך
יי באפו יבלעם ותאכלם אש : פרימו מארץ
תאבד וזרעם מבני אדם : כי נטו עליך רעה
חשבו מזמה בל יוכלו : כי תשיתמו שכם
במיתריך תכונן על פניהם : רומה יי
בעזך נשירה ונזמרה גבורתך:

roots. Despite setbacks following Napoleon's demise, during the second half of the nineteenth century all anti-Jewish legislation was eradicated in Austria-Hungary, Germany, and Italy. By the 1878 Berlin Congress, the Jews' legal acceptance and political clout had become so firm in Central and Western Europe that Germany, France, and Britain conditioned their recognition of Serbia's, Bulgaria's, and Romania's independence on their emancipation of their respective Jewish communities. Romania's initial failure to comply with this demand indeed delayed its independence.

From the Jewish end of the equation, the irony was that emancipation—and Enlightenment—first took root in countries whose Jewish communities were relatively on the margins of world Jewry. The large communities, and the great rabbinical authorities, were usually in non-egalitarian East Europe, and therefore less aware of and compelled to respond to the dramatic changes that promised, or threatened, to redefine and possibly eradicate Diaspora life as they knew it.

However, in places where Jewish conservatism did confront the new Gentile liberalism, the reflexive response was the kind of alarm that was displayed several decades earlier by the rabbis of eastern France during the Revolution. In the Habsburg Empire, which bridged between the new Zeitgeist and the bulk of nineteenth-century world Jewry, leading sages initially tried to defy emancipation. For Rabbi Moshe Sofer (1762–1839) of what today is Slovakia, emancipation was but another way in which God was testing His Chosen People. A bit farther east, the great Talmudist Rabbi Shlomo Kluger of Brody (1775–1869) ruled that Jews should not take advantage of the new permission to buy property in Central Europe because Jews should not buy real estate outside the Land of Israel.

Farther east, in czarist Russia, discrimination persisted in earnest, as the Pale of Settlement remained intact, with Jews forbidden to reside in Russia proper, their business opportunities severely limited, and their access to higher education largely blocked through punishing quotas. However, by the twentieth century even that bastion of bigotry was toppled as the Bolshevik Revolution abolished all ethnic and religious discrimination, and in fact outlawed anti-Semitism.

The Jewish masses, at the same time, usually voted with their feet in favor of emancipation's new opportunities, some by migrating from village to town, others by emigrating to Western Europe, and others yet by altogether abandoning the Old World for the New. Soon enough, rabbinical disenchantment with emancipation became irrelevant. By the end of World War I, the Jews' legal status across the world had been radically transformed. For the first time in some fifteen hundred years, most Jews were no longer victims of formal discrimination.

Galut, therefore, could have seemed well on its way to extinction had such optimism not been marred by massive anti-Jewish violence, first by the Russian government prior to the Bolshevik Revolution, then by the White Russians and the newly independent Ukrainians, and finally with the rise of Nazism. The significance of these regressions was not only in the magnitude of the destruction they generated, but also in the reminder they provided that while rulers, thinkers, and legislators embraced emancipation, there were plenty of others who had no intention of accepting the Jews as equals, or even tolerating them as non-equals.

In fact, this tension between legal acceptance and mental rejection of the Jews ultimately became a mainstay of modern Diaspora existence. That lingering insistence on rejecting, blemishing, and eventually also harming the Jews in a secular setting came to be known as anti-Semitism.

ANTI-SEMITISM: THE CUNNING FACE OF JEW-HATRED

Throughout most of the nineteenth century, anti-Jewish policy seemed like a remnant of a vanishing past, a disease that if even not yet fully eradicated was nonetheless on the decline, just as progress was on the rise. Anti-Jewish violence of the sort that surfaced in Damascus in 1840 or the pogroms that washed southern Russia in the 1880s was to be expected in lands ruled by narrow-minded czars and ineffective sultans, but not in the industrialized, enlightened, and free parts of Europe—until 1895.

That year, on a cold January day in the heart of Paris, a Jewish officer named Alfred Dreyfus was publicly stripped of his rank after being convicted by a military court of spying for Germany. The charges later proved unfounded and Dreyfus was retroactively exonerated, but as the verdict was made public that fateful day in the Ecole Militaire, the large crowd at hand spontaneously shouted hysterically, "Death to the Jews."

The Dreyfus Affair by no means sparked the return of anti-Jewishness to the developed world. During the preceding decades that sentiment had continued to ferment in newly liberal societies, gradually adapting to the changing times in a way that could have rendered obsolete much of the neo-messianic thinking that assumed the emancipated Diaspora had joined the historical mainstream. In fact, the most tragic tale of the Diaspora's history was the smooth passage of anti-Jewish prejudice from the religious Middle Ages to the secularist modern era.

As historian Shmuel Ettinger (1922–1988) demonstrated, the decline of theological accusations about the murder of Christ was soon followed by equally virulent secular accusations that were aimed mainly at the newly outgoing, accommodating, and assimilating Jew rather than his introverted, religious, pre-modern ancestor. Collectively, these new attitudes became known as anti-Semitism, a term coined in 1879 by German writer Wilhelm Marr.

(ABOVE)

THE TRUE COMPLAINT OF THE WANDERING JEW.

EPINAL PRINT. NINETEENTH CENTURY. FRANCE.

The image that originated in the biblical Cain's punishment for killing Abel was favored by Christian, Nazi, and Communist propaganda against Jews.

The common denominator among the many types of anti-Semitism was the depiction of the Jew as the stereotypical villain of varied modern, secular ideologies.

Karl Marx, for instance, saw the Jews (including, apparently, his own ancestors and relatives) as the ultimate capitalists and plutocrats. Using the "Jewish means" of finance, he claimed, the Jews had bought power and made money rule the world. "Money," he wrote, "is the jealous God of Israel, and there is no other God before Him. The banknote is the Jew's true God."

For romantic nationalists, the Jews were always insufficiently patriotic at best, downright disloyal at worst. Such, for instance, was the gist of composer Richard Wagner's attacks on the Jews, which included the statements that the Jew's only hope lies in his disappearance and that the Jewish race was "the born enemy of the human race and everything that is noble in it," or Berlin University historian Heinrich von Treitschke's (1834-1896) slogan "The Jews are our disaster," which ultimately became a famous Nazi mantra.

It was against this backdrop that another modern ideology, social Darwinism, also found an attentive ear among anti-Semites, who now claimed the Jews not only were deficient in assorted ways but also could not be "improved" since their traits stemmed neither from their old heritage nor from their new convictions but from their racial origins. The German race, claimed British political philosopher Houston Stewart Chamberlain (1855–1927) in his *The Foundations of the Nineteenth Century*, was creative, loyal, and responsible; the Jewish race was corrupt and parasitic.

Thus, the ideological underpinnings of the greatest calamity in the history not just of the Diaspora but of the world—the Holocaust—were largely in place well before the turn of the twentieth century. So were also the unique social circumstances that surrounded the rise of Nazi anti-Semitism and which made the modern Diaspora the unique phenomenon it remains to this very day.

As Europe gradually emancipated the Jews, and as they themselves increasingly embraced the values of Enlightenment, they lost no time making the most of the new opportunities that suddenly opened to them. In Vienna, Paris, Berlin, London, Budapest, Prague, and Amsterdam thousands of Jews flocked to previously inaccessible positions in commerce, academia, and the professions as if each of them had personally waited the fifteen centuries it took for Christian societies to allow them this kind of opportunity. By the latter decades of the nineteenth century the number of Jewish lawyers, doctors, bankers, entrepreneurs, and journalists far exceeded their overall shares in the local populations.

That astonishing social mobility could not go unnoticed, particularly by people who had initially inherited age-old anti-Jewish attitudes, and were ultimately dislocated by the dramatic transitions that came with the Industrial Revolution. For such people, to be treated by a Jewish dentist, to request a loan from a Jewish-owned bank, to shop at a Jewish-run department store, or to be defeated in court by a Jewish lawyer was a painful experience. And while the success of Jewish professionals made anti-Semites feel threatened from above, the mass migrations of Jews from village to town and from east to

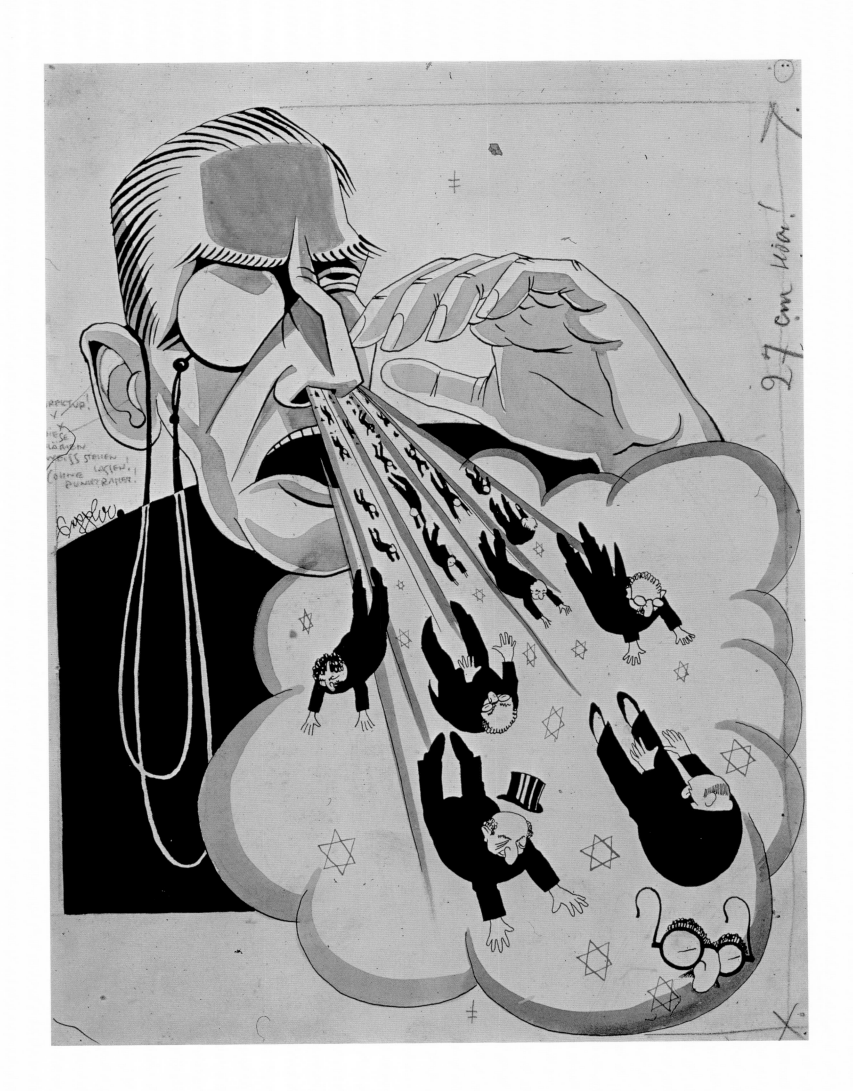

dumas
41
PARAIT LE 15 DE
CHAQUE MOIS
lisez
LE
CAHIER
JAUNE
V.v. 7140
ORAFF
138, Ch. Élysées
PARIS.

west made them feel threatened from below, as newly arrived destitute Jews crowded large parts of their cities.

Such "objective" circumstances of social dislocation have preceded anti-Semitic outbursts throughout the modern era. The 1929 Great Crash and the subsequent Depression clearly played a role in the rise of Nazism; the mid-1970s Arab oil embargo gave rise to a new wave of anti-Semitic incidents in Western Europe; since the fall of communism there has been an increase in attacks on Jewish cemeteries, schools, and community centers in parts of Europe; and in recent years, fueled by Arab-Israeli violence in the Middle East and growing Arab communities in Europe, anti-Semitism has been having a renaissance in Europe, where—in the words of historian Jacob Talmon (1916–1980)—the state of the Jews is increasingly being treated as the Jew of the states.

By 2004, the postwar eulogies of galut, inspired by the rise of the Jewish state, and by the horror of the Holocaust, seem premature at best, unfounded at worst.

TRENDS: CHANGE AND CONTINUITY

*T*hen *Jacob was greatly afraid and was distressed. And he divided the people that was with him, and the flocks, and the herds, and the camels, into two camps. And he said: "If Esau come to the one camp, and smite it, then the camp which is left shall escape."* (Genesis 32:11)

When Jacob the Patriarch returned to the Promised Land from years in Mesopotamia, where he had fled from fear of his jealous brother Esau, the Bible says he prepared himself for the worst by splitting his extensive family and many possessions, lest they all be annihilated should calamity occur. Eventually, this tactic would epitomize the Diaspora's secret of survival: Whenever calamity would strike a large Jewish community in one part of the world, Jews in other parts of the world would be safe, and ready to restore in one place what was destroyed in another. In our times, this is what happened with the rise of American Jewry and the emergence of the State of Israel, each of which offered a haven to the survivors of the European Holocaust. A similar pattern was evident with the resurgence of Sephardi Jewry, which for several generations had stepped into Jewish history's background, and the emigration of Soviet Jews, who for seventy years were systematically uprooted from their heritage and blocked from maintaining ties with their relatives abroad.

SHIFTING DEMOGRAPHICS

The rise and decline of Jewish centers was also coupled with a constant shifting of the Diaspora's geographic distribution. Four hundred years ago world Jewry was more or less split evenly between Muslim and Christian lands. That alone represented a significant change from the Middle Ages, when only a fraction of world Jewry resided in Christian Europe. However, during the modern era the Diaspora was even more radically redistributed, as Jewish geography and demographics rapidly changed in unpredictable ways.

Europe's Jews not only steadily recovered from the blows they had been dealt during the 1648–1649 massacres in the Ukraine, but in fact grew exponentially. By the beginning

of the nineteenth century, as Europe's overall population multiplied dramatically, an estimated 2 million of the world's 2.25 million Jews lived in Europe. Eight decades later, on the eve of the great immigrations to the New World and the Land of Israel, Europe had become home to 7 million Jews, while outside of Europe there were but a mere 0.5 million Jews.

By then, Middle Eastern Jewry had shrunk in size and declined in importance so that for Ashkenazi Jews, those from the Middle East seemed exotic, a dim echo of the glorious times when Baghdad's rabbis and Spain's merchants towered above the Jewish world. Yet as Jewish history's surprises go, by the end of the twentieth century Sephardi Jewry restored much of its size and clout.

One reason for this was the Holocaust, whose victims were almost exclusively Ashkenazi, with the numerically marginal exception of Greece's predominantly Sephardi community. The

(ABOVE)
THE CITADEL, OLD JERUSALEM,
SITE OF ONE OF HEROD'S PALACES.
*For the first time since antiquity the
Land of Israel is poised to become host to
the world's largest Jewish community.*

morning after the Holocaust, which shrank the Diaspora from 16 to 10 million Jews, one in ten Jews worldwide was of non-European extraction, as opposed to roughly one in sixteen in 1939.

The massive immigration of Middle Eastern and North African Jews to the newly established State of Israel also helped the non-Ashkenazim regain their prominence. Until the twentieth century, the Jewish communities of the Muslim universe were much less frequently and intensely exposed to the emancipation and enlightenment trends that secularized Jews elsewhere. Consequently, they remained more traditional, and as such were much less reluctant to embrace Zionism. Their familiarity with the Middle East also made the idea of relocating to Israel more natural to many of them.

Still, as Arab hostility to Zionism grew, the departure of Middle Eastern Jews to Zion became increasingly involuntary. Ultimately, the young State of Israel airlifted thousands of

(ABOVE)

YEMENITE JEWS WAITING AT THE
ADEN AIRPORT TO BE FLOWN TO
ISRAEL.

C. 1950. YEMEN.

*The mass immigration of Middle
Eastern Jewry to Israel, and the
Holocaust's severe blow to Ashkenazi
Jewry, eventually restored non-Ashkenazi
Jewry's prominence, after some two
centuries of being marginalized.*

(RIGHT)

A GROUP OF YEMENITE IMMIGRANTS
HOLD A FAMILY COUNCIL NEAR
THEIR TENT AT THE ROSH HA'AYIN
TRANSIT CAMP OUTSIDE TEL AVIV,
EARLY 1950S.

(LEFT)

YEMENITE IMMIGRANTS
CELEBRATING TU BISHVAT, THE
FESTIVAL OF THE PLANTS, ROSH HA-
AYIN, EARLY 1950S.

Jews from Yemen and Iraq, while others, most notably Morocco's sizable community, were brought to Israel en masse by sea.

Once in Israel, Middle Eastern Jews found themselves on the bottom of a social ladder whose top was occupied by the East Europeans who had established the state. Ironically, that was an inversion of earlier centuries' dynamics, when Spanish-Portuguese communities such as those of Amsterdam, Hamburg, or Bordeaux kept aloof from local Ashkenazi Jews. At any rate, it took a generation of hard, and sometimes harsh, struggling with Israel's European-descended elite, but by the 1990s Israel's president, chief of staff, commander of the air force, and roughly one in two lawmakers, mayors, and cabinet ministers were descendants of the Jewish communities of North Africa, Iraq, Iran, Yemen, and Egypt. In Theodore Herzl's time, such a scenario was unthinkable, not because of non-European Jews' abilities but because of their minuscule numbers.

The restoration of non-Ashkenazi Jewry took another twist as Sephardi Jews assumed a new confidence through the charismatic leadership of Iraqi-born Rabbi Ovadia Yossef. A former chief rabbi of Israel, he established in 1984 a political party, Shas, that quickly became a major power broker in Israeli politics. By the late 1980s, with their self-esteem restored, their demographics vibrant, and their power unprecedented, Israelis who originated in the Muslim world seemed well on their way to quietly taking over the leadership of the state that was conceived and established by victims of European anti-Semitism—until 1989. The unexpected demise of the East Bloc and the consequent massive exodus of its Jews turned the tables again on Diaspora demographics, as one million predominantly Ashkenazi immigrants came to Israel, thus rejoining Jewish history after having already been eulogized as a lost diaspora.

A similar happy end came to the oppressed communities of Ethiopia and Syria, which were also freed in the Cold War's aftermath, but whose numbers were far smaller than those of the former Soviet Union. By the turn of the millennium world Jewry seemed once again to be predominantly European, both by origin and by orientation. However, the state of Israel itself lies in a predominantly Muslim part of the world, and as such may have in store more cultural surprises for the future of the Jewish people.

Throughout its history, the Jewish Diaspora was never fully contiguous, and at practically every given moment it somehow distributed itself, albeit not evenly, on both sides of a major geopolitical fault line. After the destruction of the Temple, the Jews were split between the Roman and Parthian Empires. During the early Middle Ages they were split mainly between the Mesopotamian and Byzantine spheres. In subsequent centuries the Jews gradually divided themselves between Muslim and Christian domains. Then, as the modern era approached, they first split up between czarist and emancipated Europe, then between the Old World and the New, and until its recent demise, between the East Bloc and the free world.

Today, with world Jewry divided mainly between Israel and the rest of the world, the Jewish nation seems to be positioned on both sides of the emerging North-South cleavage, which some scholars, such as Samuel Huntington, warn might generate a war of civilizations. The rejection of Israel by its non-democratic and underdeveloped neighbors makes Jewish life there markedly different from what it is in tolerant and pluralistic America and Europe.

How the increasingly malignant disharmony between the Middle East and the developed world evolves in the future, and what impact that will have on Israel in particular and world Jewry in general, is likely to determine the shape of the Diaspora in future generations

(ABOVE)

RABBI OVADIA YOSSEF (LEFT), WITH RABBI SHLOMO GOREN. *Yosef's charismatic leadership helped narrow the political gap in Israel between Jews of European and Middle Eastern backgrounds.*

GALUT REVISITED

The establishment of the State of Israel was followed by mass expulsions of entire communities from Arab countries, the bulk of which ended up in Israel. Communities like Baghdad's, Cairo's, and Aleppo's, which existed since before the Temple's destruction, all but vanished by the mid-1950s along with ancient communities like Yemen's, Tunisia's, and Morocco's, raising the prospect that both galut and the Diaspora were on the verge of extinction. Such forecasts appear premature at best.

Although the Jewish state currently hosts the world's largest Jewish community for the first time at least since the days of the Maccabees, and maybe even since the times of the biblical prophets, the Diaspora, too, is showing surprising signs of vitality.

Particularly thought provoking in this regard is the astonishing re-emergence of

INTERIOR OF CONGREGATION
SHA'ARE HASHAMAYIM,
CAIRO, EGYPT.
The Arab-Israeli conflict and the establishment of the State of Israel depleted almost overnight Jewish communities that had existed for thousands of years.

Germany as a major Jewish Diaspora. Already numbering a hundred thousand, it is the fastest-growing diaspora. Surely, this trend is fed by external circumstances, namely the sudden availability of Jewish immigrants since the fall of the Berlin Wall in 1989. However, it also reflects the German government's postwar determination to not only tolerate, but actually encourage a restoration of its Jewish past. In this regard, today's German-Jewish situation resembles the medieval pattern whereby Jewish calamity in the German lands was followed soon afterwards by restoration.

A Jewish renaissance has also been taking place since the dissolution of the USSR across formerly communist parts of Europe. Cities such as Moscow, Kiev, and Prague, where less than a generation ago Jews would be arrested for being caught with a Hebrew book in their hands, today boast bustling synagogues, vibrant schools, and busy Israeli

(ABOVE)

AERIAL SHOT OF THE BERLIN JEWISH MUSEUM.
The museum, designed in 1989 by Daniel Libeskind, was visited by more than 350,000 people even before its exhibitions were installed. Half-a-century after the Holocaust, Germany has emerged as Europe's fastest growing Jewish community.

(OPPOSITE)

INSIDE A JEWISH SCHOOL, DJERBA.
Unlike other Arab states, Tunisia remained tolerant toward its Jews even well after the emergence of the Arab-Israeli conflict.

(ABOVE)

KOSHERING DISHES ON THE
CASPIAN SHORE, BAKU, AZERBAIJAN.
*Judaism's restoration in the former Soviet
Union comes while new challenges.*

embassies. In remote localities in Siberia, southern Russia, and even the Russian Far East, one finds today active Jewish communities, sometimes with ritual baths, kosher butchers, and rival synagogues. This resilience has been confounding both pessimists who had prematurely eulogized European Jewry, and anti-Semites who quietly applauded the Jews' near disappearance from Europe in the wake of World War II.

Yet the optimism generated by the post-communist Jewish revival notwithstanding, there are also forces of disintegration threatening the future of world Jewry. As the curtain rose on the twenty first century, the Diaspora seemed like a tri-continental structure dominated by American Jewry's struggle with assimilation, European Jewry's encounter with neo-anti-Semitism, and the State of Israel's elusive quest for accommodation with its neighbors.

(ABOVE)
CELEBRATING THE FIRST SEDER
IN VILNIUS, 1991.

Demographically, Israel's is by far the world's most vital Jewish community. Israeli Jews are younger, have more children, and obviously have a lower intermarriage rate than that of any other sizable community. A decade after its absorption of some one million immigrants from the former East Bloc, Israel's 5.3 million Jews are well on their way to surpassing an aging and rapidly intermarrying American Jewry's 5.4 million members. Moreover, with three times more annual births than deaths, Israel's is the entire world's only Jewish community with a positive birth rate.

Does that mean that Israel is fast establishing itself as the center of world Jewry, thus realizing classical Zionism's vision that insisted the Diaspora had no future? Perhaps. Yet Israel is also the one place in the world where Jews are still killed in large numbers because they are Jewish. Israel has also failed, so far, to fully shed the galut fate that its founders so

eagerly sought to escape. For now, the Jewish state's position within its region is not unlike that of a medieval Jewish community within its larger town. Mentally, it is rejected by its neighbors; commercially, it remains largely ostracized by them; and physically, whether actively or passively, they attack it when they can. Perhaps most metaphorically, Israel is today the only place in the world where Jews still live surrounded by a fence. Though circumstances are obviously different, the effect, at the end of the day, is largely the same as the old ghetto wall's was in its time: a pervasive sense of confinement, rejection, and menace.

THE ENIGMA OF JEWISH IDENTITY

As far as Israel's founders were concerned, the Jewish state was supposed to tower head and shoulders above the Diaspora. In many ways this has been accomplished. Politically,

(ABOVE)
ISRAELI DOCTOR IN RWANDA, 1994.
The Jewish state's desire to be "a light unto the nations" has been frustrated by its neighbors' refusal to fully accept it in their midst.

(OPPOSITE)
TENDING VEGETABLES IN THE ARAVA DESERT, SOUTHERN ISRAEL.
Israel's Jews constitute the world's most demographically vital Jewish community.

(ABOVE)
ARMY OFFICER.

(OPPOSITE)
GUARD DUTY IN THE WEST BANK.
The mobilization of a varied population,
ranging from young women to middle-
aged men of myriad social and ethnic
backgrounds, has made the Israeli army
an important player in the shaping of a
new type of Jewish society.

Israelis are much more confident of their Jewishness—whether of a religious or secular version—than most Diaspora Jews. Israelis serve in a Jewish army where chaplains are rabbis, the food is kosher, and everyone is deeply aware of the disasters that befell the Jews when they lacked the ability to defend themselves.

Culturally, however, Diaspora Jews are often more familiar with Judaism than most secular Israelis. Whose descendants will be more Jewish in future generations? Will American Jews who belong to non-Orthodox synagogues and go to Sunday schools retain more of their Jewishness and bring to the world more future Jews than the majority of Israelis who don't belong to, and seldom even enter, any synagogue at all?

The languages of the Jews have also undergone dramatic transformation. The Holocaust all but eradicated Yiddish, which on the eve of the war was the Jewish lingua

(ABOVE)

A CUBAN MAN OUTSIDE THE
ENTRANCE TO CONGREGACIÓN
HATIKVA.
*The congregation is the focus of
religious life for the eighty Jews left in
Santiago de Cuba.*

(RIGHT)

CALLE ECUADOR, HEART OF THE
JEWISH NEIGHBORHOOD OF BUENOS
AIRES, ARGENTINA.

franca. Then, the decline of Sephardi Jewish culture, which had started well before the war and continued with its massive relocation in its aftermath, has dealt Ladino blows from which it will never recover. The number of Jews who speak Arabic has also plunged dramatically, as the Middle East's communities disappeared. Today, English, Hebrew, Russian, and to a lesser extent Spanish and French are the Jewish people's main languages.

In Israel, at the same time, Hebrew has been so successfully nurtured and taught that some see in it the Zionist enterprise's most impressive success. Today the Jews' original language is spoken everyday by nearly seven million Israeli Jews and Arabs. By their mastery of the language in which generations of Judaic sages wrote law, liturgy, commentary, and poetry, Israelis possess a crucial tool with which to connect with their cultural roots—even if they do not always do so.

(ABOVE)
ASHKENAZI JEWISH CEMETERY,
BOGOTA, COLUMBIA.
Diaspora Jews are frequently more familiar with Jewish heritage than the secular majority in Israel.

Among the rest of the world's roughly seven million Jews, Hebrew is taught extensively, both for religious and national purposes, yet only a small number of non-Israeli Jews can speak Hebrew fluently. Increasingly, it is English that seems to emerge as the language of pan-Jewish communication, the way Greek and Aramaic were in the generations before and after the Destruction.

Israeli law also makes Jewishness an even trickier question than it already was prior to the state's establishment. The determination to offer a haven for any oppressed Jew made the State of Israel legislate upon its establishment the famous Law of Return, which makes every Jew automatically eligible for Israeli citizenship. While the law frequently fulfilled its aim, as millions of Jews from totalitarian countries indeed came to Israel, it also inadvertently cast a shadow on the Jewishness of many in the Diaspora. The need to define what the Law of Return means by the adjective "Jewish" resulted in an adoption of the ancient religious definition, which says that a Jew is whoever was born to a Jewish mother. Consequently, many Western people who consider themselves Jewish would not be considered such by the Jewish state should they apply for Israeli citizenship. At the same time, the influx of semi-Jewish immigrants from East Europe who even before being formally defined as Jews served in the Israeli army, and in some cases were also killed in action, is gradually making Israel seek new flexibilities in its definition of Jewishness.

(OPPOSITE)
THE ONLY MIKVEH IN BOLIVIA.

ENERGIES OF WORLDLINESS AND SOLIDARITY

Echoing the classical Zionist school of thought that maintained that Jewish existence could not be sustained in the long term outside the Jews' ancestral land, many Israelis in the early years of the state actually believed that even the most prosperous communities should ultimately immigrate to Israel or vanish. Since then, Israelis have learned to respect the Diaspora's vitality, and have shed much of the anti-Diaspora militancy that once was the hallmark of their collective outlook. The days when farming was idealized and the professions were vilified are also long gone. Today Israelis flock to the professions of law, medicine, engineering, business, journalism, and the arts exactly the same way their cousins do in America. Moreover, capitalist entrepreneurship is embraced and hailed as if the state had been established not by socialist Zionists but by the Rothschilds, who refused to finance the Zionist movement back when it was conceived. Indeed, the entire Jewish people is today predominantly a middle- and upper-middle-class nation, and Israelis see little wrong with the way their relatives in the Diaspora live. Today, even the Israeli National Security Council defines the Diaspora as a strategic asset that is indispensable to Israel's military and diplomatic needs, considering Western Jewry's proven ability to impact on world powers' decision-making processes.

Young Israelis, meanwhile, have become some of the world's best-traveled backpackers. Since the early 1980s thousands of twenty-something Israelis can be found at almost any

(ABOVE)
INTERIOR OF JEWISH SYNAGOGUE IN
BRIDGETOWN, BARBADOS.
*Due to mainly geographic and
commercial reasons, Jews have settled
even in the most remote corners of the
monotheistic world, but hardly anywhere
beyond them.*

(OPPOSITE)
WOMEN AT A PASSOVER SEDER,
PARAMARIBO SYNAGOGUE, SURINAM.
*The Central American community's
origins date back to the seventeenth
century, when Spanish and Portuguese
Jews arrived here with the original
Dutch colonialists.*

given moment roaming villages, valleys, and mountains in Peru, Chile, India, Nepal, China, Kenya, and even the South Pole. While the common explanation for this trend is that these youngsters need to let out the steam that gathered in them during several years of intense and sometimes dangerous military service, the phenomenon also raises other thoughts: Are these "New Jews" but a reincarnation of the mythical "wandering Jew," people driven by a hereditary and irresistible urge to peek beyond yet another horizon? What is clear is that while abroad young Israelis also visit established Jewish communities in America and Europe, and eventually accept much more naturally the Diaspora as part of their national existence and personal psyche than did Israel's founders.

The Diaspora's young generation, at the same time, has been going in the opposite direction, visiting Israel much less frequently than its parents and grandparents had,

following the Jewish state's affairs less closely, and also donating less money to Jewish causes in general, and Israel in particular. This diminishing interest in Israel is but another reflection of the rapid assimilation of Western Jewry in general, and North America's in particular, where one in two young Jews today is believed to be marrying out of the faith.

Faced with this weakening connection, several American-Jewish donors and Israeli politicians have in recent years launched a program aimed at exposing loosely-affiliated American Jewish young adults to the state of Israel. Called Birthright Israel, this program brings several thousand university-age Jews from North America for a ten-day trip to Israel, free of charge, every year since 1999. While such a project can surely contribute to the restoration of Jewish awareness in the Diaspora, its sponsors are the

(ABOVE)
OUTSIDE THE SYNAGOGUE WALLS, MAPUTO, MOZAMBIQUE.
The Jewish presence in sub-Saharan Africa has mostly been a by-product of the European penetration into the black continent.

(OPPOSITE)
A JEWISH GRAVESTONE FROM 1754 IN THE BRUSH AT JODENSAVANNA, SURINAME.

first to concede that their initiative first and foremost reflects a sense of alarm about the future of Jewishness in the Diaspora.

Throughout the postwar era the Diaspora displayed vocal, visible, and effective solidarity with troubled Jewish communities. In 1967 thousands of youngsters came to Israel when it faced attack by three Arab armies; in 2002 a hundred thousand American Jews rallied in Washington in support of Israel as it was facing constant attacks by Palestinian suicide bombers, and throughout the Cold War years American, British, Canadian, French, and Australian Jews constantly pressured the USSR, Syria and Ethiopia to free their Jews.

The freedom ultimately won by those oppressed Jewries, like their eventual arrival in the Jewish state, speaks volumes of the resilience of Jewish solidarity. And yet Israelis today wonder whether what in the past went without saying—namely, that in moments of severe crisis they could count on millions of Jews worldwide to rally behind them—might in the future no longer be taken for granted.

FAITH: THE TROUBLED MONOTHEISTIC NEIGHBORHOOD

Whatever the future of Israel-Diaspora relations, Jews today mainly live in areas dominated by monotheistic religions, generally shunning the Far East and sub-Saharan Africa. Indeed, that is how the Diaspora was distributed ever since the rise of Islam in the seventh century. The last time a sizable Jewish community lived in a non-monotheistic surrounding was in pre-Muslim Babylonia during the times of the Talmud.

While it is tempting to suggest that there was some design behind this pattern, it appears that the Jews remained attached to either Muslim or Christian countries due to geographic circumstances. Europe was accessible from the Middle East and North Africa, and prepared to host Jewish communities, if even only under punishing conditions. Also, Jews established communities mainly along trade routes, which in turn straddled the expansion patterns of the imperial powers. Still, the geographic correlation between the Diaspora and the other great monotheistic faiths remains intriguing. Even off-the-beaten-path Ethiopian Jewry essentially survived in a setting that was African-Christian rather than African-pagan.

At the same time, the Diaspora has itself undergone major transformation as the Jews gradually embraced, since the eighteenth century, various forms of secularism. Also, in recent decades historically troubled Judeo-Christian relations have become relatively more harmonious, while historically benign Judeo-Muslim relations seemed increasingly tense.

Christianity's attitude has changed dramatically in the aftermath of the Holocaust, for which many Christians feel guilty. The dialogue process launched in the early

(ABOVE)
MORNING PRAYERS FOR A JEW, AN AMERICAN, AND A YANKEE FAN, NEW YORK.
World Jewry's energetic struggle for the liberation of Soviet, Ethiopian, and Syrian Jewries was largely a reaction to the trauma of its earlier failure to prevent the catastrophe of European Jewry.

(TOP)
AN ETHIOPIAN MOTHER AND CHILD JUST ARRIVING IN ISRAEL DURING "OPERATION SOLOMON."

(LEFT)
JOHN PAUL II AT BEN-GURION
AIRPORT DURING THE PONTIFF'S
HISTORIC VISIT TO ISRAEL IN
SPRING 2000.
*The pope is shown between then Prime
Minister Ehud Barak (left) and
President Ezer Weizman. The pope's
unequivocal gestures of recognition of the
Jewish state's sovereignty in the Holy
Land, including his greeting by an Israeli
honor guard to the sounds of the Israeli
national anthem, were laden with
symbolism that made many hope
Judaism and Catholicism had finally
embarked on a new era of mutual
respect and tolerance.*

1960s between the Vatican and assorted Jewish organizations has gradually generated serious improvements in Catholicism's attitude toward the Jews. Pope John Paul II's visit to Rome's synagogue in 1984, the Vatican's establishment of diplomatic ties with Israel in 1994, and the pope's official visit to Israel in 2000 all seemed to herald a new era in Christian-Jewish relations. The pope's standing attention at Ben-Gurion Airport to the Israeli anthem, which echoes the Jews' age-old yearnings for their land, and his review immediately after that of rows of armed Jewish soldiers were laden with symbolism that convinced many skeptics that something had changed fundamentally since the times when Jews were routinely burned at the stake for rejecting Christ.

This rapprochement, though of course far from simple, sharply contrasts with what is happening with Islam in the Middle East. There, a rival faith's clergy increasingly attack Judaism as a religion, resorting to prewar European anti-Semitic vitriol. In this regard, the position of Israeli Jews is much more precarious than that of the rest of the Diaspora, practically all of which lives in predominantly Christian lands.

Moreover, much like Europe's classical anti-Semites, Israel's Islamic enemies also envy its economic success. The fact that Israel's per-capita income is more than all its immediate neighbors' combined figure generates the kind of feelings, and charges, that were common in prewar Europe. Whatever the reason, the fact is that two millennia

BAR MITZVAH IN RUSSIA, JANUARY
1993.
*Seventy years of communism's imposed
atheism dealt a severe blow to Judaism,
but not to Jewishness.*

after Haman plotted to "to destroy, to slay, and to cause to perish all Jews," and a mere several generations after the Holocaust, people in the same Persia deny Israel's right to exist, and are aiming a nuclear-weapons program at the Jewish state.

Considering the familiarity of this menace, is the Jewish people's current insistence to maintain a firm presence both within and beyond the Jewish state but a variation of Jacob's survival instinct? (In order to brace for Esau's prospective attack the Jewish Patriarch divided his family, so that "If Esau come to the one camp and smite it, then the camp which is left shall escape.") Do the Jews still think, as the Talmud (in Tractate

Pesahim 87B) suggested, that "God did justice to the Jews in dispersing them among the nations" because only when spread that thin their killers will always fail to reach at least some of the Jews? Will the future vindicate the classical Zionist view that the Jews' salvation lies in their becoming a normal nation, one that will shed its sprawling Diaspora and thrive in its ancestral land? Or will perhaps the Jews manage to prove that a flourishing Jewish state and vibrant Diaspora are not mutually exclusive? Time will tell.

(ABOVE)

OLD AND NEW JERUSALEM.
After having previously been split between Rome and Parthia, Islam and Christendom, America and Europe, and the free and totalitarian worlds, the Jewish people are now distributed on both sides of the twenty-first century's emerging North-South cleavage.

BIBLIOGRAPHY

Agus, I. A. *The Heroic Age of Franco-German Jewry.* New York: Yeshiva University, 1969.

Ashtor, E. *The Jews of Moslem Spain.* Philadelphia: Jewish Publication Society of America, 1973.

Baer, I. F. *A History of the Jews in Christian Spain.* Tel Aviv: Am Oved, 1965 (Hebrew).

Baron, S. *History and Jewish Historians.* Philadelphia: Jewish Publication Society of America, 1964.

—. *The Russian Jew Under Tsars and Soviets.* New York: Schocken Books, 1987.

—. *A Social and Religious History of the Jews.* New York: Columbia University Press, 1952–1983.

Bartlett, J. R. *Jews in the Hellenistic and Roman Cities.* New York: Routledge, 2002.

Bauer, Y. *A History of the Holocaust.* New York: Franklin Watts, 1982.

Beinart, H. *The Expulsion of the Jews From Spain.* Oxford and Portland, Oregon: Littman Library of Jewish Civilization, 2002.

Ben-Sasson, H. H. *A History of the Jewish People.* Cambridge, Massachusetts: Harvard University Press, 1976.

Bonfil, R. *Rabbis and Jewish Communities in Renaissance Italy.* Washington: B'nai B'rith Book Service, 1993.

Bowman, S. B. *The Jews of Byzantium, 1204–1453.* Tuscaloosa, Alabama: University of Alabama Press, 1985.

Chazan, R. *European Jewry and the First Crusade.* Berkeley: University of California Press, 1987.

Dinur, B. *A Documentary History of the Jewish People.* Tel Aviv: 1965 (Hebrew).

—. *Historical Writings.* Jerusalem: 1972.

Dubnov, S. *History of the Jews.* South Brunswick, New Jersey: T. Yoseloff, 1967.

Goitein, S. D. *A Mediterranean Society: The Jewish Communities of the Arab World as Portrayed in the Documents of the Cairo Geniza.* Berkeley: University of California Press, 1967–1993.

Gompel, B. R. Crisis *and Creativity in the Sephardic World, 1391–1648.* New York: Columbia University Press, 1998.

Graetz, H. *History of the Jews.* Philadelphia: Jewish Publication Society of America, 1956.

Gruen, E. S. *Jews Amidst Greeks and Romans.* London: Frank Cass, 2002.

Hirschberg, H. Z. *A History of the Jews in North Africa.* Leiden: E. J. Brill, 1974.

Howe, I. *Diaspora: The Immigrant Jews of New York.* London: Routledge & Kegan Paul, 1976.

Johnson, P. *A History of the Jews.* New York: Harper Collins, 1987.

Katz, J. *Emancipation and Assimilation, Richmond.* Gregg International Publishers, United Kingdom: 1972.

—. *Tradition and Crisis.* New York: New York University Press, 1993.

—. *Out of the Ghetto.* New York: Schocken Press, 1978.

Katz, N. *Who Are the Jews of India?* Berkeley, Los Angeles, London: University of California Press, 2000.

Marcus, J. R. *United States Jewry, 1776-1985.* Detroit: Wayne State University Press, 1989.

Meyer, M. A. (ed.). *German Jewish History in Modern Times.* New York: Columbia University Press, 1996.

Netanyahu, B. *The Origins of the Inquisition in Fifteenth Century Spain.* New York: Random House, 1995.

Neuman, A. A. *The Jews in Spain.* Philadelphia: Jewish Publication Society of America. 1942.

Pinkus, B. *The Jews of the Soviet Union.* Cambridge: Cambridge University Press, 1988.

Prawer, J. *The History of the Jews in the Latin Kingdom of Jerusalem.* Oxford: Oxford University Press, 1988.

Roth, N. Jews, *Visigoths and Muslims in Medieval Spain: Cooperation and Conflict.* Leiden; New York: E. J. Brill, 1994.

Sarna, S. *American Judaism.* New Haven: Yale University Press, 2004.

Sharf, A. *Byzantine Jewry From Justinian to the Fourth Crusade.* London: Routledge & Kegan Paul, 1971.

Stern, S. *The Court Jew.* New Brunswick, New Jersey: Transaction Books, 1985.

Stillman, N. A. *The Jews of Arab Lands.* Philadelphia: Jewish Publication Society of America, 1979.

Vital, D. *A People Apart: The Jews of Europe, 1789–1939.* Oxford: Oxford University Press, 1999.

Weinryb, B. D. *The Jews of Poland.* Philadelphia: Jewish Publication Society of America, 1972.

White, W. C. *Chinese Jews.* Toronto: University of Toronto Press, 1966.

INDEX

PHOTOGRAPHY CREDITS

Arizona Historical Society: 154

Art Resource/NY: Alinari/Seat: 13; Bildarchiv Preussischer Kulturbesitz: 248, 259; Bridgeman-Giraudon: 220; The Jewish Museum: 88, 173, 226 (bottom), 238 (John Parnell), 252, 265; Erich Lessing: 11, 16, 20, 21, 41, 54–55, 66, 102, 140, 218 (left), 240, 245; Foto Marburg: 241 (right); HIP/Scala: 18, 221, 227; Réunion des Musées Nationaux: 24, 226 (top), 257; Scala: 17, 223, 224–225, 229, 241 (left), 253; Snark: 261, 263, 264; George Tatge: 13

Courtesy of the Leo Baeck Institute, New York: 36

Dvir Bar-Gal: 198 (top), 198 (bottom), 199

Beth Hatefutsoth, Photo Archive, Tel Aviv: 31 (Courtesy British Museum), 35 (Dr. Paul Arnsberg Collection), 46 (Gross Family Collection), 47, 58 (bottom), 85 (top), 91, 115, 117, 123, 124 (Courtesy Marian Fuchs), 125 (Courtesy Alain Roth, Israel), 129 (Courtesy Iona Nahmias, Tel Aviv), 134, 135 (The Central Archive for the History of Jewish People, Jerusalem), 143 (Courtesy Geresh Perlov, Israel), 145 (top) (Courtesy Jewish National and University Library), 145 (bottom) (Zuskin Collection), 146 (Bund Archives, New York), 147 (Courtesy Natalia Michoels-Vovsi), 153 (Courtesy Fred Lewis, Israel), 193 (Zentralbibliothik. Zurich), 194 (top) (Courtesy Jewish National and University Library), 194 (bottom) (Courtesy Tudor Parfitt, London), 196, 197 (Amishav—on behalf of the Dispersed of Israel, Jerusalem), 203 (Chantilly, Archives des Jesuites de Paris), 210 (Courtesy Ruma Haiby, Israel), 214 (right) (Courtesy Tudor Parfitt, London), 218 (right) (Courtesy 1956 Jewish National and University Library), 255

Yaakov Brill: 219

Central Zionist Archives, Jerusalem: 48

©Andrew Cowin, Travel Inc.: 132

Rivka and Ben-Zion Dorfman: 136, 137

Stephen Epstein/PonkaWonka, Inc.: 213

Getty Images: 148 (© Estate of Raphael Soyer, Courtesy Forum Gallery), 228, 236, 237, 243 (left)

Shai Ginott: 10, 22–23, 104, 165, 183

Itmar Grinberg: 25

David Harris: 14, 19 (top), 74, 268–269

Hebrew Union College Skirball Center, Cultural Center Museum Collection, Los Angeles: 37, 44 (John Reed Forsman)

Jewish Historical Museum, Amsterdam: 127 (bottom), 181, 243 (right)

Jewish National and University Library: 166

Courtesy Library of the Jewish Theological Seminary of America: 28, 61, 67 (Suzanne Kaufman), 233 (Nicholas Sapeiha)

Joint Distribution Committee: 69, 82 (bottom), 83, 84 (Joan Roth), 204 (top), 204 (bottom) (Ted Nevins), 209 (top), 209 (bottom), 211, 212, 230, 231, 277, 279, 292 (Robert A. Cumins)

Collection of Abraham and Deborah Karp: 242

Richard Lobell: 3–4, 8, 75, 80, 82 (top), 85 (bottom), 86, 87, 149 (top), 208, 266, 276, 278, 280, 281, 290 (top), 290 (bottom), 293

Larry Luxner/Cuba News: 192, 211 (top), 214 (left), 273, 282 (left), 282 (right), 283, 284, 286, 287, 288, 289

Roy Mittelman: 149 (bottom), 151 (top), 151 (bottom), 274

New York Public Library: 27, 31, 121, 155 (Astor, Lenox, and Tilden Foundation)

Maria and Kazimiez Piechotkah: 120

Zev Radovan, Jerusalem: 12, 15, 53, 57, 70, 71, 105 (left), 167, 172, 174, 176, 177, 178 (top), 178 (bottom), 186, 215 (left), 215 (right)

Eldad Rafaeli: 73

Lawrence Salzmann: 150, 162, 190 (top), 190 (bottom)

Nahum Slapak: 51, 68, 72, 81

South African Jewish Museum: 160 (top)

State of Israel, National Photo Collection, Government Press Office: 49, 160 (bottom), 161, 164, 270 (top), 270 (bottom), 271, 272, 291

Studio Olimpic/Alberto Jona Falco: 90, 235

Malcolm Varon: 156

Courtesy Cyril Waynick: 160 (middle)

© World Monuments Fund: 119, 122 (top) (1998 Sam Gruber), 128 (Laziz Hamani), 138 (1989 Sam Gruber), 142 (top) (2000 Sam Gruber), 205 (1991 Joel Zack)

YIVO: 142 (bottom) (Roman Vishniac)

ACKNOWLEDGMENTS

This book traces the origins and maps the wanderings of the Jewish Diaspora, from the times of the Patriarch and the ancient Israelites all the way to the rise of the modern State of Israel.

The Jewish nation is famous for many things, ranging from its unique blending of religion and nationality to its survival even in the face of harsh oppression. Still, nothing distinguished the Jewish people more than their geography, which for well more than two millennia has been almost as globalized as mankind itself.

Historically, the Jewish existence in dispersal appears to have begun more than 2,500 years ago, when the First Temple had yet to be destroyed by the Babylonians. Mentally, however, there were proverbial hints to the Diaspora's emergence already in previous history, for instance in the journeys of Abraham before and after staking his claim to the Promised Land, or in the failure of Moses to ever set foot in the very land he designated for the Twelve Tribes of Israel.

When finally at the Holy Land's doorstep, some of the Israelites chose to shun it. Then, when the Israelites were forced into exile centuries later, ten of their tribes disappeared, while the rest unwittingly established the Diaspora, that uniquely Jewish formula for metaphysical national survival.

Having had the opportunity to travel around the Jewish Diaspora since my childhood, and having been educated to see in it an anomaly, I was fascinated from an early age by my nation's dispersal. Indeed, the Jews' geographic ubiquity, economic success, and intellectual excellence is not only a historical curiosity; it has also been a source of antagonism and downright hostility on the part of theological and social competitors. At the same time the Diaspora has also been the crucible of tribal survival and spiritual resilience as well as a symphony of myriad colors, customs, languages, tastes, and smells. This book is an attempt to succinctly convey the evolution, experience, mysteries, dilemmas, debates and flavors with which the loaded term Diaspora is laden.

After having studied and taught Jewish history at the Hebrew University in Jerusalem and at Brandeis University outside Boston, I knew that some day I would write about it, in one genre or another. The opportunity for that eventually arrived thanks to two things: my frequent writing about Diaspora affairs as executive editor of the *Jerusalem Post*, which deepened my familiarity with this subject, and my acquaintance with Hugh Levin, the publisher of this and numerous other high-quality illustrated books. When he pitched to me the idea of writing a history of the Diaspora I didn't even need a moment's thought for consideration: I just agreed, knowing I would enjoy every minute of working on it. For that alone I must therefore thank Hugh, but not only for that.

Hugh's staff, and particularly Ellin Yassky, who edited this book both professionally and tactfully, have been wonderful to work with. The diligence and resourcefulness with which they tracked down the diverse and exciting art and photography collected in this book have been for me an inspiration. I also owe a special note of thanks to my friend Shai Ginott, Israel's leading landscape photographer, who worked hard to locate much of this book's photography, and who introduced me to Hugh Levin in the first place.

I must also thank at this opportunity the many historians with whom I studied over the years, particularly Professors Israel Bartal, Joseph Heller, Yoef Kaplan, Immanuel Etkes, Evyatar Friesel, Elhanan Reiner, Avraham Grossman, Arthur Goren, M. D. Herr, Martin van Creveld, the late Yehoshua Arieli of the Hebrew University, and Jehuda Reinharz, Jonathan Sarna, Bernard Wasserstein, Stephen Whitfield, and Leon Jick of Brandeis University.

Equally indispensable for tackling this project was the training I received from my professors at the Columbia School of Journalism in New York: Barbara Belford, Donald Shanor, Stephen Isaacs, Nick Lehman—who has since become dean of the school—and the late Fred Friendly.

Last but not least, I want to thank my wife, Nurit, and our kids, Shira, Aviad, and Yotam, for having tolerated my frequent disappearances, whether physical or mental, while working on this book even after long days at the newspaper, where we were busy covering two wars, in one of which we also participated.

Then again, writing and fighting simultaneously is what my forebears did for centuries, while embodying what the Diaspora was all about.